Leo Tolstoy

Volumes of the *Continuum Library of Educational Thought* include:

Aristotle	Alexander Moseley
St Thomas Aquinas	Vivian Boland
St Augustine	Ryan N. S. Topping
Pierre Bourdieu	Michael James Grenfell
Jerome Bruner	David Olson
John Dewey	Richard Pring
Michel Foucault	Lynn Fendler
John Holt	Roland Meighan
John Locke	Alexander Moseley
Maria Montessori	Marion O'Donnell
John Henry Newman	James Arthur and Guy Nicholls
Robert Owen	Robert Davis and Frank O'Hagan
Plato	Robin Barrow
Lev Vygotsky	Rene van der Veer
Rudolf Steiner	Heiner Ullrich
Jean Piaget	Richard Kohler
Jean-Jacques Rousseau	Jürgen Oelkers
EG West	James Tooley
Mary Wollstonecraft	Susan Laird

See www.continuumbooks.com for further details.

Members of the Advisory Board

Robin Barrow, Dean of Philosophy of Education, and former Dean of Education, Simon Fraser University, Canada.

Peter Gronn, Professor of Education, Department of Educational Studies, University of Glasgow, UK.

Kathy Hall, Professor of Education, National University of Ireland, Ireland.

Stephen Heyneman, Professor of International Educational Policy at the College of Education and Human Development, Vanderbilt University, USA.

Yung-Shi Lin, President Emeritus and Professor, Department of Education and Institute of Graduate Studies, Taipei Municipal University of Education, Republic of China, Taiwan.

Gary McCulloch, Brian Simon Professor of the History of Education, Institute of Education, University of London, USA.

Jürgen Oelkers, Professor of Education at the Institute of Education, University of Zürich, Switzerland.

Richard Pring, Lead Director of the Nuffield Review of 14–19 Education and Training for England and Wales; Emeritus Fellow, Green College Oxford, UK.

Harvey Siegel, Professor of Philosophy, University of Miami, USA.

Richard Smith, Professor of Education and Director of the Combined Degrees in Arts and Social Sciences, University of Durham, USA.

Zhou Zuoyu, Professor of Education, Beijing Normal University, People's Republic of China.

Leo Tolstoy

DAN MOULIN

Continuum Library of Educational Thought
Series Editor: Richard Bailey
Volume 19

Continuum International Publishing Group
The Tower Building   80 Maiden Lane
11 York Road   Suite 704
London SE1 7NX   New York, NY 10038

www.continuumbooks.com

© Dan Moulin 2011

All rights reserved. No part of this publication may be reproduced or transmitted in any form or by any means, electronic or mechanical, including photocopying, recording, or any information storage or retrieval system, without prior permission in writing from the publishers.

The scripture quotations contained herein are from the New Revised Standard Version Bible, copyright © 1989 by the Division of Christian Education of the National Council of the Churches of Christ in the U.S.A., and are used by permission. All rights reserved.

Dan Moulin has asserted his right under the Copyright, Designs and Patents Act, 1988, to be identified as Author of this work

British Library Cataloguing-in-Publication Data
A catalogue record for this book is available from the British Library.

ISBN: 9781441156570 (hardcover)

Library of Congress Cataloging-in-Publication Data
Moulin, Dan.
Leo Tolstoy / Dan Moulin.
p. cm. – (Continuum library of educational thought ; v. 19)
Includes bibliographical references and index.
ISBN 978-1-4411-5657-0 (hardcover)
1. Tolstoy, Leo, graf, 1828-1910–Knowledge–Education. 2. Tolstoy, Leo, graf, 1828-1910–Career in education. 3. Education Philosophy. 4. Education–Philosophy–History–19th century. I. Title. II. Series.

LB675.T62M68 2011
370.1–dc22

2010021225

Typeset by Newgen Imaging Systems Pvt Ltd, Chennai, India
Printed and bound in Great Britain by the MPG Books Group

for my grandmother

Abstract methodology is nothing ... the best a teacher can achieve in his school comes from him personally, from the pure drive of nature.

Berthold Auerbach

Contents

Series Editor's Preface	ix
Foreword	xi
Author's Preface	xiv
Introduction	1

Part 1 An Intellectual Biography of Leo Tolstoy — 9

1	Early Experiences and Influences	11
2	Tolstoy the Educator	29
3	The Prophet of Yasnaya Polyana	48

Part 2 A Critical Exposition of Tolstoy's Educational Thought — 67

4	The Pedagogical Laboratory	69
5	The Results of the Yasnaya Polyana Experiment	81
6	The Devil of False Education	102
7	The Spiritual Nature of a Genuine Education	118

Part 3 The Legacy of an Overlooked Educator — 137

8	The Reception and Influence of Tolstoy's Educational Thought	139
9	Tolstoy's Relevance for Today's Educators	162
10	Conclusion	177

Epilogue	182
Bibliography	184
Index	193

Series Editor's Preface

The books in this series take the form of what might be called 'philosophical biography' in the area of educational studies. Their shared purpose, simply put, is to understand the thoughts and practices of certain educational philosophers.

Straight away this project is confronted with some potential difficulties. As even a cursory read of the list of thinkers whose names provide the titles within the series will testify, many are not ordinarily considered to be philosophers. Some can be more sensibly located in other areas of the academy – sociology, economics, psychology, and so on. Others seem unsuited of the label because their contribution to education is primarily in terms of its practice. In the narrow, disciplinary sense, then, many of the subjects of this series are clearly not philosophers. In another sense, however, and this is the sense employed by Jean-Paul Sartre in his own attempts in the genre, a philosophical biography can be written about anyone whose thought is important and interesting. In this sense, I suggest, each of the thinkers acknowledged in this series are philosophers.

Implicit within the *Continuum Library of Educational Thought* is an assertion that theories and the practices that follow from them (and equally, practices and the theories that lie implicitly within them) are vitally important for education. By gathering together the ideas of some of the most important and interesting educational thinkers, from the Ancient Greeks to contemporary scholars, the series has the ambitious task of providing an accessible yet authoritative resource for a generation of students and practitioners.

It will always be possible to question the list of key thinkers that are represented in this series. Some may question the inclusion of certain thinkers; some may disagree with the exclusion of others. That is inevitably going to be the case. There is no suggestion that the list of thinkers represented within the *Continuum Library of Educational Thought* is in any way definitive. What is incontestable is that these thinkers have fascinating ideas about education, and that taken together, the *Library* can act as a powerful source of information and inspiration for those committed to the study of education.

Richard Bailey, University of Birmingham

Foreword

The year 2010 marks the centennial celebration of Lev Nikolayevich Tolstoy's (1828–1910) death anniversary, and so it is befitting to remember his legacy again and reassess the impact of his life and works on subsequent generations. As a result of a resurgence of interest in this great writer, a monumental venture is underway in the Academy of Sciences, Russia, to publish an exhaustive, 100-volume edition of the complete collected works of Tolstoy. This enlarged edition is to include dedicated volumes that illuminate Tolstoy's place abroad, especially in the last half a century, and highlight his influence on writers, readers, thinkers, philosophers, freedom fighters and educators all over the world.

Tolstoy's relationship to India and India's fascination with Tolstoy's writing has been given an important place in this inquiry. Tolstoy was fascinated with India for its deep-seated spirituality and morality. Likewise, Tolstoy's description of his never-ending search for truth and the meaning of life have touched many great men in India for more than a century. Mohandas K. Gandhi is undoubtedly one of the most important disciples of Tolstoy's preaching of non-violence resistance to evil. Gandhi's understanding and complete acceptance of non-violence is largely attributed to his reading of Tolstoy's *The Kingdom of God is within You* in 1894.

Gandhi reread Tolstoy's book again in 1908 when he was jailed for his disobedience during the Satyagraha campaign in South Africa. While reading the book for a second time, he derived more strength and unbending determination to follow a non-violent path. Tolstoy's independent thinking, profound morality and truthfulness echoed with Gandhi's own inclinations and Gandhi became forever Tolstoy's disciple. Gandhi named his first commune in South Africa 'Tolstoy Farm.' In his letter to Tolstoy of 4 April 1910, Gandhi called himself 'your very devoted adherent' emphasizing the kinship. In September 1910, shortly before he died, Tolstoy wrote to Gandhi the last long letter he wrote to anyone, in which he agreed with Gandhi and reiterated the immense importance of renunciation of all opposition by force and advocated the law of love as the means to use in India's freedom struggle against British rule.

The kindred souls, Tolstoy and Gandhi, who could have been father and son, changed the course of history forever. Amazingly they have not been forgotten by leaders and intellectuals all over the world even now and their names stand together in many narrative records of India's freedom struggle against British rule. Thus a reading of Gandhi could take a researcher on to Tolstoy as it did with Dan Moulin. His curiosity took him to understanding Tolstoy as an educational thinker, a subject often overlooked. With this book Moulin has added to existing scholarship by highlighting Tolstoy's place as an educational visionary, who strove to revolutionize the school system in Russia. This book brings to our attention the series of experiments that Tolstoy undertook to teach and learn in an atmosphere of freedom and choice, criticizing the age-old system of learning by memorization and examination. Moulin's work gains significance in our times when prevailing educational methods are constantly being subjected to intense scrutiny.

Tolstoy's quest to educate young minds began in the late 1850s, as his disillusionment grew with his own fiction writing, and before he was to embark on writing his monumental novels *War and Peace* and *Anna Karenina*. Schools were being reformed in Russia at that time. German schools stood as examples for the bureaucrats, but Tolstoy dreamt of a different kind of school which could be established for the peasants and by the peasants. As a result of setting up such an experimental school in Yasnaya Polyana, Tolstoy went abroad to gain a greater understanding of modern education methods, only to dismiss them in an attempt to keep Russia from imitating the West, and guide it to return to its roots. He wrote a series of articles published in his own educational journal, based on his experiments at establishing a radically different kind of school. Despite the hostility to Tolstoy's educational practices and his publications from the government officials of the Education Ministry of Tsarist Russia, Tolstoy was a brilliant innovator and experimental schools in America and elsewhere have profited from the full accounts he left of his own experiences. Tolstoy's pedagogical articles anticipate in their intellectual quality and style the much larger body of religious and philosophical writing that Tolstoy undertook after his spiritual rebirth.

Tolstoy returned to topic of school education in 1872, when his children were growing up. An outcome was his *Azbuka* or 'ABC' book. Although the first edition was not received enthusiastically, his *New Azbuka* (1875) which was shorter, cheaper and more practical proved more popular. At the same time, Tolstoy published children's Readers with moralistic stories from many different cultures. Many simple tales from India were presented as straight-forward, easily understandable narratives. Until the end of his life, Tolstoy was to write short simple stories for a wide reading public. These stories have been widely read in Russia and abroad, especially in India where Tolstoy occupies the venerated position of a spiritual head or 'guru' in the popular Indian consciousness.

Looking back it becomes clear that just as Tolstoy's literary creations helped enlighten mankind, his educational thought is relevant to teachers all over the world. Tolstoy held his work on education more highly than his literary works and so for this reason alone it becomes important to reexamine his entire contribution to education once again for the present.

Radha Balasubramanian
University of Nebraska, Lincoln
17 June 2010

Author's Preface

Tolstoy's educational thought first came to my attention via Gandhi's autobiography, *The Story of My Experiment with Truth*. It is a fascinating, candid read. In it Gandhi describes, among other things, how Tolstoy's views on Christianity, pacifism and simplicity influenced him intellectually and practically, leading to his establishment of 'Tolstoy Farm' in South Africa. In form, Gandhi's writing follows a genre of confessional autobiography that spans one and a half millennia. Starting with St Augustine's *Confessions*, the retrospective portrayal of personal growth, and frank self-disclosure, can be traced to Rousseau, and from there – as well as to a number of other writers – to Tolstoy and Gandhi.

St Augustine, Rousseau and Gandhi all had something to say about education, and after my interest in Tolstoy's religious thought was roused by Gandhi, I soon learnt that Tolstoy spent some time as a teacher and wrote at length about his experiences. To my surprise I found that in the academic discourse on spiritual and religious education, Tolstoy's ideas had never been fully considered. In addition, I discovered that the few books and articles available about Tolstoy and education often excluded reference to his later religious thought.

This book represents an attempt to give a comprehensive account of Tolstoy's educational thinking and to relate it to his literature and other writings. I hope that the following pages draw together these interrelated aspects of Tolstoy's thought to present the reader with a coherent rendition of Tolstoy's educational vision.

It is not surprising, given Tolstoy's prodigious literary talent – and the sheer volume of material he wrote, that in relation to the task of understanding Tolstoy the artist, some biographers and critics have given his educational thought little attention. One notable exception is the work of the great Soviet literary scholar, Boris Eikhenbaum, whose thorough treatment of the relationship between Tolstoy's educational exploits and his literature seems incontrovertible. Nevertheless,

Eikhenbaum was primarily interested in Tolstoy's art and not in the analysis of his educational ideas and I am convinced that the subject of this book – Tolstoy and education – has still not been fully researched by scholars in sufficient depth and focus. This present volume can therefore only serve as an introduction to an enormous subject that demands further attention from specialists in Slavonic studies.

Anyone researching Tolstoy is confronted by a huge body of writing – his own published and unpublished work, the memoirs of those that knew him and a corpus of secondary literature. In the writing of this book, I am indebted to the work of the many Slavonic scholars who have made much of this material available in English. I have used Pinch and Armstrong's volume of Tolstoy's early pedagogical articles, and I have also referred extensively to Wiener's translations, which include, crucially, some of Tolstoy's later writings and extracts from his notebooks. In addition to this, I have used, with the help of Anya Wells and Andrey Levitskiy, the original Russian texts from the standard 90-volume complete works for other important writings which have remained altogether untranslated into English.

For biographical information, apart from Tolstoy's own autobiographical writings translated by Aylmer and Louise Maude, I have made use of R. F. Christian's selection of diaries and letters, the collection of biographical materials compiled by Tolstoy's official Russian biographer Paul Biryukov, the recollections of Tolstoy's children, Tolstoy's wife Sofya's memoirs and the accounts of visitors to Yasnaya Polyana. Where I have relied on these sources for quotations, I have cited them, as I have Tolstoy's writings, by a system of abbreviations set out in the Bibliography. The dates used when referring to Tolstoy's publications and general events within Russia are in the 'old style' as the Russian calendar was not modernized until 1917. However, events outside of Russia follow the conventional Gregorian system. With regard to the transliteration and use of Russian names and words I have attempted to render these in their most widely recognized forms in English.

I am very grateful to have had the privilege of attempting such an ambitious task as writing about Tolstoy and education. Researching his views has led me through the rich panorama of his fiction, the austerity of his religious and moral works, the polemics of his educational writings, and to my own pilgrimage to Yasnaya Polyana. I would like to thank the following people and organizations who have helped and encouraged me in a variety of ways in doing these things, although I hasten to acknowledge that any mistakes or omissions in my work remain my responsibility solely.

I would like to thank Richard Pring, Ingrid Lunt, Ralph Waller, Julian Stern, Michael Grimmitt and Terence Copley for their encouragement with the project, Katrina Malone and Sue Killoran of Harris Manchester College Library for their generous help with finding books, along with the staff at the Taylor Bodleian Slavonic and Modern Greek Library, St Catherine's College Library and Wadham College Library. I would also like thank Anya Wells and Andrey Levitskiy for their kindness in translating and discussing Tolstoy's rarer educational writings. I am extremely grateful for the support of my previous research into religious education in 2007 by the Farmington Institute; St Deiniol's Library, Wales, for a scholarship in August 2009; and the Cistercian community of Caldey Island, Pembrokeshire for their hospitality while I was writing in December 2009. I would also like to thank Galina Alexseeva of the State Museum of Leo Tolstoy at Yasnaya Polyana; the staff at the Centre for Dewey Studies, Southern Illinois University, Carbondale; Radha Balasubramanian for her foreword; Bertram Jörg Schirr for his help with the translation of extracts from Auerbach's *Neues Leben*; Chris Moulin, Richard Foord and Nathan Munn for their comments on the manuscript; Hannah Grainger Clemson and Mairéad McKendry for their advice on the project; and especially Faith Moulin, who kindly helped with the laborious task of proof reading.

Dan Moulin
Harris Manchester College, Oxford
30 April 2010

Introduction

From the white gate-towers of Yasnaya Polyana, up the avenue of slender silver birch trees, a fair distance beyond the estate buildings, in a wooded grassy glade, lies the grave of Leo Tolstoy. As he requested, there is no memorial, cross or gravestone; just a raised block of turf cordoned from the path by bent willow wands. The grave, dug by one of Tolstoy's former pupils, is located 'at the place of the green stick' at the edge of a gully in the Zakaz wood. This is where Tolstoy and his three brothers would play. The game, recounted by Tolstoy throughout his life, consisted in finding a green stick on which Tolstoy's elder brother, Nikolai, had written the 'secret' of how everyone on earth could live in a world without illness, anger or conflict.

Tolstoy's estate, Yasnaya Polyana, approximately 200 kilometers from Moscow, is now a national museum. It is kept as it was when Tolstoy secretly and fatefully last left it in the early hours of 28 October 1910. The gardens, farmland and woods are preserved as Tolstoy managed and worked them, as is his house, painted white and partially covered by vines. Inside the house, Tolstoy's books, bed, desk, paintings and personal belongings sit as they were in the last years of his life. Outside, across the grounds from the house, through some maples and larches, is the building that once housed Tolstoy's experimental school.

Tolstoy (1828–1910) is one of the greatest literary figures of all time. His work as a teacher and educational thinker, however, is less well known. Yet education was one of Tolstoy's perennial interests, inextricably linked with his literature, aesthetic philosophy and his own spiritual development. He believed that the education of children was of prime importance to social amelioration and the moral regeneration of society, but he also saw education as a two-way process. He was fascinated with, and inspired by, the moral reasoning and spiritual understanding of children. For Tolstoy personally, teaching was a formative experience. It had its part in the development of his wider thought; it fueled his intellectual, artistic and spiritual growth. Tolstoy's conversations with peasant children at school incited his burdensome inquiry into the meaning and purpose of religion, literature, art and life itself. The idea of writing *War and Peace* (WP, 1864–1869) was first conceived while teaching a history lesson in his school, and his interest in the philosophy of history, which is such an important part of that great epic, was first aroused as part of his consideration of educational issues.

In the 1860s, following the Russian defeat in the Crimea at Sevastopol, a battle in which Tolstoy took part, the new Tsar, Alexander II, launched the 'Great Reforms.' As part of this attempt to modernize the nation – and emancipate the serfs – a system of local government known as the *Zemstva* was instituted. During these reforms Tolstoy became a Justice of the Peace, a position established by the new legislation to settle disputes between peasants and landowners. Around the same time, Tolstoy also opened a school for the peasantry at Yasnaya Polyana. Once he had established this school, and as his interest in educational methods and their implementation grew, he traveled to Germany, France and England to survey modern educational theory and practice.

Tolstoy was concerned at what he saw in the schools of Europe, particularly the influence of the government and Church, and the widespread use of corporal punishment. He was critical of learning by rote and a 'one-size-fits-all' system of education that treated children as though they were all the same, and he became increasingly skeptical of the worth of contemporary pedagogic science. On his return, according to his reaction to European methods, Tolstoy continued experimental work at his own school and set about organizing other schools in his district. Drawing on his experiences of his 'pedagogical laboratory' and using some of his pupils' work, he wrote and published his own educational journal, the eponymous *Yasnaya Polyana*, which set out his tentative ideas on curriculum, and the purposes and aims of education. These pedagogical articles were radically progressive. He approached pedagogy in the same frank and earnest way as he later would religion, partly looking to the lives of the peasants for his solution. Tolstoy set out to understand what curriculum content and teaching methods would interest pupils. He saw the freedom of pupils as an essential condition for genuine education to take place. Otherwise how could a teacher know that what they taught was neither harmful for the student, nor pointless? For Tolstoy, true education could not be a form of induction into a preconceived conception of life, or for instrumental ends. Rather it should be a humanistic enterprise, based on each child's individual motivation and an educator's desire for them to become 'equal' in knowledge with their teacher. It is interesting to think what it would have been like in Tolstoy's school. He made no lesson compulsory and described it as a lively, fun, living organism.

Tolstoy's period of teaching between 1859 and 1862 left him exhausted and, in the fervor of the reforms, under the suspicion of the government. In early July 1862, when Tolstoy went away to recover from his exhaustion by taking the kumys cure, a concoction of fermented horse's milk made by the nomads of the Steppes, the school was raided by the police. This outraged Tolstoy who, on his return, wrote to the Tsar in protest. The school continued into 1863, but Tolstoy, newly married, took less interest in it. Tolstoy's pedagogical experiments had deepened his artistic and spiritual quest, and with his literary creativity renewed, and a hiatus in his pedagogical work, Tolstoy immersed himself in writing *War and Peace*.

After the success of *War and Peace*, Tolstoy, now more famous, restated his views on the prospect of a national education system and embarked on writing his Russian primers, the *Azbuka* (AZ, 1872), *New Azbuka* (1874–1875) and the *Russian Books for Reading* (1874–1875). These textbooks were an attempt to provide materials for teaching basic literacy and reading comprehension suitable for children of all classes. They had their genesis in Tolstoy's earlier pedagogic experiments, and to aid in their writing, the experimental school at Yasnaya Polyana reopened. Tolstoy subsequently became embroiled in a national debate over literacy which culminated in a controlled test between his pedagogical approach and those of leading contemporaries. After a well-publicized debacle and the disappointing reception of his Russian primers, Tolstoy returned to literature and wrote *Anna Karenina* (AK, 1874–1876). However, both literature and Tolstoy's work in education were leading him to confront religious questions that had bothered him since his adolescence. *Anna Karenina* was a disappointment; the lack of an ostensive moral purpose to his literature began to trouble him. As a famous author, Tolstoy felt he was confronted with the same conundrum that he had felt with school teaching: even though he communicated compellingly with his audience, he did not know the truth of what he was communicating. The project of education and literature had led Tolstoy to the burning question which had troubled him since his youth: to understand the very purpose and meaning of existence. Neither the business of educating the young, nor the art of storytelling, was viable without awareness of 'the truth.'

In the latter half of the 1870s and the early 1880s, Tolstoy went through his most intense spiritual search or 'crisis.' He read widely on world religions, learnt Hebrew and Greek and made his own translation of the Gospels. Tolstoy came to the conclusion that the Christianity of all major denominations had perverted the true meaning of the Gospels, which had been, and would continue to be, the greatest source of inspiration for him. Attempting to live out the message of the Gospels, as he understood them, led Tolstoy to seek a life of simplicity. He abstained from alcohol and tobacco, became vegetarian, dressed like a peasant and worked on the land. As a gesture of self-sufficiency he learnt shoemaking. In an attempt to renounce all property, he gave his estate over to his wife and family, and no longer retained copyright on his writings published after 1881. He began to walk with the pilgrims on the road to listen to the 'age-old wisdom of the people' which was to become a source of inspiration for his morally saturated folk tales. As elucidated by the revelations of Levin in *Anna Karenina*, the insight of the ordinary people into 'how to live' became championed in contrast with the decadent, parasitic lives of the aristocracy. In his attempt to lead a simpler, moral life, Tolstoy also became involved, both as a spokesperson and activist, with various social causes such as famine relief and the plight of the urban poor.

Tolstoy wrote a number of religious essays aimed at explaining his views and exposing the errors of orthodox Christianity, particularly the established Russian Orthodox Church. In Russia and abroad these didactic essays were derided by critics. G. K. Chesterton was horrified at the 'emergence of Tolstoy with awful and simple ethics' (1903, 418) while Bernard Shaw wrote a scathing criticism of Tolstoy as an ethicist and religious thinker, quipping that everything else that he did except literature 'he played at and soon got tired of' (Shaw, 1929, xii). The Russian philosopher Shestov also criticized him for 'moralising' and making a philosophy of life 'compulsory for all' (1900, 387). Yet Tolstoy's frank and powerful writing influenced many and a whole movement, the 'Tolstoyans,' came into being, although never gaining the approval of Tolstoy himself.

Tolstoy's obsession with finding out the meaning of life was something that spurred him on from his own childhood and lay behind his lifetime's artistic, religious and educational endeavors, as well as his interest in social issues and family life. However, Tolstoy was no saint; he was lord of the manor. As a young aristocrat he drank and gambled away his money, used prostitutes and had a relationship with a peasant from his estate, for which he felt remorse all his life. His marriage was notoriously stormy, culminating in the old man leaving his wife and home before dying at a rural railway station. His mature religious and educational thought bears the hallmark of this aristocratic authority, but as his writings became more didactic and prescriptive, his assertions became more challenging and revolutionary.

Tolstoy's conception of education was always related to his religious and political views. Influenced by Rousseau in his youth and Kant in his middle age, throughout his life Tolstoy maintained a firm belief in the natural moral law. Because of the innate goodness of every child, allowing children to follow their natural impulses to learn could only lead to goodness. Tolstoy believed that as all humans have a capacity for good, society could easily be so much better – and it was through the transformation of the individual, not democratic or socialist government that such change could come about. Education, but only of the free kind, has its part to play in this vision. Each child should be able to realize their innate goodness, rather than being corrupted by the coercive and ideological manipulation of the Church and government.

Once Tolstoy had worked through his spiritual crisis and felt that he did know, to some extent, the purpose of human life, his views on education became more centered upon spiritual and religious values – although he never abandoned the child-centered, heuristic approach he had advocated in the *Yasnaya Polyana* journal. With regards to his fiction, however, the form of the novel was abandoned in favor of folk stories that were meant to morally instruct adults and children alike. Furthermore these fables often looked to children for their inspiration. The parable, 'Little Girls Wiser than Men' (1885) serves as a good example of this genre. Two girls dressed in their Easter best play in the melted snow waters that run down the main street of their village.

Careful not to dirty their new dresses, they pick up their skirts and wade in the water. But out of fun, one splashes the other, getting her clean dress muddy and wet. When one girl's mother sees this, a quarrel breaks out in the village between their families. Meanwhile, the girls begin to play again, digging in the mud to channel the water, which eventually runs between the feet of the two girls' fathers who had joined the fray. At this moment, an old woman points out that the two girls were again playing happily with each other. The fighting adults become ashamed of not being able to forgive as easily as the children. Characteristically of his later period, Tolstoy ends the parable with a Bible verse – that of Mark 10.15 – which encapsulates much of Tolstoy's view of childhood and religion: 'Truly I tell you, whoever does not receive the kingdom of God as a little child will never enter it.' For Tolstoy, human endeavour should be based upon the simple moral truths of human existence, as received in the heart of every child, and given their clearest exposition in the teachings of Jesus. These same eternal and universal truths can be demonstrated through the pedagogic device of a simple narrative based on the lives of the Russian people.

The story of Tolstoy's own life has been told in many guises, and for many ends. His life has been examined by scholars seeking to understand the development of his literary form, and by those who have sought to understand the nature and course of his religious conversion. This book, however, aims to present a portrait and exposition of Tolstoy's thought which has often been overlooked: that of Tolstoy the educator and educational thinker. This story winds through all periods of Tolstoy's life. It begins with his experience of being a child and adolescent, incorporates his travels in Europe, his views on the purpose and nature of art and literature, as well as his experiences of teaching in his experimental school for peasants. It ends with his prophetic old age.

When Tolstoy read other thinkers' works he was always concerned with the validity of their ideas, rather than their place in history. Likewise, the principal task of this book is to examine Tolstoy's educational thought with respect to the perennial questions of education. The historical context of Tolstoy's educational thought within nineteenth-century Russia has been given brief treatment in favor of relating Tolstoy's educational ideas to his own unique intellectual and artistic achievement. It is hoped that this approach will demonstrate, faithfully to Tolstoy, how his life-experiences, literature, and developing political and religious beliefs interacted with his views on education. As previous Anglophone educationists have seldom consulted the writer's thought beyond the 1860s, a major part of this undertaking has been to accurately present Tolstoy's educational ideas in their entirety.

Part 1 of the book is given over to an intellectual biography of Tolstoy which outlines Tolstoy's story as an educator, identifying prevalent themes in his life and work and placing the development of his educational ideas and activities in the context of his wider thought. *Part 2* is given over to a critical exposition of Tolstoy's educational writings. Because Tolstoy's essays on education are relatively unknown, I give a close examination of each major text, from the 1860s to 1910, relating them to recurrent themes in his literature. In *Part 3*, I give an overview of the reception of his educational views, and some of examples of their influence. I then go on to highlight some aspects of Tolstoy's thinking on education that may still be relevant to educators 100 years after his death.

It is intended that, although only an introduction, this book reliably represents Tolstoy's wrangling with educational issues and therefore plays its part in securing Tolstoy as an important figure in the history of educational thought. I have not intended to advocate Tolstoy's ideas as such, but I do hope that by considering Tolstoy's views and experiences, readers, particularly teachers, researchers, school managers and policy makers, will be given the opportunity to ask afresh the simple but perplexing questions that Tolstoy did in the early 1860s: how do we know what we should teach? And how should we go about teaching it?

Part 1

An Intellectual Biography of Leo Tolstoy

Chapter 1
Early Experiences and Influences

Leo Nikolayevich Tolstoy was born on 28 August 1828 at Yasnaya Polyana in the Tula district of Russia. The leather sofa on which his mother labored, and on which Tolstoy's own children were later born, still sits in the writer's study next to his writing desk. The Levin of *Anna Karenina* keeps a comparable item of furniture, with a similar history, in his study. This is just one of the many autobiographical similarities, such as being orphaned, that Tolstoy shares with his fictional heroes. Countess Marya, Tolstoy's mother, died when Tolstoy was only a year and a half old; Tolstoy's father, Count Nikolai, seven years later. Tolstoy, his three older brothers, Nikolai, Sergei and Dmitri, and a younger sister, Marya were brought up by two aunts. No portrait of Tolstoy's mother survived, and Tolstoy had no memories of her. In later life, he reflected that his conception of his mother was beautiful as she was 'purely spiritual' in his mind's eye.

Tolstoy's memories of early childhood, in contrast to the exploits of his debauched youth, tell us much about his idealized view of childhood, a time of innocence and spiritual understanding. He explains in his *Recollections* (1902–1908):

> I will [only] tell of one spiritual condition which I experienced several times in my early childhood, and which I think was more important than very many feelings experienced later. It was important because it was my first experience of love, not love of some one person, but love of love, the love of God, a feeling I subsequently experienced only occasionally, but still did experience thanks it seems to me to the fact that its seed was sown in earliest childhood. (RE, 42)

This important experience occurred while Tolstoy played the 'ant brothers.' Tolstoy and the other children had heard of the 'Moravian

Brothers,' a Protestant Christian movement, but the name had become innocently corrupted in their childish parlance, as it sounds similar in Russian, to 'ant hill.' In the house, the ant brothers would hide under chairs and tables, barricading themselves in with blankets, sitting still in the dark. While in this state, the children would enter another world of quietness, contemplation and companionship. They would sometimes talk about what and who they loved, and what would make them and others happy. Outside, in the forest, the ant brothers played another game with a similar theme. Nikolai, the eldest of Tolstoy's brothers, would ask the other children to find the green stick, the inscription on which would explain how to make all men happy. In later life Tolstoy would often recall this story to his own children when he rode past the ravine in Zakaz wood, where the green stick was said to be buried, and where he would finally be laid to rest.

Along with the origin of his religious views in childhood, it would seem that Tolstoy's pedagogical instinct also began at a young age. At the age of 5, Tolstoy attempted to teach his younger step-sister, Dunechka, the French alphabet. The lesson began well, but when Dunechka began to give the wrong answers, to Tolstoy's frustration, she began to cry as did her young teacher.

Education in Tolstoy's early literature

Tolstoy's first published work, *Childhood* (CH, 1852), is indicative of the early educational interests of the young writer. Tolstoy's aim in *Childhood* was to write an account, in first-person detail, of the experiences and development of Nicholas Irtenyev. Although *Childhood* was never intended as autobiography, many of Nicholas' experiences are drawn from Tolstoy's own childhood, as he clarified later in life. The book therefore gives some insight into Tolstoy's own experiences of education, and the origins of his later thought.

Much of the book is given over to a vivid description of the emotional experience of learning. Little attention is paid to the subject content of lessons in favor of a thorough examination of the inner psychology of the young narrator. Tolstoy's belief in the importance of a good, friendly relationship with pupils is exemplified in Nicholas' warm relationship with his German tutor Karl Ivanych, a character based entirely on Tolstoy's own much loved tutor, Fedor Ivanovich Kessel.

Karl Ivanych's leaving is a key episode in *Childhood*. In it Tolstoy juxtaposes the banality of the formal lesson – learning dialogues off by heart – with the honest heartfelt emotion of a reluctant separation. As he thinks about his tutor's leaving, Nicholas cannot concentrate: 'For a long time I looked senselessly at the dialogues but could not read because of the tears that gathered in my eyes at the thought of the approaching parting' (CH, 20).

For Nicholas the important lessons of life are learnt outside his formal lessons. His relationships with adults and other children, playing games and his experiences of nature are particularly valuable. During one game, reminiscent of the ant brothers, Nicholas makes an imaginary horse and carriage out of a shawl and chair with the other children, and reflects, 'If one goes by reality there can be no games. And if there are no games – what will be left?' (CH, 38). The importance of a child's liberty and the playing of games, later endorsed in Tolstoy's pedagogical articles is also emphasized by the form, as well as the content of the novel. The reader is presented with a stream of consciousness, freely exploring the candid observation and moral sentiment of the child, often in contrast to the strict disciplinarian attitudes of adult figures, such as Princess Kornakova, who extols the virtue of corporal punishment.

Childhood was followed by its sequels, *Boyhood* (BH, 1854) and *Youth* (YO, 1857). The trilogy was originally intended to be called the *Four Stages of Development* with a fourth part, never completed, dedicated to later adolescence. The two later books, like the first, share similarities with Tolstoy's own life, and continue to contrast Nicholas' personal development with the worthlessness of formal education. Both are therefore germane to understanding Tolstoy's own experiences as an adolescent, and his views on education.

A key episode, which tells much about Tolstoy's view of discipline and assessment, is described in *Boyhood*. Nicholas can hear the arrival of guests downstairs, but has to await the history teacher to complete a test. For Nicholas, the history lessons consist of pleasing the teacher, rather than learning anything of use to him. While waiting for the teacher to come, Nicholas looks at the page in an attempt to revise his homework. He realizes that he will not be able to learn any of it, especially because he is excited at the prospect of meeting the visitors who awaited him. In the ensuing history lesson, which he finds the 'dullest and hardest' subject, Nicholas receives the lowest mark possible, including a cause for concern over his effort. Tolstoy describes the humiliation of this event in lengthy detail as the harsh tutor records the grade in the ledger, with apparent disregard for the young boy's feelings. Nicholas' brother lies to St Jerome, Karl Ivanych's strict replacement, about this grade, and the boys go free to play. However, the poor report is eventually found by St Jerome, who prompts a violent struggle by seizing Nicholas' arm. Nicholas resists this physical intervention and as a punishment is locked in the furniture store room for a day and a night. While incarcerated, he hears St Jerome whistling overhead, which he considers is merely to goad him in what has become a battle of wills. Tolstoy describes the inner turmoil and psychology of this event which results in Nicholas being scolded by his grandmother.

After this incident, and the humiliation of the punishment that was given to him, Nicholas fails to have a good relationship with his tutor, and they give up on each other. Hatred defines Nicholas' feelings for St Jerome, who although conscientious and well informed as a teacher, fails to build as good a relationship with his young students as Karl Ivanych did. It is not known whether the scuffle between Nicholas and St Jerome was autobiographical, but the character of the French tutor was based on Fyodor Ivanovich's real-life replacement, St Thomas. According to Tolstoy's daughter, Alexandra, Fyodor Ivanovich was loved by Tolstoy, and although he 'did not hold any educational theory,' he loved his pupils. In contrast, the affected Frenchman St Thomas had his 'own theory of education and discipline' (AT, 21). Such an appraisal, reflecting Tolstoy's later criticism of the pomposity of theory-based pedagogical practice as opposed to a more humane, personalized approach, is preempted by Nicholas' evaluation of the two teachers.

> St Jerome was a proud self-satisfied man for whom I felt nothing but the involuntary respect with which all grown-up people inspired me. Karl Ivanych was a funny old usher whom I loved from my soul ... St Jerome, on the other hand, was an educated and handsome young dandy, who tried to put himself on a level with everybody. (BH, 188)

Rather than his formal education, Nicholas' experience of the natural world and his inner reflections provide the real drive of his learning and development. For example, a whole chapter of *Boyhood* is devoted to the passing of a storm. In this episode, joyfully described, the child freely experiences nature, despite getting himself dirty and wet:

> the delicious scent of the wood after the spring storm, the odour of the birches, of the violets, the rotting leaves, the mushrooms, and the wild cherry, is so enthralling that I cannot stay in the brichka [a wooden cart] but jump down from its step, run to the bushes and, though I get sprinkled with the rain-drops that shower down on me, break off wet branches of the flowering wild cherry, stroke my face with them, and revel in their exquisite aroma. Heedless even of the fact that large lumps of mud stick to my boots and that my stockings have long been wet, I run splashing through the mud. (BH, 141)

As *Boyhood* progresses, however, Nicholas' feelings become less innocent, even if they remain natural. Nicholas narrates his feelings about Masha, the servant whom he realizes he is attracted to. He also feels pangs of teenage self-doubt and loathing as he becomes self-conscious about his appearance. Nicholas' problems concentrating, which began in childhood, become worse during adolescence. When thinking about Masha, he paces up and down, his imagination taking control of him.

Youth is preoccupied with Nicholas' life at university and his desultory experiences of attempting to become an adult. It begins with the university entrance examinations. Tolstoy disagreed with formal methods of assessment throughout his career as an educator. In *Youth* he gives a negative portrayal of them, based on his own experiences at university. Tolstoy recounts Nicholas' entrance exams in history, mathematics and Latin. The examinations consisted of queuing with other candidates and drawing questions at random, and then being orally examined by a professor on that question. In these three episodes, Tolstoy, through Nicholas, narrates the emotional experience of the student in what seems a process of favoritism, luck and guile as much as academic ability. He also exposes the perceived vindictive nature of some of the educators, in particular the Latin professor who was considered by students 'a beast who delighted in ruining young men, especially paying students, and who was said to speak only in Latin or Greek' (YO, 257). Nicholas' experiences of his Latin exam confirm the professor's reputation. He favors a student who lodges with him and then reduces the sensitive protagonist to tears, giving him the lowest pass mark.

During his time at University, Nicholas' reflections highlight the pretence of adult life, from the perspective of the innocent bravado of an adolescent trying to grow up. For example, Nicholas attempts smoking. He buys his pipe and paraphernalia and retires to his room. Tolstoy explains the resulting experience in humorous detail as Nicholas' face turns white and he lies on the sofa expecting to die. In a vignette with a similar theme, Tolstoy describes Nicholas' first experience at a drinking party. Nicholas confusedly attempts to fit in, only to be ashamed and disappointed the next day, particularly when he finds his fellow drinkers bragging to other students. Tolstoy would later condemn drinking and smoking and also declare that universities, rather than promoting intellectual growth, merely allow the moral corruption of the young.

An important stage in Nicholas' development at university is his self-diagnosed snobbish fascination with being *comme il faut* or doing things 'properly.' Here we can see the origins of Tolstoy's later indictment of the idle and decadent lives of the upper classes, and the education provided for them. For Nicholas, being *comme il faut* involved projecting himself as someone with class and panache, to speak the best French, to know how to dance and make conversation. He subsequently divided all people into two classes, those who were *comme il faut* and those who were not. Nicholas later saw this phase as illusory, a hallmark of the false education of the superficial upper classes: 'one of the most pernicious and fallacious ideas with which education and society inoculated me' (YO, 338). He reflects that it is strange, given his incapacity for being *comme il faut* and that the obsession hindered his application to developing a profession, and developed contempt for 'nine-tenths of the human race' and ignoring the 'beauty that existed outside of the circle of the *comme il faut*' (YO, 341).

These developments run alongside Nicholas' equally superficial experiences of formal teaching at the university. He describes his first lecture as jovial, but ultimately desultory. The experience of being among so many people of the same age is described more powerfully than the ensuing lecture. 'As soon as I entered the auditorium I felt my personality disappearing' explains Nicholas, but as the lecture begins he is disappointed by the professor's opening comments and spends the rest of the time doodling in his notebook (YO, 362). Nicholas often feels sad: disappointed that real intimacy had not been forged between his educators and his classmates in this context. Tolstoy would later attempt to preserve the personalities of his students in his school, and always favored small classes for this purpose.

After spending winter in an unclear state of mind, getting caught up in imagined love affairs, socializing, focusing on being *comme il faut*, Nicholas suddenly realizes that he will be examined in eighteen subjects, which he has not studied at all. The book ends with Nicholas' failure in these exams, in which he feels humiliated and disgraced. After spending three days morosely without leaving his room, Nicholas begins to write some new 'Rules of Life,' as Tolstoy himself did when faced with the same failure, as a 'moment of repentance and moral expansion' came over him and he firmly resolved never to 'spend another moment idly' (YO, 403).

Tolstoy's early adulthood

The account given in *Youth* of Nicholas' time at university bears some similarities with Tolstoy's own, although the reality of Tolstoy's life was actually far more salacious than the events of his fiction. Tolstoy moved to Kazan with his aunt and brothers, where all the Tolstoy boys would eventually enroll in Kazan University. Here, at the age of 14, Tolstoy was encouraged to visit prostitutes by his older brothers. During his teenage years and early adult life, Tolstoy regularly, even if with regret, continued to use prostitutes and serf girls. His first surviving diary entry of 17 March 1847 is written as he convalesces in a university clinic for sufferers of gonorrhea. The subsequent pages document his strong sexual urges on the one hand, and his desire for moral development and a life devoted to wholesome enterprise, on the other. According to one commentator, LeBlanc (2009), the battle between the sins of the flesh and the life of the spirit continues into Tolstoy's old age, resurfacing in his attitude toward food and its treatment in his literature. Tolstoy certainly felt lifelong self-reproach for his early sexual misdemeanors. Tolstoy's son, Ilya, tells how his father wept when he learnt of his son's sexual innocence, apparently out of remorse for his own moral corruption years ago.

Tolstoy, after two attempts at the entrance exams, entered Kazan University in 1844 to study oriental languages. His absence from lectures soon became habitual and he found it difficult to fit in with his classmates. He failed his end of first year exams because of a family quarrel with a professor, and changed to study Law. In this subject he also achieved low marks, but he was noticed by one professor who encouraged him to study aspects of the theory of law. Tolstoy studied this in earnest, but true to the views later articulated in his writings on education, not so as to achieve success in the exams but out of his interest in the subject. This reinforced Tolstoy's view that what really interested him academically could be more easily studied outside of university, rather than being constrained by a given curriculum. Tolstoy recollected later in life that studying the theory of law had 'opened up for me a new sphere of independent mental work, but the university with its demands not only did not assist such work but hindered it' (RE, 45).

Tolstoy's disillusion with university, artistically rendered throughout *Youth*, remained with him all his life. In her biography of her father, Alexandra Tolstoy provides an anecdote of Tolstoy's sophomore year, which affirms his disenchantment. Tolstoy had been put in the University lock-up with a fellow prisoner, Nazariev, who reported that while incarcerated, Tolstoy had complained bitterly about the worthlessness of the university: 'you have no right to assume ... that we are to go forth from this temple as useful persons in possession of some knowledge. Actually what are we carrying away from this university? ... What are we fitted for?' (AT, 34). In 1847, Tolstoy left Kazan University without taking his exams, and after a second brief dissolute attempt to study Law in 1849 at the University of St Petersburg, he gave up on university completely.

On his return to Yasnaya Polyana in 1849 at the age of 20, Tolstoy first opened a school on the estate, which he had inherited two years earlier. Nothing is known about the school at this time. Tolstoy's early essay 'Temporary Method for Learning Music' (1850) demonstrates his interest in music and harmony and how they may be learnt, but the essay is philosophical in nature and does not appear to be directly linked to any pedagogical enterprise. The school must have been short lived. In the spring of 1851, Tolstoy left Yasnaya Polyana and went to the Caucasus with his brother Nikolai to begin military service, first as a volunteer and then as a Cadet. Tolstoy's novel, *The Cossacks* (TC, 1863), completed a decade later when he was in need of money, is based on his experiences in the region. Its protagonist Olenin, like Tolstoy, is 'a youth who had never completed his university course' (TC, 10).

During his free time in the Caucasus, Tolstoy first began to write. In July 1852 he sent the manuscript of *Childhood* to the journal *The Contemporary* with a letter asking the editor if it were publishable. *The Contemporary* was founded by Pushkin in the 1830s and was the foremost journal of Russian literature at the time. In August Tolstoy received a letter from the editor confirming that it had been accepted. On its publication in the same year, *Childhood* was well received by the literary set, including the famous author Turgenev.

Tolstoy became a commissioned army officer in 1854. During the Crimean war he served on the Danube and then acted as a commanding officer of an artillery battery during the siege of Sevastopol. His experiences prompted him to write more well-received pieces – the Sevastopol 'sketches' (1855–1856). Following the success of these publications and others, Tolstoy was accepted into the Russian literary intelligentsia. A photograph, taken on 15 February 1856, shows Tolstoy in military uniform with the famous group of authors who also published in *The Contemporary*: Grigorovich, Goncharov, Turgenev, Druzhinin and Ostrovsky. Tolstoy left the army later in 1856 and after spending time traveling in Europe during 1857, with Turgenev and alone, he again returned to Yasnaya Polyana. The accounts of Tolstoy's lifelong friend, Fet, describe how during this period Tolstoy would drink, gamble and visit prostitutes all night long – only to then sleep like a 'dead man' until mid-afternoon. Tolstoy's diaries are also testament to his prodigious habits of gambling and fornication. The debts he incurred with these pastimes even necessitated the sale of the original residence at Yasnaya Polyana in which he was born. The house was sold for 500 rubles and moved and erected on another landowner's estate. Tolstoy later laments of his early adulthood in his spiritual autobiography, *A Confession* (AC, 1879).

> I cannot recall those years without horror, loathing, and heartache. I killed people in war, summoned others to duels in order to kill them; gambled at cards; I devoured the fruits of the peasants' labour and punished them; I fornicated and practised deceit. Lying, thieving, promiscuity of all kinds, drunkenness, violence, murder ... there was not a crime I did not commit. (AC, 22)

During this period, despite his numerous indiscretions, Tolstoy was looking for direction. And by the end of 1859, much to the despair of his literary mentor Turgenev, Tolstoy had found it not in literature, but teaching. This contributed to the friction between the two authors, which eventually ended with Tolstoy challenging Turgenev to a duel in 1861. An argument had erupted between them at their mutual friend Fet's house concerning the moral education of Turgenev's daughter. Tolstoy took objection to her father's encouragement for her to repair poor people's clothes and then return them to their owners. Tolstoy remarked that a 'richly dressed girl who manipulates dirty, ill-smelling rags is acting a false and theatrical farce' (BK, 300). This enraged Turgenev who then, over the dining table, threatened to punch Tolstoy. Both the writers left Fet's and Tolstoy later demanded a duel via post, which never took place. Later in his life, the immorality and hypocrisy of acts of charity – while supporting the inequalities of a corrupt social order – would continue to be a matter of passionate conviction for Tolstoy.

Early influences on Tolstoy's educational thought

Despite his lack of success in formal academia, Tolstoy's diaries and letters demonstrate his keen lifelong interest in philosophy and the writings of great thinkers. From his teenage years, Tolstoy was an ardent fan of Rousseau and attributes *The Confessions* (1781) and *Emile* (1762) as having a powerful influence on him – so much so he even replaced the Orthodox cross around his neck with a medallion of Rousseau. Tolstoy was particularly fascinated by Rousseau's *Confessions* which he reread while writing *Childhood* in the Caucasus and which no doubt influenced that work. Indeed, the experiences of Nicholas in *Childhood*,

Boyhood and *Youth* and Olenin in *The Cossacks* have clear parallels with those of Rousseau in *The Confessions*, and with the young protagonist of *Emile*. In his early novellas Tolstoy explores the existence of a natural religious and moral sentiment and champions the innate goodness of the child, or the primitive lives of the Cossacks, in opposition to the corrupt nature of human society.

With regards to pedagogy, for Rousseau, and for Tolstoy, the child must be left to learn naturally. The exercising of a child's volitions coincides with what is necessary for that child's development. Rousseau suggests a position similar to that later endorsed by Tolstoy. In the preface to *Emile*, Rousseau stresses that the 'particular application' of each educational method will depend on the unknowable countless situations that 'other men will be able to concern themselves with' (1762, 35). It would seem that this is exactly the challenge that Tolstoy would later concern himself with at the experimental school at Yasnaya Polyana. At his school, however, Tolstoy did not blindly follow Rousseau. He believed Rousseau's educational thought to be just another abstract theory with no basis in actual practice and experience. This criticism did not stop Tolstoy including an abridged translation of Daniel Defoe's *Robinson Crusoe* in his pedagogical journal – significant because Rousseau refers to the novel in *Emile*.

In addition to Rousseau, Tolstoy was well acquainted with the educational thought of Pestalozzi and Froebel. Although some comparisons can be made between each of these earlier educationists and Tolstoy's views, Tolstoy positioned himself against them. He did not approve of their attempts to formulate theories of learning. Furthermore, he was horrified by the attempts to implement some of these theories in the schools of Europe. Tolstoy believed that teachers who followed a certain method would not act in the interests of their students. It would be better if they acted in accordance to the needs of the students as they arose than on the prescription of a theorist removed from the actual context in which they were teaching.

Rather than Rousseau, Pestalozzi and Froebel, who despite his censure, Tolstoy is often likened to, Tolstoy was more enamored by a writer who, in his fiction at least, denied the value of educational theory – the now obscure German author Berthold Auerbach. Tolstoy read Berthold Auerbach's novel *Neues Leben* (1871) first published in 1851, during May 1860. The novel enshrines many of the same pedagogic principles that Tolstoy later endorses in his educational writings. The American diplomat Eugene Schuyler, a visitor to Yasnaya Polyana in 1868, recounts that during his visit Tolstoy recommended that he should take the book to bed with him to read, claiming that 'it was owing to this that I started a school for my peasants and became interested in popular education' (SL, 274). No translation of this obscure novel exists in English, and given its influence on Tolstoy, it is worth considering certain passages of Auerbach's work in some detail.

The story starts with two strangers meeting, one of whom is planning to take up a new office as a teacher in the German village Erlenmoos. The other one, for now, is known as a refugee who has escaped from prison and is about to flee the country. The teacher wishes to emigrate to America so they decide to switch lives. The 'refugee' now takes the name Eugen Baumann combining his name and that of the teacher, who in turn goes to America. To prepare Eugen for teaching, the teacher Baumann explains an anti-theoretical pedagogical position, which echoes the main thesis of Tolstoy's journal *Yasnaya Polyana*:

> The art to become a proper educator – this book we lack. Remember this above all: when you come to a school, there are children combed and uncombed behind the desks, then you clear your throat and interpret silently for yourself: All that you know is not useful, all your methods from Adam to Wurst and Becker are useless and you are now the best teacher. Ask your children, look in their notebooks and go on. Develop your method together and it will work just fine. All abstract methodology is nothing but system-raging mirror-fencing [*systemwütige Spiegelfechterei*]; the best a teacher can achieve in his school comes from him personally, from the pure drive of nature. (1871, 14)

When Eugen begins to teach, he puts these ideals into practice. He allows the pupils to vote to decide who is the most capable representative to assist the teacher, and he encourages his students to sing to get away from the 'abstract method' (1871, 153). Auerbach further expounds anti-theoretical, child-centered pedagogical views through Baumann's letters and the advice of Eugen's teacher colleague, Deeger. Deeger explains the significance of students acquiring and developing vernacular speech as a means of empowerment: to enable a child to become his or her own master and teacher. Accordingly, to allow pupils to learn for themselves and to become equal to their teachers, the main principles for education, for Deeger are 'love and patience' (1871, 39). Baumann corroborates the importance of such pedagogical principles, writing to Eugen:

> You are executing something hallowed, never hesitate, and when you become anxious, think, that to all who know of you or will once hear of you, you will give the faith in mankind and the finest act of sacrifice, you must not, you cannot wear down and desert, you would destroy the finest faith and would become a traitor to the hearts which will be edified by you. Never forget your holy profession, which reaches far, far beyond the closed space of a school room. (1871, 139)

The religious nature of education is further explained by Deeger, who asserts that although the final ends of education can be religious, the process must be heuristic, free and natural, building 'bottom-up' from personal experience to religious understanding, rather than vice versa. These views again preempt Tolstoy's later religious and educational thought, making reference to the passage in Mark 10 on which Tolstoy would also later draw for his story 'Little Girls Wiser than Men':

> Religion is the copestone on the construction of education which you cannot make into the cornerstone. A child which only yet begins [in] the knowledge of life, can not stand already at its end, where faith lends itself; one wants a surrender of knowledge, before the knowledge was even there but did not merely start. The master of all of us has spoken the highest principle of pedagogy in the simple words: let the children come to me and do not stop them – yes, let them come, let their drive to higher knowledge [come], but don't thrust nor push them; let them come with their artless [natural] questions, but don't snatch them or catechize a foreign world into them. (1871, 63)

The advice of his mentors leads Eugen to develop a humanistic concept of religious education based on the natural experience of the child to freely comprehend and negotiate their way to the truth. Like Tolstoy, Eugen romanticizes the spiritual intuition of the child and suggests that the child's uncorrupted innocence can be both a metaphor and paradigm for the spiritual development of adults:

> We have to overcome the oppositions and the destruction of the old to win new and beautiful forms for our actual thinking and feeling. We need to become naïve enough again for the new and innermost lifted sentiments to make festive garments and to wear them. Religion has its symbols put on the turning points of being, where man thrives to outwardly express his interior, at the birth of a child, at the chosen entry into life ... it must [come to] be that humanity wins the like-minded, who are the living and personal expression of the highly aroused heart. Only then will freedom become reality. (1871, 75)

Eugen's understanding of piety again echoes the Rosseauian deistic, universalism of Tolstoy's later religious expositions and the spiritual revelations of major characters in his novels. He explains how all humans are subject to the same interior religious instinct:

> Everybody must worship something greater, be that written inside a catechism or elsewhere ... Every man, whoever it may be, no one is too small, has moments, shines, and there are people in whom this noble sentiment spreads over their entire lives. To worship the majesty within ourselves and outside of ourselves, that [is what] I call being pious. (1871, 99)

Eugen Baumann also shares other similar views with Tolstoy. He dislikes the village's Countess speaking French as it appears snobbish and he disagrees with the death penalty. The parallels are more than matters of principle, however, as the novel later proves to be prophetic of Tolstoy's life story. As *Neues Leben*'s main narrative device unfolds, we learn that Eugen the 'refugee,' is actually Count Eugen Falkenberg. The Count had rid himself of his aristocratic life because he believed that the aristocracy was morally corrupt and that such a difference between rich and poor was unacceptable. In the conclusion of the story, the case of life imitating art becomes even more striking. As Tolstoy did later, Eugen decides to marry, builds his own house, and founds a school for the people in which the boundaries between master and servant are ignored, and where Eugen intends to use the act of teaching to perfect his personality.

The tour of Europe

In 1859 Tolstoy set up a school at Yasnaya Polyana for the second time. As he taught, his interest in educational thought grew, and he read widely on the subject. To further his knowledge of contemporary educational methods, Tolstoy returned to Europe between the summer of 1860 and the spring of 1861. In the south of France he witnessed the death of his consumptive brother, Nikolai, which had a profound effect on him. In spite of this, he devoted a large proportion of his time and energy observing, and reflecting upon, the pedagogical practices of Germany, France and England. Tolstoy had a negative impression of the urban, industrial nature of the leading nations of Europe, and developed what he describes as 'a loathing for civilisation' (TD, 160). He was also horrified by the stupefying effect of the public education instituted in modern European countries, particularly Germany. He records in his diary many of the views later articulated in his educational writings. Education should promote equality and be based on freedom – the opposite of what Tolstoy observed in Germany and France. The schools he visited there, Tolstoy records in his diary, were terrible. The children lived in fear of corporal punishment and were taught solely by rote and dictation. Consequently they became 'morally deformed.'

While abroad Tolstoy met a number of leading intellectuals and political figures, including the exiled Russian revolutionary Herzen, the French socialist Proudhon and Julius Froebel, the nephew of the famous pedagogue Friedrich Froebel. Of meeting Tolstoy, Froebel noted in his memoirs that Tolstoy had remarked that at that time, unlike the population of continental Europe, the Russian people had as yet not been corrupted by a damaging system of national education. Tolstoy had hinted at his hopes to provide an alternative:

> Progress in Russia must emanate from national education, which will give better results in our country than in Germany, because the Russian people are not yet perverted, whereas the Germans resemble a child has been for several years undergoing a wrong education. (BK, 274–275)

During his trip, Tolstoy spent 20 days in London, where he claims he was 'in a fog literally and metaphorically' (TL, 143). With a letter of introduction from Matthew Arnold, then an official at the Education Department, Tolstoy visited a number of schools. At one of these, the Practicing School attached to the College of St Mark in Chelsea, he asked the boys to write a composition about what they had done in the morning on the way to school. Tolstoy took these compositions home with him to Russia, where they are now part of the Tolstoy archive. They are reproduced in Lucas' book *Tolstoy in London* (1979). Tolstoy seems to have collected samples of children's work from other schools. One account of a teacher in Germany, included in Biryukov's compilation of biographical resources, tells of how Tolstoy watched a lesson in Weimar and then asked to take the children's exercise books. When the teacher insisted that he could not give away the students' notebooks, Tolstoy returned with some notepaper and asked for the students to copy out the work – which they subsequently repeated. He then rolled up their work and took it with him (BK, 292–294).

It is sometimes recounted by biographers, such as Troyat (1968, 203), Yegorov (1997, 649) and Simmons (1973, 59), that while in London, Tolstoy heard Dickens speak on education. This would seem to rest on an account by Apostolov that quotes Tolstoy as reporting: 'I have seen Dickens in a large hall. He was lecturing on education. At that time I did not understand spoken English well' (1926, 71). However, Lucas has argued convincingly that it is likely that Tolstoy did not see a lecture on education but a reading by Dickens of his *Christmas Carol* and *The Boots of the Holly Tree Inn* held at St James' Hall Piccadilly as advertised in *The Times* newspaper during Tolstoy's stay.

Tolstoy's negative impressions of contemporary European methods of instruction led him to think about his own pedagogical convictions. On 3 April, while in Germany, he writes in his diary that he could not sleep due to his desire to 'solve the problem of upbringing and education.' Two weeks later, Tolstoy's views were beginning to set. Of a school he visited in Weimar, Tolstoy jotted down two criticisms that would later become central to the arguments articulated in his pedagogical journal: his dislike of abstract theory and the meddling of government in education: 'A very stupid school, showing what institutions imposed from above can lead to. Theory without practice' (TD, 160). On the same day after enjoying a walk in the woods Tolstoy reflected that the job of the school is not 'to impart knowledge' but to 'impart the respect for and the idea of knowledge.' Tolstoy writes that after having this consoling thought, he was again able to sleep peacefully.

In Berlin on the last leg of his journey, Tolstoy had another experience that confirmed the direction his educational ideas should take. On 21 April 1861 Tolstoy met his favorite author, Berthold Auerbach. Without giving the author his real name, Tolstoy introduced himself to the writer as Eugen Baumann – the fictional aristocrat-turned-teacher of the novel *Neues Leben*. The impact of the visit on Tolstoy is clearly recorded in his enthusiastic diary entry of the same day: 'Auerbach!!!! A most charming man' (TD, 161). Auerbach later confessed of the incident to Schuyler, the American diplomat who met both writers, that he was shocked at the 'strange-looking man' who claimed to be Eugen Baumann because he was worried the man was going to sue for libel (SL, 275).

Tolstoy's dislike of educational theory, something he shared with Auerbach's Eugen, had been confirmed by his negative observations of the German education system. Such a view of the German national character later becomes part of *War and Peace*, personified in the German military 'theorist-general' Pfuhl. As Tolstoy explains in a famous passage comparing the conceit of the European nations, all the nations have different reasons for their self-confidence but Germans are by far the worst, for 'only Germans could base their self-confidence on an abstract idea – on science, that is, the supposed possession of absolute truth' (WP, 757). In contrast, according to Tolstoy, a Russian draws his confidence from knowing that he does not know anything: 'he does not believe that it is possible to know anything completely' (WP, 757–758). Such a 'Russian' view is a significant component of Tolstoy's educational thought: a teacher should eschew theoretical presuppositions, in favor of instigating an ongoing experiment, in constant search of innovation, sensitive to the needs of the students. On his return to Russia, Tolstoy, spurred on by his experiences abroad, would set out such thoughts and his reasons for them, in his own educational journal *Yasnaya Polyana*.

Chapter 2

Tolstoy the Educator

After the harvest of 1859, Tolstoy decided to start a school for the peasants of Yasnaya Polyana. On its opening day, 22 peasant children in their best clothes, some accompanied by their parents, arrived outside Tolstoy's house. To greet his new students, Tolstoy walked into the small crowd asking the boys and girls if they wanted to study. Straightaway he nicknamed one of the students 'Vasska,' Russian for 'tom-cat' – a pet name later to be used for Denisov in *War and Peace* much to Natasha's amusement. The student's real name was Vasily Morozov, and is given the pseudonym 'Fyedka' in Tolstoy's pedagogical articles.

In his reminisces, Vasily Morozov describes his experiences at the school. On the first day the children went up the stairs of the estate house, for many the first time they had seen inside a nobleman's home. Tolstoy took down their names in a ledger, and then wrote the beginning of the Russian alphabet on a blackboard. After this, he dismissed the children with the instruction to return tomorrow.

The next day the children returned. The first lesson consisted of the instruction in the Russian alphabet as a whole class, with Tolstoy prompting the students if they had problems remembering. According to Morozov, Tolstoy spoke kindly, made jokes with the children and refused to be called 'Lordship' preferring his first name and patronymic Lev Nikolayevich. Tolstoy believed that the most important quality of a teacher was to respect the students and the conditions in which the peasants lived, and above all, to be honest. Such is the description Tolstoy would later give of Levin in *Anna Karenina*:

> Pretence about anything whatever may deceive the cleverest and shrewdest of men, but the dullest child will see through it, no matter how artfully it may be disguised. Whatever failings Levin had, there was not an atom of pretence in him, and so the children showed

him the same friendliness that they read in their mother's face. (AK, 288)

There is evidence that Tolstoy was not always an approachable and kind teacher, however, as recounted by Maude (1917). One visitor to the school in 1862, Ouspensky, read some of the students' compositions while Tolstoy was out of the room. In one of them a student had written an account of Tolstoy losing his temper with another child, Savoskin. It described Tolstoy calling Savoskin to the board to answer a question regarding arithmetic. When he did not give an answer, Tolstoy pulled the child's hair. Ouspensky challenged Tolstoy about this when he returned, to which Tolstoy replied 'Life in this world is a hard task' (1917, 253).

The number of children attending the school fluctuated, depending on parental circumstances, agricultural necessities and the changing reputation of the school. In November 1861, Tolstoy claims that the total number of enrolled students was 40, with around 30 students attending on any given day. These students, mainly boys, between the ages of 6 and 12, were split into 3 classes by age and ability: Class 1, the senior class, Class 2, the intermediate and Class 3, the junior. In the senior class there were 10 pupils who were Tolstoy's favorites. During the winter when there was no agricultural work to be done, adult students would also attend the school, although according to Tolstoy they were often subjected to the derision of their friends, family and the younger pupils of the school.

Although secondary literature sometimes stresses the extreme libertarian nature of the school, there was clearly some semblance of organization at Yasnaya Polyana. It had a bell on the porch and a timetable hanging in the hall. The 12 subjects studied, as listed by Tolstoy at the beginning of his essay 'The School at Yasnaya Polyana' (TSYP, January, March and April 1862), written during the months of November and December 1861, were Reading, Writing, Calligraphy, Grammar, Sacred History, Russian History, Drawing, Technical Drawing, Singing, Mathematics, Talks on the Natural Sciences and Divinity. Tolstoy also refers to the 'daily routine' which was followed from the first lesson at 8 in the morning, a long lunch break beginning at 2, followed by evening lessons which ended at 8 or 9 at night. The lesson activities were changed during the course of the day according to the mood and alertness of pupils, and the natural or candle light available in the classroom. In the evening lessons, singing, experiments, storytelling, reading and essay-writing were favored. Tolstoy and the other teachers would plan their lessons together for each week on a Sunday, although their plans would be altered according to the perceived needs of the students and the opinion of the students with regard to their own needs as they went through the week.

Pyotr Morozov, of no relation to Vasily Morozov the student, was a teacher who worked at the Yasnaya Polyana school. He had fond recollections of it and later returned to help Tolstoy with his renewed pedagogical experiments in the 1870s. In his memoirs he describes how, when he first arrived at the school, he thought Tolstoy was the boiler-stoker as he was wearing a peasant's sheepskin jacket. He tells of how the students were noisy when he walked through the door on his first day, shouting about how the other teachers had not survived long. The students were sitting in groups, tackling whatever tasks they wanted to, all asking for Tolstoy's attention, shouting 'Lev Nikolayevich!' Morozov comments that the school was different from others; it had an unusually 'straightforward atmosphere' where 'each person felt at home' (PVM, 187). Vasily Morozov (Fyedka) corroborates this view. He claims that Class 1, to whom Tolstoy was particularly attached, would stay long after the juniors had gone. Tolstoy had a captivating, authoritative presence that 'seemed to penetrate to something deep in the heart of the pupil' (PVM, 210), but at the same time was patient and good humored: 'he would miss no opportunity of a joke and of having a laugh' (PVM, 213).

During the early 1860s, Tolstoy endeavored to set up similar schools around the district modeled on Yasnaya Polyana. In October 1861 Tolstoy writes that three such schools were opened and operational, with another ten pending. As Justice of the Peace, he applied to the Tula Provincial Bureau of Peasant Affairs with a proposal for setting up village schools throughout the area. For this purpose he recruited teachers, mainly ex-gymnasium students, whom he would mentor, meeting every Sunday to discuss pedagogical practice and the contents of the *Yasnaya Polyana* journal. Biryukov (1906) lists the names of ten teachers employed by Tolstoy in such a capacity in Tolstoy's jurisdiction.

By mid-winter 1861, Tolstoy claimed in a letter to his friend Botkin that there were twenty-one such schools in the area.

As the Yasnaya Polyana school itself became more popular and Tolstoy's experiments more adventurous, he moved the school from his own house to the annex. Here it occupied three rooms, one room serving as a museum of natural history specimens where Tolstoy's German assistant, Gustav Keller – whom Tolstoy had recruited on his travels in Europe – would perform experiments on Sundays. In the summer, lessons were held outside and the students would also go once a week into the woods, looking for flowers and mushrooms as part of their botany studies.

The Yasnaya Polyana school and the origins of Tolstoy's literature

Tolstoy's experiences teaching at the Yasnaya Polyana school are well documented in his pedagogical articles. These give much insight into his views on education and the influence the school had on his literary development. In the evenings, Tolstoy describes how he found the mood of the children quite different. He regarded this as a good time for scientific experiments, which for him took on a fairy-tale quality, as he later retells as 'natural science stories' in his textbooks. Members of the senior class would stay with Tolstoy throughout the evening listening to his stories while, in exchange, they told him the local folklore of witches and wizards in the forest. In these frank exchanges Tolstoy discussed with his students thoughts of giving up his property and his plans to marry. After their imaginations had been kindled by reading stories, Tolstoy would sometimes take his students out walking at night. The outside environment, Tolstoy explains, made an excellent place for learning to take place, as opposed to the formal constraints of the classroom:

> Outside the school, in the open air, there establish themselves, despite all the liberty granted there, new relations between pupils and teachers, of greater liberty, greater simplicity and greater confidence, – those very relations, which, to us, appear as the ideal of what the school is to strive after. (TSYP, 247)

Tolstoy describes a key moment for himself and his students taking place on one such walk, that would have a long-lasting influence on his fiction and wider thought. One particular evening after reading Gogol, Fyedka decided that he wanted to walk in the woods and so Tolstoy and some of the senior boys went out into the forest. During this walk, Tolstoy told them stories about the Caucasus which he would eventually publish as *The Cossacks* and 'Hadji Murad' (1896–1904). One of the stories included, as Tolstoy describes in the final pages of *The Cossacks*, a guerrilla fighter singing before he died. This prompted an important question for Fyedka, 'Why sing?' This was not meant as why the fighter should sing before he dies, but rather why sing at all? The boys and Tolstoy then began to discuss the nature and purpose of art. Tolstoy describes the ability of the children to discuss these great issues with complexity and with sensitivity. However he felt unable to answer the children's questions satisfactorily at the time. He recounts of this conversation with Fyedka: 'What he was asking me was what art was for, and I did not dare and did not know how to explain to him' (TSYP, 251). Tolstoy was not to give his final answer to this question until his late essay on the topic, *What is Art?* (1898).

In another important episode with the senior class, as the evening gloom set in around the classroom, Tolstoy, frustrated with his previous attempts to teach Russian history, began telling the story of Russia, starting with the most recent history, with some success. He writes:

> I have also made other experiments in teaching modern history, and they have been very successful. I told them the history of the Crimean campaign, and the reign of Emperor Nicholas, and the year 1812. All this I told almost in a fairy-tale tone, as a rule, historically incorrect, and grouping the events about some person. The greatest success was obtained, as was to have been expected, by the story with the war with Napoleon. This class has remained a memorable event in our life. I shall never forget it. (TSYP, 327)

Tolstoy goes on to describe the children's interest as they engaged with the familiar story of the French advance, the burning of Moscow and the eventual Russian victory. Tolstoy did not feel that this was historically accurate, it was 'not history, but a fanciful tale rousing the national sentiment' (TSYP, 330). As Eikhenbaum (1982b) documents in detail, this lesson was nothing other than the oral prototype of *War and Peace*. Indeed, such patriotic and romantic sentiments, the successful elements of the lesson, are still evident in the novel.

Pupils as coauthors

As well providing an impetus for his subsequent literature, Tolstoy's work in the classroom also led him to write short stories in collaboration with his pupils. In his composition class, Tolstoy suggested to his students that they should write stories based on proverbs. One such proverb was 'he feeds you with a spoon and pokes you in the eye with the handle.' Although members of the class seemed interested in the task at first, they soon asked Tolstoy to write the story himself. Tolstoy rose to the challenge and began to write a narrative based on the saying. As Tolstoy did this, the children became interested in what he was writing and began to crowd around him. Tolstoy read out what he had written. This prompted a discussion about the direction of the narrative and its internal coherence. Now drawn in, Fyedka and his friend Syomka began to finish the story, enthused by the prospect of the story being published as a collaboration with Tolstoy, and they worked well into the night. This evening was an important moment for the boys and yet another revelation to Tolstoy:

> I cannot convey the feeling of excitement, joy, fear and almost repentance which I experienced in the course of that evening. I felt from that day onwards a new world of delights and sufferings had opened for him [Fyedka] – the world of art. It seemed as though I had been prying into something which no one ever has the right to see, the birth of the mysterious flower of poetry. (SWTP, 227)

Tolstoy believed that he had unlocked something innate in the children and allowed them to flourish; he explains how the details of the composition work and how the moral of the story is conveyed through artistic description of the events. Although he was a published author of some merit, he could only just understand the creative powers of the two semiliterate peasant boys.

In an ironic twist that also illustrates much about Tolstoy's school, the original manuscript of the story ended up being burnt. A craze for making paper bangers had taken over the school. The students themselves became so annoyed at this that all the paper bangers were placed in a burning stove. With the papers went the manuscript for the story. Tolstoy laments that he 'never felt any loss so hard as the loss of those three closely written sheets; I was in despair' (SWTP, 231). Seeing the disappointment of their teacher, Fyedka and Syomka came to Tolstoy's house and in his study wrote the story again from the beginning.

The experience of writing the story was also an important one for Fyedka. He writes in his memoirs that he was incredibly excited at the prospect of printing his article under the names of Makarov, Morozov and Tolstoy, a conversation recorded in equal detail by Tolstoy. Later one page of the original manuscript was found. The final version of the story, printed in the *Yasnaya Polyana* journal was Tolstoy's edited amalgamation of the two.

'He Feeds You with a Spoon and Pokes You in the Eye with the Handle' by Makarov, Morozov and Tolstoy (May 1862) can be seen as a prototype for Tolstoy's later didactic folk stories. It has a clear Christian subtext, reminiscent of the biblical story of the Good Samaritan, of a peasant wanting to do good – along with a child hero whose innate goodness allows him to see the error of the anti-hero – the peasant's wife. The peasant's wife was Fyedka's idea, and she bears many similarities to his own step-mother.

The story line is simple. An old man is found laid out in the cold snow. The peasants think he could be dead and fear touching the dead body. Semyon, the peasant hero of the story, checks the body against the advice of his neighbors and the will of his wife. The man is alive and he is taken into Semyon's household. His wet and cold clothes are taken off to dry and he is given food and rest, all begrudgingly by Semyon's irritable wife. The old man is an old decorated soldier from the Caucasus, and forms a friendship with the peasant's son, Seryozhka, and begins to teach him to read. Both summer and autumn come and Semyon still does not send the old man away. Semyon's wife becomes increasingly annoyed with the extra mouth to feed, and one day when Semyon is out, she angrily criticizes the old man for not working to help the family. The old man accidentally knocked over a cooking pot, and then the samovar, breaking it. The woman shouts again at the old man and he leaves for good. He meets the disappointed Seryozhka, gives him his ABC book, and answers the question, 'Why are you going?' by explaining that 'they fed me with a spoon and poked me in the eye with the handle.' The story ends with Seryozhka's inconsolable weeping as Semyon shouts at his neighbor, who takes his wife's side in the ensuing argument.

Another story printed in the *Yasnaya Polyana* journal is 'The Life of a Soldier's Wife' (Morozov, September 1862). This was written by Fyedka over the summer break with Tolstoy's encouragement. Tolstoy amended the work slightly, claiming them to be 'vulgar' additions. The story is a simple narrative told from a child's perspective, based on Fyedka's own experiences. His father drinks all that he earns. The family has no money, and as his father does not contribute toward the taxes, he is sent off to be a soldier. His sister marries; his grandmother and newborn sibling die of poverty and malnutrition. However, when Fyedka's father returns, he brings with him a significant amount of money, declares that he has given up drinking, and talks of plans to begin to work, buy a cottage and some animals. In the article 'Should We Teach the Peasant Children to Write, or Should They Teach Us?' (SWTP, September 1862), Tolstoy claims that this story was like nothing else he had encountered in Russian literature. He commends it to critics as an example of a touching story relayed in powerful and simple, natural language. Such insights into the psychology of children and the moral power of narrative were an important influence on Tolstoy, and his experiences while teaching brought him closer to understanding the lives of the peasants.

The end of the experiment

On 6 July 1862, while Tolstoy was taking the kumys cure in Samara, as he did at other times in his life when suffering from exhaustion, three carriages of senior officials, soldiers and police under the command of Colonel Durnovo, arrived at Yasnaya Polyana. They arrested the student teachers who were staying on the estate during the vacation, and for two days searched the house and school. To Tolstoy's annoyance, fully expressed in a letter to Tsar Alexander II, they went through all of Tolstoy's papers and diaries. Tolstoy explains to the Tsar that such treatment was unfair due to his conscientious service in the field of public education, and that consulting the *Yasnaya Polyana* journal, which expressed his 'sincere convictions' could have proved that such a search was unnecessary. He laments the effect of the police's search on the peasants' opinion of him, which he considered 'essential' to his 'chosen occupation – the founding of schools for the people' (TL, 164). The raid is not mentioned by Vasily Morozov in his memoirs, but its effect was as Tolstoy suspected. Of the following autumn of 1862, Morozov reports:

> it was as if a sort of silent strike had been declared: instead of the former seventy pupils only fifteen turned up. Practically nobody came from the distant villages and nearby districts. Many of our Yasnaya Polyana children held off because of their parents. (VSM, 218)

In his letters describing the raid, Tolstoy protests his innocence and that of his student teachers, although it is likely that these young men did harbor revolutionary ideas – something which Tolstoy claimed he had eradicated through the process of teaching at his school. Tolstoy's letter to the Tsar states his bafflement as to the reason for the search but his daughter Alexandra gives some explanation in her biography. One of the teachers had been under surveillance for his revolutionary ideas and a detective Michael Shipov, also known as Zimin, had been tracking him. Zimin had been arrested for drunkenness and tried to appease the authorities by making up evidence against Tolstoy, claiming that there was a concealed printing press at Yasnaya Polyana (AT, 143). Biryukov in his treatment of the raid argues that Tolstoy had angered local landowners by favoring the newly emancipated peasants in his role as a Justice of the Peace. Tolstoy's enemies had therefore made a false accusation in an attempt to undermine his position, which he soon resigned.

After the raid the school persisted until 1863 but Tolstoy rarely came to it, leaving his teachers to continue the work he had started. The *Yasnaya Polyana* journal continued to be heavily censored, delaying its publication by months, and Tolstoy also soon abandoned this enterprise. There had been another development in his circumstances that led to the waning of his interest in the school. He had fallen in love with Sofya Behrs and married her in Moscow at the end of September 1862.

Tolstoy's experience teaching had a profound effect on him. Eikhenbaum concludes his analysis of this period that 'the Yasnaya Polyana School turned out to be not so much a school for the peasant children as it was for Tolstoy himself. It 'formed' him; that is, it returned him to writing' (Eikhenbaum, 1982b, 62). It would seem that Tolstoy's educational endeavours also relate to the evolution of his religious and political ideas. The school from its outset had been, in part, politically motivated. Tolstoy wrote to a friend in January 1862 that 'until there is greater equality of education there won't be a better system of government' (TL, 153). Furthermore, the education of the people would never take place if the government controlled the schools, which would only 'deform' pupils' moral faculties through indoctrination. Indeed, the great art that Tolstoy's school produced – the stories by the peasant children, that Tolstoy loved so dearly and wished to distribute widely – had political implications. The stories side with the plight of the humble poor and are in that sense, evocative of the Christian ethic of Dickens.

The school clearly provoked Tolstoy's interest in religious issues. Tolstoy's reading on pedagogy brought him into contact with theologians, in particular Luther and Schleiermacher, and his journal featured articles on religious figures of interest written by Sofya Behrs' sister – one on Luther, and another on the Prophet Muhammad. Tolstoy's experience teaching 'sacred history' gave him greater insight into the Bible and its reception by children. Preempting Tolstoy's later interest in reconciling scientific materialism with religion, Tolstoy clearly believed that the Bible's pedagogical efficacy was relevant to the debate between atheists and believers. Only when the materialists had a textbook of equal power could religion be declared dead: 'Let those who deny the educational value of the Bible, who say that the Bible has outlived its usefulness, invent such a book' writes Tolstoy (TSYP, 311). Tolstoy's correspondence at this time also demonstrates his perception of the effect the school had on his religious views. In a letter to his first cousin once removed,

Countess Alexandra Tolstaya, dated 7 August 1862, Tolstoy explains about the police search and how it spoiled his sacred enterprise:

> You know what the school has meant to me ever since I opened it: it has been my whole life, it has been my monastery, my church, in which I sought and found refuge from all the anxieties, doubts and temptations of life. (TL, 160)

In an earlier letter to Countess Alexandra, Tolstoy writes how the religious instruction of the school followed the real life events in the village. He states that he taught about the last rites when an old peasant died and about the saints on their respective saints' days. He claims that he was so successful in such lessons, that he even taught the priest how to teach. To this Tolstoy remarks to his relative, known for her piety, 'and you still think I'm a godless fellow' (TL, 150).

Tolstoy also claimed that his school reeducated the university students whom he mentored, even suggesting that it promoted the conversion of 11 of the 12 university students he employed, from revolutionary tendencies to good Christians:

> Everyone arrived with manuscripts of Herzen in his trunk and revolutionary ideas in his head, and everyone without exception burned his manuscripts within a week, discarded revolutionary ideas, and taught the peasant children Bible history and prayers, and handed round the Gospels for reading at home. (TL, 161)

The reopening of the school

During the rest of the 1860s, with the school closed, Tolstoy focused on writing *War and Peace*. Despite this lull in educational activity, it is clear that Tolstoy did not doubt his skills as a teacher and educator. In November 1865 he wrote to Countess Alexandra giving advice on how to teach. She had been appointed as tutor to Alexander II's daughter, the Grand Duchess Marya, who would subsequently marry The Duke of Edinburgh. In his letter Tolstoy writes that teaching is a frightening task – as he realized when he taught at Yasnaya Polyana. The job of a tutor carries a sacred responsibility, but this should be matched with feeling rather than cold rationality:

> The tutor is the first person very close to them on whom they make observations and draw conclusions which they then apply to all mankind. And the more a person is endowed with human passions, the richer and more fruitful these observations. (TL, 202)

In the letter, Tolstoy endorses views similar to those of Auerbach's Eugen: the teacher should act on instinct because such human, passionate influence is good for children but 'rational, logical influence has a harmful effect' (TL, 202). 'To educate by reason' is a mistake as no child is purely rational. Rather, it is the personality of the teacher – their very humanity – that is crucial. It is better to admit mistakes than to put oneself on a pedestal and make out that one is infallible. As children are more intuitive than adults, it is not possible to deceive them.

After *War and Peace*, Tolstoy's next major project was to return to education. This time his concern was to write a textbook for learning Russian – an 'Azbuka' or Russian primer. This was partly inspired by his opinion of the unsuitability of the textbooks available for teaching his son Sergei. It was also the result of his rekindled desire to create suitable literature with which all social classes could learn to read. Tolstoy first drafted the *Azbuka* in 1868. In the same year he asked Eugene Schuyler, of the American embassy, to acquire materials from America on basic literacy, which he consulted in preparation for his textbook.

Tolstoy reopened the school in the early 1870s for the purpose of testing his ideas. As with the school of the 1860s, the lessons took place in the annex, what the family called 'the other house,' or sometimes in the front hall of the main family residence. Tolstoy involved his own children in teaching the school at this time, which Sergei attributes to the influence of the Lancaster Method – of which Tolstoy had learned in the 1860s. Aged 6 at the time, Tolstoy's son Ilya writes in his memoirs of the peasant children and the smell of their sheepskin jackets:

> Lesson time was very gay and lively. The children did exactly as they pleased, sat wherever they liked, ran about from place to place, and answered questions simultaneously, interrupting in their eagerness to

help one another remember what had been read. If one of them left something out, another promptly sprang up with an answer, then a second, and a third, and the story or sum was reconstructed by their joint efforts. Papa particularly valued the colourful and original language of the pupils. (IT, 18)

Ilya recounts that one day at the school a child ran past Tolstoy in the classroom. Tolstoy asked him where he was going, to which the child replied 'to uncle, to bite off a piece of chalk.' When the boy had gone, Tolstoy reminded the teachers of the aim of the school: 'It's not for us to teach them, but for them to teach us' (IT, 18).

Tolstoy intended his *Azbuka* to be compatible with a number of different teaching strategies and is in this sense atheoretical. Yet the very structure of Tolstoy's text demonstrates his conception of learning to read. First the students are to learn the alphabet, then common words and their constituent syllables. Once known, the commonly occurring syllables can then be applied by the student to understand new words as they occur in the texts provided – which become progressively longer and contain increasingly complex words and sentences. Tolstoy's approach was a contrast to the popular 'new' or phonetic method. This approach involved students first learning phonemes, the smallest particles of sounds, and then using them to form words.

The *Azbuka* was published in 1872. Tolstoy believed that the first edition would sell out quickly. However, the book was a flop. It was comparatively expensive, ineffectively marketed and most importantly, the Ministry of Education did not endorse it. The Tsarist regime was still suspicious of Tolstoy's 'free' pedagogy and many of the stories, whether based on foreign sources or Tolstoy's original ideas, were considered strange. The lack of a clear system of instruction, the result of Tolstoy's views on theory, also made the *Azbuka* appear methodologically weak.

Despite these criticisms, Tolstoy continued to value the primer highly and worked on a new improved edition, the *New Azbuka* with four supplementary reading books, *Russian Books for Reading*. On 16 December 1873, Tolstoy's wife wrote in her diary:

> He has compiled four books for children, proudly working on them with the firm conviction that the work is good and useful. His ABC

book is a terrible failure, and this, especially at first, grieved and annoyed him considerably. (ST, 59)

Like his earlier pedagogical works, Tolstoy's *Azbuka* had a political agenda. The textbook did not just have the aims of literacy at its heart. It was intended, from its inception, as a way of bringing the different social classes together, through a universal literature and education. The *Azbuka* remained important to Tolstoy throughout his life. Tolstoy's son Sergei recounts that Tolstoy would never recommend any of his own books for his own children except the *Azbuka* and the *Russian Books for Reading*. During the controversy and redrafting of his will in 1908, Tolstoy wanted to make sure that even if all his works would not be publicly available without copyright, the textbooks would. They belonged to the Russian people. Nevertheless, on its publication the *New Azbuka* also failed to be approved by the Ministry, but the accompanying *Russian Books for Reading* were recommended as a reading supplement for school libraries.

The 'great battle' with the pedagogues

Tolstoy's involvement with education in the 1870s led him to observe contemporary pedagogic practice in Russia. This provoked criticism similar to that levied at the schools of continental Europe a decade earlier. Tolstoy writes that when visiting schools in Moscow, he felt as though he was watching drowning children: 'Oh my, if only I can pull them out, and whom shall I save first, whom next. What is being drowned is that most precious thing, that spiritual something' (AT, 202). The failure of the primer, and Tolstoy's concern with contemporary methods of education, particularly the phonetic method, led to what Eikhenbaum describes as the 'great battle' with the pedagogues. This public confrontation is well documented by Eikhenbaum in his study *Tolstoy in the Seventies* (1982a), and the summary below is based on Eikhenbaum's account.

In June 1873 Tolstoy had written a letter, published in the *Moscow Record*, criticizing the phonetic method. After this public criticism, Tolstoy was invited to speak to the Moscow Committee for Literacy to present and defend his ideas. To the subsequent meeting, on 15 January 1874, more than one hundred people attended to listen to the debate. True to his arguments against theory in education, Tolstoy refused to give any theoretical justification for his views claiming that theory was useless. The superiority of his methods could only be demonstrated practically. Tolstoy was taken up on his challenge, and he agreed to give two model lessons. He failed to turn up to the first lesson, and the second did not convince his observers. It was then considered that a test should be carried out between Tolstoy's approach and the phonetic method. P. V. Morozov, the teacher who had taught at Tolstoy's first school at Yasnaya Polyana, would teach one class, and a leading proponent of phonetics, M. A. Protopopov, would teach another.

The test took place on 6 April 1874 and the board decided that the phonetic method was superior. Unsurprisingly, Tolstoy argued against the findings of the committee the following week, claiming the test was unfair. Tolstoy argued that the pedagogues were merely imposing a Western conception of education on the Russian people based on an ideologically biased view of 'development.' This aroused popular sentiment among the audience at the meeting, and the Moscow Literacy Committee wrapped up the discussion on the experiment by claiming that there was no conclusive evidence for either method. The argument had shifted, Eikhenbaum observes, from one being concerned with the mechanics of literacy, to one concerning the ideological issue of how the Russian nation should progress.

Tolstoy's response to this battle was a restatement of his educational views 'On Popular Education' (PE, 1875) which repeats many of his concerns aired in the 1860s. The essay, like its counterpart of the 1860s, is really about social and historical issues: the problem of 'progress,' the validity of the scientific method and the legitimacy of the academic establishment to dictate to the people. As Eikhenbaum concludes of this episode, Tolstoy's battle with the pedagogues had led him 'into a controversy over the significance of science and the meaning of human life' (1982a, 117). He thus compares the origins of Tolstoy's subsequent work, *Anna Karenina* with those of *War and Peace*. Both great novels were preceded by intense pedagogical activity. And both novels changed their form as Tolstoy wrote them; from trivial narratives to epic works of literature which tackle the great social and philosophical questions that bothered Tolstoy in his educational writings. Eikhenbaum argues in both cases that pedagogy became the 'bridge leading to other pursuits' (1982a, 119).

However, Tolstoy's 'great battle' did not stop him from attempting to further his pedagogical ideas through a teacher training college. In 1876 he applied to Minister of Public Education to found a peasants' teacher training college – 'a university in bast sandals' – with the aim of training teachers who lived the same life as the children. However, this plan stalled due to a lack of approval by the authorities and interest from prospective teachers. Furthermore, his interest in education as a sole preoccupation was waning. In 1875 he wrote to Fet:

> I'm now setting to work again on my tedious, vulgar Karenina with only one wish to get it out of the way as soon as possible and have the leisure for other occupation – not pedagogical, however, which I love but intend to give up. It takes too much time. (IT, 99)

Although Tolstoy was never again to try to take up education as a priority occupation, his interest did not end in the 1870s. He continued to meet and address children from his estate and surrounding villages into his old age and his daughters set up schools in Yasnaya Polyana in 1891 and 1905. During 1907, he regularly taught religious education to a group of young peasant children who would, out of their own volition, arrive at seven o'clock in the evening to listen and talk with Tolstoy. It was from these classes that Tolstoy drew his inspiration for 'The Teaching of Jesus' (TOJ, 1908). Tolstoy continued writing on the subject of education in his diaries, and as he became older, the boundaries between his literature and educational writings became increasingly blurred – as he began to believe that the very work of the writer and artist was essentially pedagogic.

The education of Tolstoy's own children

Some further insight into Tolstoy's character as a teacher can be gleaned from accounts of how he attempted to educate his own children. It was common for the aristocracy, as Tolstoy illustrates in his novels, to be educated at home by tutors and members of the household. In *War and Peace*, for example, Maria Bolkonsky teaches her nephew 'Little Nikolai.' At times she finds this difficult, as Tolstoy describes in a vignette similar to that described earlier of the young author teaching his step-sister at the age of 5:

> No matter how often she told herself that she must not lose her temper when teaching her nephew, almost every time that, pointer in hand, she sat down to show him the French alphabet, she so longed to hasten, to make easy the process of pouring knowledge into the child – who was always afraid that at any moment Auntie would get angry – that the slightest inattention of the little boy would make her tremble, become flustered and heated, raise her voice. (WP, 638)

According to his son Ilya, Tolstoy was natural with children. He enjoyed their company and easily gained their attention and affection. Yet alongside this aspect of Tolstoy's personality was his imposing authority. Ilya describes how when his father taught him arithmetic, he was 'so scared that he could not learn' and Tolstoy made his other son Sergei cry by telling him that he deliberately did not learn. Similar to the accounts of Fyedka of Tolstoy's presence and authority, Ilya writes that his father's 'great strength as a parent was that one could no more conceal anything from him than one could conceal one's own conscience' (IT, 204). Such views are corroborated by Tatyana, who explains that when he was at leisure, spending time with her father was a great joy, as though 'a life force [was] radiating from him,' but at the same time he carried stern authority without needing to give punishments (TT, 35).

In his memoirs, Sofya's brother, Sergei Behrs, who was a regular visitor to Yasnaya Polyana, describes Tolstoy's approach to educating his own children. He claims that under the influence of Rousseau, Tolstoy believed that education should impress on a child the 'consciousness of its powerlessness in the presence of nature' (BS, 32). For this reason he hired an English governess for the children because he believed that these principles were best captured by the English attitude to education. However, Behrs observed that Tolstoy's belief in the freedom of the child, as expounded in his pedagogical articles, was only adopted to a certain extent in Tolstoy's own household. In practice, Behrs explains 'the universal application of this principle was found to be inconvenient and even impossible' (BS, 36).

Ilya, Sergei and Tatyana's accounts of their upbringing corroborate this. Although Tolstoy did not believe in violent or severe punishment, he devised a rigid, traditional curriculum for his children and developed strenuous programs of study for them, often utilizing his own innovative techniques. Tolstoy taught them arithmetic, Latin and Greek, whereas Sofya would teach them French and Russian. This, combined with the efforts of private tutors, turned the Tolstoy household into what Ilya considered a 'private university' (IT, 49). Ilya gives a description of Tolstoy's exacting standards as a teacher at this time:

> He was a wonderful teacher and made everything clear and interesting but as with the horseback riding, he always proceeded at a brisk trot and one had to struggle to keep up with him. It was probably due to this good start he gave me that I made excellent progress in mathematics and always enjoyed it. (IT, 48)

Tolstoy's sense of humor, and fun, evident in his *Azbuka*, is also recalled by Ilya's recollections of life in the Tolstoy household. One such memory is the 'postbox.' The Tolstoy family and their resident guests devised a system where children and adults could place any piece of writing – verses, articles, stories – anonymously in a box in the house. The postbox would then be opened in front of everyone and read out. Ilya records some of the preserved deposits by Tolstoy, which shed light on family jokes and some of his religious and political views. One such posting, was the sentence: 'Question: which is more dreadful, a case of cattle plague for the farmer, or the ablative case for a schoolboy?' (IT, 103). Another interesting entry was Tolstoy's mock history of Yasnaya Polyana seen from the perspective of people living in the year 2085:

> From the April issue of Russian Antiquity in 2085 we are able to reconstruct life in 19th century Russia. 'Enlightened families' lived in a narrow street working all the time. Two families were taken care of by forty people who did nothing other than pampering them [... who spent their time] learning the most inane and useless rules, and sometimes studying very blasphemous works known as sacred

histories and catechisms . . . the amazing thing is that the people of these two barbarian families called their most profligate forms of idleness work and often considered them burdensome, yet were always proud of their ignorance and idleness. (IT, 104)

For the early part of his childhood, Ilya describes how he was brought up traditionally as an aristocrat. He was shielded from outside influences in the home and taught that he was better than the peasants. Ilya describes how at Christmas the family would give small gifts to the village children, but at the same time they would proudly display their own gifts to the village children, never thinking that they might make them jealous. However, after his religious crisis of the late 1870s, Tolstoy's attitude to his children's education changed. Although Tolstoy's wife continued to employ foreign tutors and governesses, the 'private university' was abandoned for his younger children. Tolstoy's wife noted with disapproval, that Tolstoy would not become involved with their education because he did not agree with the religious instruction of children. Such a view corresponds with the memoirs of Behrs, who describes how Tolstoy mentored him. Behrs stresses the free and heuristic attitude Tolstoy had to discussing religion: 'he always managed to avoid expressing his own opinion, as if he knew what authority he had over me, and did not wish to bias me, or in any way, hamper my freedom' (BS, 63).

Behrs also noted a change in Tolstoy's religious attitudes from the latter half of the 1870s. Upon his conversion Tolstoy asserted that education was only worthwhile if it contributed to 'the good of one's neighbors'; therefore, education for the purposes of seeking a life of luxury or securing a higher position in society was wrong. Ilya reflects on the harm that the change in his father had on his development, claiming that as Tolstoy said scholarship was unnecessary he would go tobogganing with the village lads rather than studying. Such views became increasingly difficult for Tolstoy's family, particularly his wife, as Tolstoy became more and more famous for being a religious teacher, with people visiting Yasnaya Polyana from all over Russia, and abroad, to hear his advice. And as his fame grew, Tolstoy himself became progressively more perturbed by his own wealth and wished for a simple, spiritual life of seclusion.

Chapter 3

The Prophet of Yasnaya Polyana

The period of Tolstoy's life directly after the writing of *Anna Karenina* is sometimes referred to as his 'spiritual crisis.' After publishing his masterpiece, with the exception of *Resurrection* (1899) Tolstoy turned his back on writing novels in favor of religious essays and moral fables. A stream of religious writings, heavily censored or banned in Russia, such as *A Confession*, *On Life* (OL, 1887) and *The Kingdom of God is within You* (1893) along with many shorter open letters, were eagerly printed and distributed across Europe by Tolstoy's followers. Yet Tolstoy's religious 'conversion' was not as sudden as his critics often made out. As Medzhibovskaya (2008) and Gustafson (1986) demonstrate, the quest for religious truth is a persistent feature of Tolstoy's fiction and personal life – present throughout all his literature. It is also a theme within Tolstoy's educational writings.

To understand Tolstoy's educational thought it is necessary to understand his religious views. Tolstoy's work as an educator and novelist can be considered as different stages or facets of the same endeavor of seeking and living the truth. In *A Confession*, his spiritual autobiography, Tolstoy explains that he temporarily left the business of writing, or what he calls being a 'literary teacher' for the more 'noble' job of school teacher, because he felt that although he could influence many through his art, he did not know what message he should teach through it. However, he found that in school teaching he was faced with exactly the same issue:

> [At school] I was confronted with same insoluble problem of how to teach without knowing what it was I taught ... It amused me to recall how I side-tracked in order to fulfil my ambition of teaching, while knowing very well in the depths of my heart that I could not possibly teach what was needed because I did not know what it was. (AC, 27)

Tolstoy's experiences as a teacher and artist led him to the same destiny: to find the meaning of life or 'what was needed' as a solution to life.

A corollary of Tolstoy's religious conversion was his changed conception of the nature and purpose of the arts. In his concluding statement on the topic, the essay, *What is Art?*, Tolstoy declares that art has primarily a moral and religious purpose. Art should communicate those eternal truths necessary for the betterment of humankind. Literature should concern itself with morality, differentiate between what is good and what is bad, and ultimately lead the reader to 'the will of God.' In a mechanical sense, this is to take place by the artists' work 'infecting' the consciousness of another.

Along with this didactic view of the purpose of art came a more austere aesthetic, demonstrated in the simple folk fables of Tolstoy's later years – some of which bear many similarities with the stories included in the *Azbuka*. Genuine art should not need any frivolous, superfluous, stylistic features. Unnecessary aesthetic content, particularly if sentiments were distorted through poetry, could confuse the reader. For example, when commenting on Matthew Arnold's poems, Tolstoy is reported as saying that it was 'a pity they were not written in prose' (Maude, 1902, 192–193). Such a view is even more bluntly asserted in *A Calendar of Wisdom* (1904–1908) as Tolstoy compares real art to marital fidelity, and false art to harlotry: 'Like a true wife who loves her husband, real art does not need any decorations. Like a prostitute, false art needs to be decorated' (CW, 244).

Religious conversion in Tolstoy's literature

Tolstoy's emerging religious views are at times artfully explained in his literature. One crucial episode, also highly relevant to Tolstoy's educational thought, is Levin's epiphany in *Anna Karenina*. None of Tolstoy's novels are free from autobiographical content and Levin, like Tolstoy's other single male protagonists, is often thought to represent Tolstoy himself: he is a lonely landowner who goes through a difficult search for the meaning of life. Indeed, the writing of *Anna Karenina* corresponded with Tolstoy's own crisis of the 1870s and can be seen to mirror Tolstoy's own conversion.

Toward the end of the novel, after getting married, Levin becomes suicidal. He thinks to himself: 'I cannot live without knowing what I am and why I am here. And that I can't know, so therefore I can't live' (AK, 823). Here, as we shall see in Tolstoy's last thoughts on the nature and purpose of education, knowledge and living are equated, and they cannot be separated. Living correctly is a form of knowledge and knowing how to live comes as a direct intuit from the experience of living and existing in itself.

Levin had been drawn to a materialistic view of life but dismisses it. Life cannot be a mere biological accident. He rereads the great philosophers Plato, Spinoza, Kant, Scheling, Hegel and Schopenhauer, only to find his questions better answered in the following days by a casual conversation with a serf, Fiodr. Fiodr extols the virtues of a selfless, upright and relatively well-off peasant, Platon, who helps other peasants by letting them off debts they cannot pay. Levin questions Fiodr further, excited by his easy, effortless articulation of life's meaning given as though it were a truth that everyone already knows. He answers the landowner's questions on the meaning of life, stating 'Why, that's plain enough: it's living rightly, in God's way' (AK, 829). These words become an epiphany for Levin as he walks back to his house. The effect of the conversation with the peasant indicates Tolstoy's view of the psychology of learning implicit in his pedagogical writings. People are often corrupted by false understanding, but the process of *true* learning involves relating the words of others to our own individual emerging worldview. This then leads to a unified conception of reality that has not been hitherto recognized consciously:

> The peasant's words had the effect of an electric spark, suddenly transforming and welding into one a whole series of disjointed, impotent, separate ideas that had never ceased to occupy his mind. They had been in his mind, though he had been unaware of it. (AK, 829)

As a result of this conversion experience, Levin contrasts the view of a selfless godly life practiced by the peasant, with the rational, selfish view others of his own class had subscribed to. He thinks that it is rational to live for oneself, but we should live for what is good. Levin concludes that goodness is over and above philosophical understanding: it cannot be reduced to reason.

Commentators have mistakenly classified Tolstoy as a rationalist because of his renunciation of the supernatural elements of religion. This is a gross misrepresentation of Tolstoy's views. By saying that goodness is outside reason, Tolstoy means that if goodness is caused by something it becomes arbitrary and is not done because it is good; if it has reward it is not goodness for goodness' sake. This view is restated in his later essays. In 'Religion and Morality' (RM, 1894) Tolstoy argues that morality cannot be reconciled with 'non-Christian science.' It is also reflected in Tolstoy's description of Levin's revelation. Not only had Levin known the truth all along as part of his 'mother's love for him,' but reason and studying had been part of the gross deception which he had been under. As Levin consolidates his realization of the purpose of life, he comes to understand that 'reason is incommensurable with the problem.' Rather, the answer had been given to him by 'life itself', through his 'knowledge of what is right and what is wrong' (AK, 832).

After this profound realisation, Levin reflects on his experiences with his sister, Dolly, and her children. Levin recalls how Dolly grew impatient with them for inventing a game which involved making jam by putting cups of raspberries over candles and pouring milk into each other's mouths, making fun out of something ordinary because they could not fully comprehend the goodness of life that they enjoyed daily. Levin sees this as analogous to his own pursuit of the purpose of life, and the futility of the project of philosophy in determining how to live. Philosophers know the truth, as does Fiodr the peasant, but the philosophers contrive a 'dubious' system of thought to stress things we already know intuitively. The vignette about the jam making uses children's ignorance as an analogy for spiritual ignorance. As Levin contemplates the simple, honest truth revealed by the peasant, he compares himself with the children. Even though he has been living a life graced by God, he does not recognize it and fights against it. The episode is temporarily concluded by Levin tearfully looking at the sky asking himself if he has discovered God.

Pierre's conversion to freemasonry in *War and Peace* is another episode in Tolstoy's literature that preempts some of the views of Tolstoy's later religious essays. Pierre, considering his mistaken marriage and duel with

Dolohov, sits in a station waiting room and considers 'What is life for, and what am I? What is life? What is death? What is the power that controls it all?' (WP, 407). He meets the freemason, Osip Akexeyevich Bazdeyev, who makes him reconsider his atheistic position through a heuristic dialogue. Pierre begins the conversation by asserting that his atheistic worldview would not admit freemasonry. Bazdeyev, in contrast to this dogmatic materialism, states that he would never be so bold as to confidently assert that he knows the truth. For Bazdeyev, as Tolstoy would later proclaim in his repudiation of theology, God exists but trying to understand him is difficult.

Pierre, is drawn into a discussion that makes him reconsider his whole conception of the universe. Pierre's treatment of freemasonry takes on a Tolstoyan nature: it is not a club for social advantage but the 'teaching of Christianity freed from the fetters of the State and Church: the doctrine of fraternity and love' (WP, 454). This draws on the Tolstoyan principles of self-perfection and diary writing with the aim of moral improvement. We see here again a criticism of rational knowledge in contrast to the importance of religious sentiment. The religious view is an 'all-embracing teaching' whereas 'human sciences dissect in order to comprehend and destroy in order to analyse' (WP, 519). Pierre's beliefs take the form of experiential monism, as Pierre later describes to Andrei while pointing to the sky:

> If there is a God and a future life, then there is truth and goodness and man's higher happiness consists in striving to attain them. We must live, we must love, we must believe that we have life not only today on this scrap of earth but we have lived and shall live forever, there in the Whole. (WP, 456)

The ideas expounded in this episode of *War and Peace* resound with Tolstoy's project of revising Christianity. Pierre wanted to find the 'original' meaning of Freemasonry, as Tolstoy did with Christianity. Similarly, Pierre, like Tolstoy, finds science to be fragmentary and ultimately deceptive, while God is unknowable and ethereal in contrast to the tangible nature of the moral imperative. Furthermore, Pierre's conversation with Bazdeyev demonstrates a founding principle of Tolstoy's educational and spiritual thought: that communication, particularly of spiritual truths, should progress through a heuristic dialogue that supports an individual's own search for what is right, rather than a systematic exposition of those supposed truths.

Tolstoy's famous short story, 'The Death of Ivan Ilych' (DII, 1886) again demonstrates Tolstoy's religious views. It is a story not of conversion, but the opposite: the life of a man who does not realize the spiritual depth of existence until too late. After describing the funeral, Tolstoy retrospectively plots the banal life of Ivan Ilych, a man who had done everything that he was supposed to do as dictated by middle-class society, but who in his slow painful demise, reflects that his existence had lacked real meaning. His whole life had actually been wrong. Part of this realization is that rational thought, and his education in deductive reasoning as a lawyer, had not been conducive to making sense of his existence. On his death bed Ivan Ilych realizes that it is not rational thought that is essential to understanding life at all. He recalls reading a logic text book with the simple syllogism, familiar to all logic students: 'Caius is a man, men are mortal, therefore Caius is mortal' (DII, 147). Yet in the face of death, this logic was redundant and non-sensical. Ivan Ilych knew what mortality was, he understood that all men die, but that was very different from actually *being* a dying man. What he needed during his lifetime was to understand what it was to *be* a living man and to direct his life to proper meaning. A parallel to this realization is the form of care that ultimately brings some comfort to Ivan Ilych. It is not the professionalism and application of deductive, rational thinking of the doctor that provides solace. The only person who actually helps Ivan is his kind peasant-servant, who is compassionate and does not participate in false hopes and denial like the doctors and his family. This illustrates Tolstoy's criticism of the scientific method and the sole use of analytic reasoning to pursue the true meaning of life. As Tolstoy asserts in his religious essays, belief in science could itself become a superstition. Furthermore, it was such false beliefs, supported by erroneous forms of education, that had led directly to the unjust structure of society.

In his later essay, 'Religion and Morality', Tolstoy endorses a conception of religion and morality that places prime importance on the experience of individuals. He argues that anyone who has experienced religious feelings in childhood knows that God and the moral law exist because of that person's 'inner consciousness.' Religion is natural; it is not something that has its basis in culture or 'degree of education' but in a person's experience. Even so, true conversion requires a repudiation of the natural animalistic state of humans and an aspiration toward spiritual ideals. As Olenin, the main protagonist in *The Cossacks* ponders on a hunting expedition in the forests of the Caucasus, happiness can only be achieved by a renunciation of the selfish 'animal' existence of rational egoism. In his own life, the renunciation of 'animal' existence led Tolstoy to give up gambling, tobacco and hunting, and advocate manual labor, temperance, celibacy, vegetarianism, and above all, pacifism, which he powerfully articulated in his famous and influential essay *The Kingdom of God is within You*.

Tolstoy's definition of religion

Tolstoy's religious views have not been accepted by any mainstream Christian denomination. They do not fit into neat categories, yet Tolstoy believed them to be simple and easily comprehended. Tolstoy defines religion as a relation to life, the direction of intention prior to rational justification, dependent on the universal experience of humankind. He states in 'Religion and Morality', 'Religion is a certain relation established by man between his separate personality and the infinite universe or its source' (RM, 198). It follows, therefore, that it is impossible *not* to have a religion, in the sense that every individual must have a relation to the universe, even if this is an unconsidered or erroneous one. Tolstoy bluntly asserts, 'A man without a religion – i.e., without any relation to the universe – is as impossible as a man without a heart' (RM, 177). For Tolstoy, establishing the correct relationship with the universe involved following the moral teachings of Jesus. However, in his view, following the teachings of Jesus did not require belief in miracles, the resurrection or the sacraments of the Church. A genuine conception of 'religion' should not appeal to, or depend upon, any belief regarding supernatural events or adherence to a human organization. Religion was about living out the correct relationship with the world.

An important aspect of Tolstoy's view of religion is the role of reason in determining the correct relationship between ourselves and the universe. Belief in God is ultimately reasonable and justifiable but, in an individual's spiritual quest, purely rational inquiry into the nature of God is unfruitful. True religion is simple and not dependent upon abstract theorizing: 'to attain full and clear understanding of one's belief, no special mental gifts are required' ('Reason and Religion', 203). Tolstoy confirms this view as he writes about his own search for God in *A Confession*. He became dissatisfied by rational knowledge: 'having realized the errors in rational knowledge I found it easier to free myself from the temptation of futile theorizing' (AC, 63). He concludes his studies in theology with the criticism that the discipline was 'destroying the thing it should be advancing' (AC, 74).

Tolstoy claims that the investigation of phenomena independently of the investigator's position or experiences will necessarily lead to a false, distorted understanding of human existence as it does through the methodologies of science and philosophy – a view as pertinent to his educational thought as it is to his religious beliefs. However, despite his repudiation of rational thought as a means to understand the truths of human existence, religion in its true form can be compatible with reason, unlike what Tolstoy considered to be the superstitions of Orthodox Christianity. Given God's revelation in human experience, it follows that supernatural beliefs are not required to justify belief in God. As Tolstoy states in 'What is Religion and Wherein Lies Its Essence?' (1902), religion and science are not really in opposition, religion can easily be 'accordant with reason and contemporary knowledge' (WR, 281).

Tolstoy read widely during his middle age and Kant became a major influence on his religious thought. Tolstoy's essay *On Life* begins with a lengthy quotation from the opening paragraph of the conclusion of the *Critique of Practical Reason* (1788). In this famous extract, reminiscent of Psalm 8, Kant states his awe and wonder at the appreciation of the inner moral law and the glory of God's creation: the starry heavens. The experiences of characters in Tolstoy's literature poetically illustrate such views – and although we cannot be sure they are directly attributable to Kant's influence, particularly in Tolstoy's earlier literature, they can be considered as an important, reoccurring motif of Tolstoy's fiction. In *War and Peace*, looking up at the clear, frosty night sky from Arbatsky square, Pierre experiences communion with the universe as he watches a comet. Similarly, as *Anna Karenina* ends, Levin stands out on the terrace looking up at the stars considering the world's religions as he ponders the awesome power and unfathomable nature of the Deity. He reflects how rational knowledge of God is impossible but intuitive knowledge of life is possible. Again in *Youth*, written 20 years earlier, Nicholas looks up to the moon and feels the presence of God in the power and grandeur of nature:

> the moon that seemed to stand at a high uncertain spot in the pale-blue sky and yet was present everywhere and seemed to fill an immeasurable space, and I, an insignificant worm already defiled by all sorts of mean, paltry, human passions but with a boundless, mighty power of love – at those moments it seemed to me that nature, the moon, and I, were all one and the same. (YO, 348)

Tolstoy believed genuine religious belief is based on personal experience rather than enculturation or education but he also believed religious truths to be partially communicable between humans. This is reflected in Tolstoy's view of scripture. Tolstoy had been strongly influenced by the Gospels from a young age and his later moral fables and religious essays are littered with biblical quotations. When his biographer later asked about his major influences between the ages of 14 and 21, Tolstoy placed the Gospel of Matthew, in particular the Sermon on the Mount at the top of the list (BK, 97).

However, for Tolstoy, religious knowledge does not rest purely on scripture. In his translation of the Gospels, the culmination of his foray into biblical exegesis, 'The Four Gospels Harmonised' (FGH, 1881–1882), Tolstoy explains scripture is just a human rendition of the encounter with God's eternal truths, revealed to the human heart and then written down. He argues against any form of fundamentalism that puts the authority of a text before that of an individual's conscience. God cannot be constrained by a book: 'to say that the revelation of God is expressed on 185 pages of paper, is the same as saying that the soul of such and such a man weighs fifteen hundredweight' (FGH, 13). Tolstoy considered the holy books of other religions as expressing the same eternal truths as the Gospels. His last major work, *A Calendar of Wisdom*, attempted to demonstrate the unity of religious and philosophical truths from all the world's cultures throughout time by quoting diverse sources from a number of the world's religious traditions.

Tolstoy's religious views are given their most formal argument in *On Life*. Tolstoy begins the essay with an analogy of a miller who relies on the mill to make a living. As the miller becomes interested in the workings of the mill, he traces the power source from the flour between the mill stones, to the shaft, through the various cogs, to the river. He thinks to himself that as the river is the source of power, it must be the most important aspect of the mill. However, because of this belief, he soon neglects the real purpose of the machinery and the mill: to grind good flour that he can sell and people can eat. This leads to the mill machinery becoming dilapidated and not producing good flour.

Tolstoy argues that in one sense the miller's reasoning is correct and logical. Without the river there would be no power or flour. Yet, in another sense, Tolstoy points out, the miller is mistaken. The *direction* of the miller's thought is wrong. The miller should have first considered the purpose of the mill, not the source of power. Tolstoy argues that life is like the mill, and the miller's mistake is like that of science and philosophy. If we answer the wrong question correctly, the actual meaning and purpose of the investigation is still lost. The purpose of life is to live it well; the purpose of the mill is to produce flour. This is how Tolstoy conceives science and philosophy; they are like the miller's distraction. For Tolstoy any 'argument is not so much the argument itself as the place it occupies ... it is not what we call science that supplies our conception of life; it is our conception of life that determines what ought to be regarded as science' (OL, 12). Philosophy and the empirical sciences are therefore grossly limited in helping find the meaning of life; they can only support a prior direction of thought. Furthermore they can act as powerful illusions and diversions. Before embarking on any such systematization it is essential that we should first find the direction of our thought by establishing the 'correct relationship' or attitude between ourselves and the universe, and this cannot rely on rational thought alone:

> philosophy always has been and always will be simply the investigation of the consequences that result from the relation religion establishes between men and the universe, for until that relation is settled there is nothing on which philosophy can work. (OL, 179)

The analogy of the mill can be compared to a teaching of Buddha that much impressed Tolstoy regarding the 'unanswered questions'

(TD, 224). According to traditional Buddhist teaching, the Buddha refused to answer some questions, such as whether there is eternal life. A man dying from an arrow wound would be foolish to not want to be healed until he knows who wounded him. First he must seek the solution of the most immediate problem. Similarly for everyone else, we must ask questions about how to act, before we speculate on the unknown. For Tolstoy, as it was for Buddha, the most immediate question was a moral one: how should we live?

The Scribes and the Pharisees

Tolstoy was an outspoken critic of the established political and economic order, and he saw the prevailing belief systems of materialism and Orthodoxy as false views which perpetuated the immorality of society and the exploitation of the people. In 'Religion and Morality', Tolstoy uses the analogy of music to explain the difference between the doctrines of scientific materialism, the Church and his own view, which he believed to be the truth (RM, 168–169). Religion, according to the teaching of the Church, is like a definition of music which says music is a particular tune 'that [it] ought to be taught to as many people as possible.' The scientific materialists' view of religion, however, is like defining music as the 'production of sounds with one's throat or mouth, or by applying one's hand to certain instruments, and that it is a useless and even harmful occupation.' For Tolstoy then, the correct view of music consists in understanding its essence: the communication and expression of emotion through sound. Correspondingly, the correct view of religion is understanding its essence: the subjective experience of human beings in their interactions with God and the world around them. Secular morality is problematic: understanding how to live correctly must involve the apprehension of life's essence, God.

In *On Life* Tolstoy attacks what he considers are the prevailing ideologies of his day, the Church and the materialists. Comparing them to the enemies of Jesus in the Gospels, he dubs the former the 'Pharisees' and the latter the 'Scribes.' The Pharisees are the Christian Church, in particular the Orthodox Church but also the other main denominations. They are guilty of preaching doctrines which no reasonable person could assent to, and insistent on sacraments which shield people from their true moral and religious duty. The Scribes, on the other hand, are a more recently powerful but equally misleading group who base their lives on the myths of science and improvement. They do not see Christianity as a reasonable belief system because they have been presented with a false version of it (RM, 183). The Scribes, therefore, having used their reason, reject the doctrines of the Pharisees as superstitious nonsense, but only to create their own superstition – the belief in progress.

Tolstoy was concerned about the influence of the Scribes' ideology on the spiritual life of the people and the material change that technology had on people's way of life. Such criticism of 'progress' is evident in his pedagogical articles of the 1860s and as Tolstoy grew older he became more critical of the inventions of the early twentieth century, and the lack of implicit good in them. He compared the dominance of scientific modes of thought with the Church in its promulgation of mass delusion and reflected that awareness of God was being eroded by the mistaken belief in the advance of technology. He also felt that the instruments of mass communication and education associated with modern society were corruptive because of the lack of worthwhile knowledge they distributed. For Tolstoy, society had come to be controlled by enslaving industry, institutionalized religion, education and mass media which made millions suffer in physical pain and spiritual ignorance. The authorities promulgated the 'lie of religion' and the 'stupefying effect of drunkenness and education' and where these did not control the masses, the government had to rely on brute force in the form of prisons and executions (AT, 485). Tolstoy predicted the dissatisfaction and terror that such a society would yield in the twentieth century.

Related to Tolstoy's fear of a technological and godless dystopia, and his criticism of the Orthodox Church, was his view that education by both parties was harmful. The doctrines of the Pharisees and Scribes obscure the truth; they do not demonstrate how to aspire to the good and live beyond the 'animal' state of selfish desire. The Scribe cannot advocate any basis of morality or education other than egoism. The Pharisees on the other hand do not demonstrate moral living through their actual behavior. Tolstoy writes in *On Life*:

> A child is born in want or in wealth and receives the education of the Scribes and Pharisees. For the child or the youth neither the

contradiction of life nor questions about them as yet exist, and so neither the explanation of the Pharisees nor of the Scribes is necessary to him, nor can they guide his life. He learns only by the example of the people around him, and this example, whether of Pharisees or Scribes, is the same: both live merely for the satisfaction of their personal life and teach him to do the same. (OL, 29–30)

In addition to concerns about a secular education, Tolstoy was a vehement critic of Orthodox catechesis. Tolstoy believed that the nonsensical dogmas of orthodox Christianity could not form the basis of education because they could not be demonstrated to be reasonable. Initiation in such a faith could only make people less moral, since receiving doctrine on authority would lead a man to believe he should be not guided by his reason and intuition, but by what he is told. Tolstoy therefore concludes that such an education produces 'a terrible perversion of man's spiritual world' (WR, 268). Indeed the reliance of the Church on enforcing its doctrines through formal education revealed the sham of institutionalized religion itself. Tolstoy declares of the Orthodox Church:

If they had a real religion they would know that religion is an understanding of life – the relation each man established to God – and that consequently you cannot teach a religion but only a counterfeit of religion. ('Church and State,' 335)

Tolstoyanism

Tolstoy believed himself to be a Christian in the sense that he followed the moral teachings of the Gospel, which for him were the fullest expression of the will of God. However, on principle, he did not adhere to any Christian denomination or dissenting group. He saw the mere existence of these divisions as a reason not to believe in any of them. He writes in *A Confession*, there is a 'contemptuous, self-righteous, invincible manner of rejection with which the Catholics behave towards the Orthodox and the Protestants, and the Orthodox towards the Catholics and the Protestants, and the Protestants towards them both' (AC, 74). He notes that these divisions can only cause people, particularly the younger generation, to ask the question why the truth is to only be found in the Orthodox faith and not the other denominations.

Tolstoy saw any form of religious exclusivity as limiting the true divine command to love God and neighbor and unify humankind. Subsequently he denounced the absurdity and vanity of nurturing a religion of his own. However, as his religious ideas spread, Tolstoy 'colonies' were founded around the world in which devotees, the Tolstoyans, attempted to live out his views as communities of followers. Although he wanted to disseminate his ideas and influence the world, Tolstoy was skeptical of this movement. He wrote to Percy Redfern of the Manchester Tolstoy Society on 15 August 1901, setting out of why he disapproved of such organizations: 'to be a member of the old Society started by God at the beginning of conscious humanity is more profitable . . . than [being] a member of the limited [Tolstoy] societies' (TL, 601). However, of one commune, founded in South Africa by Gandhi, Tolstoy was more sympathetic: 'Gandhi is a man very much akin to us, to me' reflected Tolstoy when talking about his correspondence with Gandhi to his daughter (AT, 484).

During the last thirty years of his life, Tolstoy attempted to live out his creed and championed a number of national and international social, political and religious causes. In January 1882 he took part in a three day census of Moscow. This experience led to the writing of 'What Then Must We Do?' (1886) in which he set out his views on the plight of the urban poor. In the same decade Tolstoy also became involved with famine relief in rural areas. Tolstoy saw the solution to poverty not through charity and philanthropy, which only demonstrated inequality, but through the transformation of the unjust socioeconomic system and the renunciation of the privileges of the landed gentry. His son, Ilya, who helped Tolstoy during the famine relief, reported Tolstoy's analogy for this: 'if a horseman sees that his horse is exhausted, he should not remain seated on its back, but should simply get off' (IT, 223). Tolstoy wished for a radical restructuring of society. However, he was no revolutionary in the normal sense of the word; he sought spiritual transformation of the individual rather than violent political upheaval. Indeed, Tolstoy did not see any form of human authority in the form of the state as valid, but rather saw God's Kingdom as a possibility on earth, if humans could only follow the moral code of the Gospels.

Tolstoy felt strongly about the persecution of dissidents in Russia and the increasing use of the death penalty as the Tsarist establishment tried to maintain the status quo. On 11 May 1908, he read in the morning newspaper of the sentencing to death of 20 peasants and this led him to write 'I Cannot Be Silent' (1908), an essay strongly stating his opposition to capital punishment. Tolstoy also came to the aid of the Doukhobors, a persecuted Christian sect. He wrote the novel *Resurrection*, which is also concerned with the immorality of the penal system, to raise funds for the mass emigration of Doukhobors from Russia to Canada. Aylmer Maude, Tolstoy's English friend and translator, on behalf of Tolstoy, helped coordinate the exodus and traveled to Canada to liaise with the Canadian government. His wife, Louise Maude, translated the novel into English and gave over the proceeds to the cause, as did Tolstoy with the Russian editions.

The term 'Doukhobor' is a nickname that was coined by the Orthodox Church meaning 'spirit wrestler' because the established Church dismissed the sect's heretical views as being against the work of the Holy Spirit. Although not a completely homogeneous group in terms of doctrine, the movement can be considered a form of dissenting group, monotheistic but stressing the Christ 'within' and rejecting the need for a priestly order and Church hierarchy. It is obvious why Tolstoy, the Tolstoyans and Quakers took interest in their plight. As Maude observed, the 'Doukhobors were, in the eyes of the Tolstoyans, a folk who had well-nigh realised the Christian ideal' (1904, 59).

In 1895, the Doukhobors had begun to refuse Army service due to their pacifist leanings. Those serving in the army were incarcerated, tortured and one inmate died. Those outside the military were persecuted, the army began to attack settlements and disperse them resulting in the deaths of 1,000 Doukhobors. Following the dispersion, their villages were occupied and those who were left were forced to live in other villages, away from their communities, where their freedom of movement was severely restricted. Chertkov, Tolstoy's publicist and disciple, went to petition the Tsar, which resulted in his banishment and exile to England. In 1898, permission was given by the Russian government for the Doukhobors to leave, provided that it was not at the cost of the government. As a result of the work of the Maudes and others, steamships were chartered direct to the Black Sea and by the winter of 1899, 7,363 Doukhobors were settled in Canada.

Excommunication and death

Despite his constant clashes with the establishment, the censorship of his religious essays and the banishment of his associates, Tolstoy was not excommunicated from the Orthodox Church until 1901. This finally came about because of the satire of the Orthodox Church in the novel *Resurrection*. The story, autobiographical in its main themes, is based around the lengthy, harmful consequences of the sexual misdemeanor of a young aristocrat. It is morally didactic, in keeping with Tolstoy's aesthetic principles, and derides the Orthodox Church and its place in the established social order. Particularly offensive to the Church was Tolstoy's description of the communion rite administered to children in prison. It is retold in sarcastic detail revealing the hypocrisy of the Church endorsing a place of torture, punishment and degradation. Tolstoy uses psychological power to attack the Church through an insightful description of the corrupt priest's mental state as he conducts communion.

Tolstoy responded to his excommunication with another powerful statement of his convictions, 'A Reply to the Synod's Edict of Excommunication' (RSE, 1901). He explains his religious evolution by reference to Coleridge's dictum that 'He who begins by loving Christianity better than truth will proceed by loving his own sect or church better than Christianity, and end in loving himself better than all' (RSE, 214). Tolstoy rephrases this with his own view of his conversion: 'I travelled the contrary way. I began by loving my Orthodox faith more than my peace, then I loved Christianity more than my church, and now I love truth more than anything in the world' (RSE, 225).

The Orthodox Church sought reconciliation with Tolstoy on a number of occasions. Maude recounts how in 1902 when Tolstoy was thought to be dying he received a telegram from a bishop of the Orthodox Church asking him to return to the Church, to which Tolstoy replied: 'tell these gentleman that they should leave me in peace ... how is it that they do not understand that, even when one is face to face with death, two and two still make four' (Maude, 1918, 296).

Despite his own repudiation of the Church, Tolstoy did not wish to undermine the common people's faith but to challenge the hypocrisy of the aristocracy in upholding it, and the Church's vested interest in the corrupt social order. He was sympathetic to the monastic tradition within Orthodoxy and made a number of retreats to monasteries, in particular just before he died, to visit his sister who had become a nun. Alexandra recounts that when visited by the Bishop of Tula in 1909, Tolstoy received the blessing of the priest and read passages of *A Calendar of Wisdom* to him. Tolstoy felt this work demonstrated his desire to strengthen people's belief in God and show unity between religions, explaining to the priest that when he saw peasants praying he felt this was true and honest prayer, but that the so-called 'educated' people seemed to have no faith at all (AT, 471).

Tolstoy's religious views were problematic for those closest to him. Family members noticed a change in Tolstoy after he wrote *Anna Karenina*. Tolstoy's son Ilya blames his own instability on his father's spiritual quest and its negative effect on family life. He describes how difficult this was for the family at the time. Tolstoy's wife, Sofya, makes a similar observation with regards to the deterioration of their marriage following her husband's spiritual crisis. She describes how she saw his stubborn, countercultural views as responsible for his low moods:

> A spirit which rejected the existing religions, progress, science, art, family, everything which mankind had evolved in centuries had been growing stronger and stronger in Lev Nikolaevich and he was becoming gloomier and gloomier. (ST, 52)

Tolstoy left his home and wife on the morning of 28 October 1910. His daughter Alexandra describes how she was woken in the early hours, as Tolstoy asked her to help him pack. After traveling by train to visit his sister in her convent, he rose early in the morning and fell ill. He was diagnosed with inflammation of the lung, and the stationmaster at a station he was passing through, Astapovo, gave Tolstoy a bed in his house. Tolstoy did not leave it alive.

The reasons for the final twist of the novelist's life, his 'going away,' are apparent in the accounts of those close to him. His wife, his children, his secretary Bulgakov and his publicist Chertkov all later published versions of the story. Tolstoy's diaries themselves speak of the increasing guilt of his worldly wealth that plagued him. He desired the spiritual release of leaving behind his worldly belongings. Twelve years before his flight, on 1 June 1897, he had written to Sofya, in a letter he never sent, explaining why he wished to leave. He wrote that he had long been troubled by his worldly wealth in comparison with those around him and he wished to retire into the forest in solitude as Hindus do in later life (IT, 219–220). In addition to his spiritual yearnings, Tolstoy had also found living with his wife increasingly difficult because of her nervous and odd behavior, particularly her jealously toward Chertkov. In one bout of rage she shot at the photograph of Chertkov that Tolstoy had hanging in his study with a toy gun that she had bought. After shooting it to no avail, she tore if from the wall and ripped it up. She also went through Tolstoy's diaries and letters and followed him out of fear that he would sign away the rights of his work in collusion with Chertkov. This was a genuine fear. On 27 March 1895 Tolstoy had written a letter asking his family to give his works to the public domain. Chertkov believed that it should be made formal and in October 1909 a new will was made in secret, and another in June 1910 in the forest near Chertkov's estate.

Tolstoy left the house for his final journey without telling his wife, leaving a letter asking her not to follow him. When she found the letter, she ran out of the house and jumped in the estate pond in an attempt to commit suicide, only to be retrieved by her daughter and Tolstoy's secretary, Bulgakov. Sofya was able to get to Astapovo before Tolstoy died, but she did not see him while he was conscious. Around the stationmaster's house, crowds had gathered. Chertkov read extracts from *A Calendar of Wisdom* to soothe Tolstoy, while a media maelstrom ensued. While still conscious Tolstoy dictated notes to his daughter Alexandra, affirming the beliefs articulated in his great works, fiction and non-fiction: 'God is that infinite All of which man recognizes himself to be a finite part. Only God truly exists' (AT, 520).

Part 2

A Critical Exposition of Tolstoy's Educational Thought

Chapter 4

The Pedagogical Laboratory

The most well-documented and intense phase of Tolstoy's educational activities at Yasnaya Polyana took place between 1859 and 1863. During this time Tolstoy taught in his school – first in his own house and then, as it grew – in the building adjacent to it. In the summer of 1860 he left Russia to travel to Europe to observe educational practices. On his return he began to write about his ideas and experiences in the *Yasnaya Polyana* journal. The journal ran editions from January 1862 to December 1862, although the release of these was delayed by the government censor. The journal contained articles which stated the aims and methods of Tolstoy's experiment, work by his students, some of his tentative findings, as well as articles by other teachers. It is important to note that Tolstoy's essays in the journal, although assertively written, do not constitute a definitive statement of Tolstoy's view of education. As he wrote in the first edition of *Yasnaya Polyana*:

> In entering what is for me a new field, I am apprehensive about myself and those ideas which I have worked out over the years and which I hold to be right. I am convinced in advance that many of them will prove mistaken. (AT, 137)

Such a view is confirmed in the last edition of the journal when Tolstoy states in exasperation: 'It is so easy to talk a great deal in this field, without convincing anybody!' (PDE, 181). Despite this acknowledgment of the lack of conclusive answers, and his greater concern with spiritual education in his later writings, Tolstoy never fully repudiates the views expressed in his earlier pedagogical articles. Rather he develops the themes and arguments found in them, as an examination of his other statements on education, written as late as 1909, confirm.

The first edition of *Yasnaya Polyana* began with Tolstoy's first essay titled 'On the Education of the People' (OEP, January 1862). In this article, Tolstoy is preoccupied with providing a rationale for his school, which he describes as a 'pedagogical laboratory.' The essay was written around the time of the emancipation decree, and this is critical to understanding Tolstoy's argument. Like others, he wished to enable social reform through education, but he believed that this should be done through consultation with the Russian people, not through the diktat of government or the imposition of European methods. Tolstoy therefore argues in 'On the Education of the People' that the problem of public education, at this critical crossroads in Russian history, should be approached without any preconceived theories or theoretical assumptions: it should be solved practically.

The problem

'On the Education of the People' begins with Tolstoy setting out the as yet unsolved 'problem' of education for the people. All humans, particularly children, desire to increase their knowledge, skills and understanding. Across Europe, the more educated classes, the ruling elite, want to improve the education of the people by instigating varying forms of national educational provision for the general population. Yet, Tolstoy observes, in almost every case, the people, rather than being pleased with the attempts to educate them, resist these efforts, and in the main do not become educated. Tolstoy claims that the coercion of educators and the resistance of learners has been a problem that has dogged education throughout time and in every culture and has persisted into modern times. He cites the education system of Germany as a pertinent example.

Tolstoy continues his argument. Given that resistance to education is universal, as is the ubiquitous use of force necessitated by it, which is more justifiable – the people's resistance to education, or the pressure of governments on the people to become educated? Tolstoy notes that according to history the answer to this question has always fallen in favor of the government. This is because education has always been based on a conception of truth. According to Tolstoy, the Chinese justified making students memorize the sayings of Confucius because they were considered indubitable. Similarly, learning Greek in the Middle Ages was justified because it was the language in which the truth was revealed by Aristotle and the Scriptures. In the modern age of progress, Tolstoy argues, these foundational 'truths' are no longer valid. However, neither is the 'truth' of the modern era – that determined by science. Tolstoy argues that science cannot form the basis of the curriculum because scientific theories are often disputed, and are also too complex. As there are an enormous amount of subdivisions within the sciences, just determining which branch of knowledge to teach would be problematic. Furthermore, Tolstoy continues, not only is there uncertainty in determining the basis of the curriculum, but there is also a similar problem in deciding on the best pedagogical methods to use, particularly for the peasantry, who have hitherto been uneducated. Given the lack of a firm base on which to rest education, teachers are therefore left with the quandary of not knowing what to teach or how to teach it.

Tolstoy considers four possible answers to this impasse. First, he weighs up a religious argument: a teacher should teach the truths revealed from God and bring children up according to those principles. Secondly, a teacher could explain the foundation of education in term of a philosophy, such as those of Kant, Fichte or Hegel. Thirdly, one could base education on the empirical fact that schools are coercive and that this kind of system must therefore be a necessary, appropriate condition of them. Fourthly, Tolstoy considers an historicist argument: schools are as they are because religion, philosophy and the experience of educators has led them to be as such, and these 'historical' forces must be rational.

Having considered these four possibilities, Tolstoy then argues why none of them can form a satisfactory basis of pedagogy, nor legitimize the use of coercion in schools. Firstly, religion cannot form the sole foundation of schooling because in the modern age it only comprises a small part of the knowledge of humankind. Philosophy is also insufficient. Philosophers, Tolstoy muses, have each come up with different ethical theories. Pedagogy could be based upon one of these ethical systems because each of them purports to show humankind right from wrong. However, not only are there rival incommensurable theories to choose from, but each thinker only expresses ethical theories appropriate to their era. Thus, if a foundation to pedagogy is based on a philosophical system, it could easily become anachronistic.

The problem, continues Tolstoy, with using philosophy as a foundation of pedagogy, is that the aims and limits of education are dictated before a teacher actually knows what innovation is possible. Here Tolstoy discovers another paradox. Thinkers such as Rousseau, Pestalozzi and Froebel all wished to free schools from traditional forms of education, yet ironically in doing so they merely prescribed a new set of laws based on their own conception of freedom. In addition, pedagogical theories encourage teachers to think that 'no matter what the teacher and pupil are like, the [teaching] method should be the same' (OEP, 74). Theories, by definition, are not based on the experience of any particular given group of students; they therefore constitute 'guesses.' The educational ideas of Rousseau, Pestalozzi and Froebel are, consequently, in Tolstoy's view, 'extremely strange, quite unfounded theories' (OEP, 70).

In answer to the third argument, that coercion is justified by the fact that it is a natural, necessary condition of schools, Tolstoy extends his polemic to his experiences traveling to schools abroad and to an evaluation of traditional education in terms of pupil experience: 'Let us look at these schools . . . by [getting] to know the schools and their influence on the people in actuality' (OEP, 71). Tolstoy notes that in his entire journey through Europe he rarely found students who could answer the questions he posed to them without giving answers that were learnt by rote. Students in European schools were brain washed and traumatized, succumbing to:

> a strange psychological state which I should call the school state of mind, which we all, unfortunately, know so well, all the higher abilities – imagination, creativity, understanding, give place to some sort of other, semi-animal capabilities. (OEP, 75)

Tolstoy thought that the schools he visited in continental Europe taught things pupils did not understand, deprived children of freedom of movement, speech and happiness and subjected them to disproportionate corporal punishment. Children's natural place in the order of society and their relationships with adults were also strained: parents resented the schools because they deprived them of the extra labor of their children, whereas teachers were only pleased when their domination over their pupils was complete. Tolstoy observed a morally counterproductive power-play in the classroom: 'as soon as the child has reached this state [of fear and mindlessness] and lost all independence and self-reliance ... the teacher is pleased with him' (OEP, 75).

Of the overall effect of schools in Germany, Tolstoy states it is ironic that in Germany the common people have a 'mechanical ability to read and write' but because of schools they attended 'have such a strong distaste for the paths of learning that they never pick up a book again' (OEP, 72). Part of this problem was the unnatural environment of the classroom. In the homes, fields and workshops of their communities, children were able to learn from their environment and elders. In school, however, rather than learning naturally from their parents and their own experiences, pupils were subjected to 'a long drawn out perversion of the intellectual capacities' (OEP, 73). The curriculum did not deal with questions 'posed by life' which naturally came to children from their lives outside school, such as 'How was the earth made?' but focused on unimportant content selected by adults to be learnt off by heart. Tolstoy concludes that the aim of these kinds of schools must not be to educate as such, but to educate according to a certain method. He sums this up in a pithy pastoral analogy: 'schools are organised by governments as flocks for a shepherd not shepherd for a flock' (OEP, 74).

With regard to the fourth possible justification of contemporary schools, popular in nineteenth-century Russia, that history has acted as a 'rational' process to create them in their most efficient form, Tolstoy argues that all previous schools have been unsound in their coercive nature and in their epistemological foundations. Moreover, over the years each kind of school has been modeled on a previous one, teachers have been discouraged from thinking about what their pupils really need and non-coercive methods have never been tried. In the modern age of progress, Tolstoy reasons, knowledge has become more complex but the methods of transmitting that knowledge in schools have remained the same.

The solution

Given the failings of traditional methods of education, and the inadequacies of the 'theories' suggested by Rousseau and the progressives, Tolstoy argues that a new form of education should be instigated. This should be devised by studying the 'conveniences' of the pupils as well as those of the teachers. To progress in education, the school should become 'an experiment with the younger generation which constantly yields new conclusions,' a 'pedagogical laboratory' with which to lay 'firm foundations for a science of education' (OEP, 76).

Tolstoy gives a number of arguments for this view. A school should 'answer the questions which life poses to man' (OEP, 77). Yet, evidently different ways of life will yield different questions and different educational needs. People living in urban districts will already have a level of sophistication that village dwellers will not. Tolstoy uses the example of his trip to Marseilles where he evaluated the schools by talking with teachers and pupils. Here, as elsewhere in Europe, he discovered bad schools which predominantly taught by memorization. However, he also noticed 'unconscious education' which was acquired from the cafes, theatres, public libraries and cheap novels available across the city. He observed that rather than being the catalyst for the improvement of society, the schools did not keep up with the development of the people. In comparison with the culture of the city, the content of the curriculum was trivial and uninspiring.

The diversity of pupils' needs is not limited to the difference between rural and urban populations, Tolstoy observes: it is also cross-generational. As it cannot be known in advance what future generations will need to know, it is essential that the emerging needs of each generation be understood. Hence, Tolstoy states that the basis of his educational experiment is the freedom for pupils to express what they are naturally inclined to learn. Education should be an evolving, dynamic process that should address the needs of each individual and each generation. The educator should be sensitive to, and address the dissatisfaction of the pupil and constantly seek to engage the younger generation in new and innovative ways. Education should move forward in kilter with the progress of every generation and individual.

Tolstoy gives an analogy of a mother and young child to illustrate his view of this educational experiment. A mother teaches her child to speak instinctively by coming down to the level of the child and using simple words to aid his or her progress. Yet simultaneously the child tries naturally to rise up to the level of the mother to understand her. The mother has a natural tendency to teach and the child a natural tendency to learn. Tolstoy reflects that the same situation is found with an author and reader, and with a teacher and class of pupils. One party has the natural tendency to rise to the level of the other, and the other has the innate inclination to stoop to assist this. The science of education, therefore, is simply to see how, and in what conditions these two tendencies come together. Tolstoy's view of the innate goodness of the child is also a factor in his belief in the worth of his educational experiment. Students are well placed to know what and how they should be taught because of the natural basis of morality. They are naturally drawn toward the good. Teachers need only study such inclinations and the problem of education will dissolve.

Tolstoy recognized that an argument against his desire to provide education for the masses was that it might interfere with the peasants' natural way of life. Indeed, it was unlikely that the manual work of the peasants would require the ability to think and read, so why raise their expectations and awareness of inequality through education? In answer to this, Tolstoy claims that the motivation of the peasant children, like Fyedka, to learn, is not based on economic interest but on the desire to consider moral questions. This is fundamental to his conception of a universal education based on the common questions 'that life poses to man': the process of learning should come from the questions that arise in children naturally, not from the need of the children to learn a trade or improve their employment prospects.

In the peasant children Tolstoy felt that he saw a genuine thirst for understanding born out of free inquiry and contemplation that had hitherto only been available to the upper classes. In another essay 'The school at Yasnaya Polyana,' Tolstoy addresses an imaginary adversary – a liberal philanthropist member of the aristocracy, his criticism of charity preempting the views espoused in his later moral essays:

> Fyedka is not vexed by his tattered kaftan but moral questions and doubts torment him, and you want to give him three roubles, a catechism, and a tract about the usefulness of labour ... He does not need your three roubles: he will find and take them when he needs them, and he will learn to work without your aid ... he needs that to which life had brought you, your own life and that of ten generations not crushed by work. You have had leisure to seek [and] think. (TSYP, 255)

Thus, the goal of Tolstoy's experiment was to find out how a teacher could educate without impinging on a child's free development, harnessing their naturally inquisitive natures, and to infer, in consultation with peasant children, what would constitute a suitable education for them. To sum up this view, Tolstoy asserts a pithy maxim: 'the only method of education is experience and its only criterion freedom.' 'Freedom' in the sense that learners' innate tendency to progress is realized naturally; 'experience' because teachers' understanding of pupils' needs is best tried and tested, rather than predetermined by theory, ideology or philosophy. Tolstoy concludes the opening article of the *Yasnaya Polyana* journal, 'On the Education of the People,' by claiming that although his ideas may sound like a 'visionary dream,' he will prove their worth 'fact after fact' by publishing the results of his pedagogical laboratory in the successive editions of the journal, its motto affirming Tolstoy's aims: 'You mean to push, but in reality it is you who are pushed' (BK, 325).

Some characteristics of the experimental school

In the essay 'The School at Yasnaya Polyana,' published in three parts in the January, March and April editions of the *Yasnaya Polyana* journal, Tolstoy artistically describes the school and its pupils. His descriptions stress the importance of a non-coercive atmosphere and champion the natural inclination, and innate goodness of children. At first, Tolstoy explains, any order was very difficult to obtain, even to organize break times, but as time went on, the students themselves wanted the timetable to be followed. This is because pupils themselves want to learn:

> Schoolchildren, small men though they be, have the same needs as we, and they reason in the same manner; they all want to learn, coming to school for this only, and so they will naturally arrive at the conclusion that they must submit to certain conditions in order to acquire knowledge. (TSYP, 234)

Tolstoy goes on to describe how, on the whole, his faith in students' natural desire to learn paid off. For example, the students ran to school in the morning and were never late. Similarly, Tolstoy did not tell children where to sit, but allowed them to naturally settle into their work. This method also worked satisfactorily. After a short time, the children began to enter the correct mental state to study. He declares, when beginning a lesson 'the martial spirit takes flight [scuffling and play fighting] and the reading spirit reigns' (TSYP, 231).

Tolstoy explains that his school is a 'living being' (TSYP, 227) which grows as a result of the mutual influence of its constituent parts. He repeatedly refers to this complex interaction of social factors as the 'spirit' of the school. By this he means something that is not traditionally understood by pedagogical science but something that is essential to the educational transaction. It exists as a relationship between the teacher and the students, and in relationships of the students with each other. It is elusive and difficult to obtain, but a positive 'spirit' is imperative to foster if children are to be in the correct state of mind to learn:

> This spirit of the school is something that is rapidly communicated from pupil to pupil, and even to the teacher, something that is palpably expressed in the sound of the voice, in the eyes, the movements, the tension of the rivalry, – something very tangible, necessary, and extremely precious, and therefore something that ought to be the aim of every teacher. Just as saliva in the mouth is essential for digestion, but is disagreeable and superfluous without food, even so this spirit of strained animation, though tedious and disagreeable outside the class, is a necessary condition for the assimilation of mental food. (TSYP, 299)

Tolstoy argues that this psychological state is necessary for the unlocking of learners' minds, and is subject to the negative influence of the teacher. The necessary conditions for the promotion of the 'spirit of the school' are damaged by the teacher if he or she attempts to constrain pupil's thinking, if the class size is too big or if the lesson goes on for too long.

Perhaps unsurprisingly, Tolstoy's favored pedagogical strategy was storytelling followed by a question and answer session. He notes that when doing this, students began to all talk at once. To remedy this, he suggests that teachers 'regulate' the children, but do not stifle them:

When there are too many voices speaking at the same time, the teacher stops them, making them speak one at a time; the moment one hesitates, he asks others. When the teacher notices that some have not understood anything, he makes one of the best pupils repeat it for the benefit of those who have not understood. This was not premeditated, but grew up naturally, and it has been found equally successful with five and with thirty pupils if the teacher follows all, does not allow them to cry [shout out] and repeat what has once been said, and does not permit the shouts to become maddening, but regulates that stream of merry animation and rivalry to the extent to which he needs it. (TSYP, 293)

Another method of 'regulation' that Tolstoy advocates is to leave the room while the children quieten down. He notices that in the absence of the teacher, the students do not get worse, but soon settle for the next part of the lesson. Tolstoy states that this free method of allowing students to contribute to the class is useful for the teacher, as it encourages pupils to participate. He strongly condemns the practice of picking on students to answer questions individually, as this emphasizes the unequal relationship of power between the teacher and student and makes lower ability or shy students less likely to join in.

Tolstoy did not intend his school to be a model school. The *Yasnaya Polyana* journal was anticipated to be a record of what had not worked, as well as what had proved successful. In the journal Tolstoy explains how at times teachers did try to coerce their students by shouting, and how this proved counterproductive. Tolstoy's desire not to interfere, but to encourage children's growth by natural development, at times also led to disaster. Once, a boy was found guilty of stealing. Tolstoy then asked his pupils what punishment should be devised – a decision which he would later regret. It was agreed that a label saying 'Thief' should be worn by the child. This prompted jeering and exclusion from the group, and weeping from the child. After the boy stole again and the same punishment was dished out, Tolstoy began to feel that this mob-rule element of his educational experiment was wrong, and he resolved not to subject children to such punishments.

Despite being a 'free' school, it is clear that the teacher had a very important role to play in the pedagogical experiment. In a later article in the *Yasnaya Polyana* journal, 'Training and Education' (July 1862), Tolstoy confirms the views he sets out at the journal's outset, but also explains how teachers' own personal views become a legitimate way of determining what and how to teach. For example, although Tolstoy rejects the possibility of a theoretically demonstrable curriculum plan, he claims, some subjects would be clearly unsuitable in a Russian village. Just as there would be no point opening a shop that sells surgical instruments in a Russian village, argues Tolstoy, similarly there would be no point opening a school that does not teach what experience has corroborated there is a demand for. Nevertheless, Tolstoy asserts that if a teacher can teach any subject in an absorbing and relevant way, this does not go against the principles of the school. Any subject, which was not compulsory, would become naturally integrated into the knowledge of the learner.

In 'Training and Education' Tolstoy explains that a school should be the site of an ongoing, dialogic process where teachers are encouraged to experiment and develop their art. The practice of teachers should rest upon what works. Tolstoy defines 'what works' as what a teacher wishes to teach, and what pupils wish to learn. Thus the process of education is not merely dictated by the whims of the pupils, it is set into motion by allowing a number of people who have a vocation – teachers, to impart knowledge in as many different kinds of innovative and creative ways as they can. In return for the teacher being able to use his or her intuition or skill to aid learning, the pupils have the right to accept or not accept the knowledge on offer.

Tolstoy claims that the urge to bring children up into one's own fold is natural and it is from this that a teacher's enthusiasm and efficacy originates, and where the moral influence of the curriculum lies. It would be foolish to forbid an enthusiastic teacher to give his own point of view, or to deny that there was a moral consequence to his teaching. It is here that real pedagogical freedom is given. Tolstoy writes that only when a 'teacher passionately knows and loves his subject; only then does that love communicate itself to the pupils and work upon them as moral training' (TE, 324).

Tolstoy conceived his pedagogical laboratory as an ongoing experiment based on the needs of students. If the needs of each student can be understood sensitively by teachers, and if teachers are able to use their initiative, it would be possible to create an education system where students can attempt subjects which they wish to study, and where the teacher is able to cater for their needs. Tolstoy adds by way of conclusion, to 'Training and Education,' however, that readers should not be too alarmed by his radical ideas. They will perhaps take over a hundred years to come into being, at which time freely formed institutions will give freedom to a new generation.

Chapter 5

The Results of the Yasnaya Polyana Experiment

Tolstoy's experiences teaching at the Yasnaya Polyana school had a far-reaching influence on his own literary religious and intellectual development. The school was the closest contact Tolstoy had had with the lives of the peasants, and it consequently had an important impact on his understanding of society and its inherent inequality. Of the effect of the school on Tolstoy's awareness of injustice and subsequent desire to challenge the existing social order, Tolstoy's daughter Alexandra observes: 'the fire was kindled and never went out' (AT, 116).

The school also confirmed a number of Tolstoy's views on education. The principal purpose of Tolstoy's school was to allow students a free rein to determine what they needed to learn. Once this had been ascertained, courses of study could then be devised that would fulfill the 'will of the people.' On the basis of his experience, therefore, Tolstoy endorses certain pedagogic strategies and curriculum subjects and rejects others that he considers failures.

In the article 'The School at Yasnaya Polyana,' Tolstoy describes the students' responses to various methods and subjects. To tackle the essential task of teaching reading, Tolstoy devised a system called 'mechanical reading' where students would read out of one book that was passed around the class. This idea was conceived because it was impossible for a teacher to listen individually to all the students in a class at once. The method soon seemed to fail. It lost the interest of students and the relationship between teachers and students soured. Tolstoy notes that in introducing such a method he had broken one of his own pedagogical rules, which he reiterates: '*The more convenient the method is for the teacher, the more it is inconvenient for pupils. Only that manner of instruction is correct with which the pupils are satisfied*' (TSYP, 264; translator's italics). Following this realization, Tolstoy and the teachers at his school then left the students to their own devices as a means of ascertaining the best way of learning to read.

Given a chance to use their own initiative, Tolstoy observes that the students began to read in pairs, the stronger reader often helping the weaker. Soon the school had dropped the practice of 'mechanical reading' altogether, as every pupil began to use whatever approach he or she found best, be it reading with the teacher, or reading communally, or reading with the purpose of learning by heart. Tolstoy concludes his thinking on this experiment with a simple pedagogical maxim: the teacher's task is to offer students a range of learning approaches and strategies that make the process of learning easier. He argues this point passionately, claiming that the military conception of students working in an organized manner under strict discipline fails to recognize that 'each pupil represents a separate character, putting forth separate demands, which only the freedom of choice can satisfy' (TSYP, 269).

Tolstoy's belief in collaboration between students, and the primacy of the child's own exploration of a subject, is also demonstrated in his description of how students learnt to write at Yasnaya Polyana. Tolstoy argues that this should begin by the students first associating the sounds of letters and whole words, and then learning how to trace out their shapes. Tolstoy would write on the walls in chalk and the children would take it in turns to write and then check each other's work. He notes that this process was particularly successful, in that the class educated itself. He says that this activity became like a game and that through it students learnt about grammar, pronunciation and reading. He did not coerce the students to write in cursive form, and argued that prescription was not necessary. The traditional practice of copying out model writing was easy and undemanding for the teacher, but boring and uninspiring for the pupils. Rather, Tolstoy argues, just as adults eat bread, but children may refuse, the students would naturally progress to using cursive writing rather than a mixture of cursive and print.

The importance of children's freedom to form their own concepts

Tolstoy's conclusions with regard to reading and writing demonstrate his view of the psychology of learning, which rests on the natural way students form new concepts. He describes in detail how during a reading comprehension of Gogol, the class did not comprehend the use of specific words but only gathered the general meaning of a passage. As he felt that they had not grasped the particular use of poetic language, Tolstoy set them about the task of reading it again, only to find that their understanding and forming of concepts and interpretation was different from his own, perhaps less detailed, but valid. He did not feel it was legitimate to consider these as incorrect. Another example of this, Tolstoy explains, was how, in a drawing lesson, the children objected to writing 'A drawing by Romashka' under their drawings of a picture originally by the artist Romashka, as they themselves had drawn the picture. The reasoning of the children was that Romashka had only invented the pattern, so the pictures should be labeled as a composition by Romashka but a drawing by the pupil. Tolstoy believed that students must be left to form their own concepts from experience and the general sense of any text read, and these could not be predicted or dictated by the teacher, but only facilitated:

> When he [the pupil] hears or reads an unintelligible word in an intelligible sentence, and then meets it in another sentence, he dimly begins to grasp a new idea . . . ; once used, the word and the idea become his property . . . But consciously to give the pupil new ideas and forms of a word is, in my opinion, as impossible and fruitless as to teach a child to walk by the law of equilibrium. (TSYP, 278)

Such a view of learning resonates with the experiences of Tolstoy's fictional characters, such as Levin in *Anna Karenina*, Olenin in *The Cossacks*, Pierre in *War and Peace* and Nicholas in *Youth*. All these characters change their views according to their experiences as they negotiate their way through significant life events. It also accords with Tolstoy's religious views on the importance of personal interpretation and experience.

Tolstoy's belief in the natural ability of students to form concepts themselves led him to repudiate the Socratic method. He describes in 'The School at Yasnaya Polyana' an unsuccessful history lesson in which he tried to teach concepts such as 'law' or 'Russia' by its use. Teaching by the Socratic method did not enable any of the students to explain in his or her own terms what Russia, or a law was. Tolstoy reflects on this experience, commenting that the Socratic method can be seen as a way of surreptitiously attempting to influence the responses of students, without actually allowing students to form their own new conceptual understanding.

Tolstoy's disapproval of the Socratic method is again apparent in his account of *Anschauungsunterricht* or 'visual instruction,' a German implementation of Pestalozzi's theory. In his parody of it, Tolstoy combines his distaste of the Socratic method and his dislike of the phonetic method in teaching the alphabet. A teacher holds up a picture of a fish and asks the class what they can see. The children come up with various correct responses such as 'it's a fish' or 'it's a picture,' but the answer the teacher is looking for is 'it's a picture of a fish.' This pedantry exemplifies Tolstoy's dislike of conceptually constraining children by applying an educator's own standards, particularly if the children are following an equally valid line of thought. In Tolstoy's vignette, after eliciting the desired response, the teacher goes on to teach the children how to read the word by taking three parts of the sound for the German word for fish: 'f,' 'i,' 'sch.' Tolstoy mocks this breaking up of words, which results in the children being unable to recognize the actual word: 'the poor children writhe, and hiss, and blow, trying to pronounce the consonants without vowels, which is a physical impossibility' (OTR, 49). Tolstoy continues his diatribe claiming that all over Europe he found proud pedagogues in the mold of Pestalozzi, whose claims amounted to nothing but empty, unnecessary terminology. Tolstoy then reaffirms his plea that Russia should not try to impose European methods.

Given his view of the individual nature of each child's understanding and ability to form concepts, it is no surprise that Tolstoy is skeptical of the need for assessment. In the *Yasnaya Polyana* journal he argues that the teacher, who knows and understands each student because of the hours they have spent together, is best placed to judge a child's understanding and progress. Tolstoy argues that if children are no longer required to learn passages off by heart, a practice of which he strongly disapproved, assessment becomes redundant. Examinations only confuse a child as to what real learning is. They begin to equate preparing for examinations with learning.

Tolstoy's criticism of examinations is also present in his literature. The theme of failure in examinations and testing, and the despair it can cause, clearly semiautobiographical in Tolstoy's early works *Boyhood* and

Youth, reoccurs in *War and Peace*, written after Tolstoy's main phase of teaching. When Rostov returns from war he finds life much more pleasant than before enlisting, a time when he was in 'despair at failing in a scripture examination' (WP, 353). Elsewhere in *War and Peace* exams are also criticized as a means of preparing the workforce. Members of high society question the reforms of Alexander's reign as examinations are introduced for posts in the civil service. The critics wonder what use examinations can have in comparison to experience.

Because of his belief that the teacher is best placed to judge an individual's progress, Tolstoy is also skeptical of inspectors and other visitors' abilities to gain the measure of a school's worth in a short visit. It is impossible to make a résumé of all that a pupil knows, Tolstoy argues, just as it is impossible for anyone to make a summary of what Tolstoy knows. Examinations can only be based on a limited amount of knowledge learnt by rote, and this does not equate with genuine knowledge. In order to know what an individual really knows, reflects Tolstoy, you would have to live with that person for months. Furthermore, Tolstoy argues, if examinations are introduced in any subject, it merely creates a new subject: 'preparation for examinations' (TSYP, 296). Tolstoy does not consider that such a subject is based on any form of genuine knowledge. It is therefore not worthy of being taught, as it limits students' creativity and ability to form their own ideas naturally. He concludes that:

> all attempts at examination are only a deception, a lie and an obstacle to instruction. (TSYP, 296)

History, geography and sacred history

With regard to the curriculum subjects experimented with at Yasnaya Polyana, Tolstoy is critical of his attempts to teach history and scathing of geography. He describes vain attempts to explain the seasons of the year and the continents of the world. He recounts the boredom of his students during such lessons:

> I could see the question 'Why?' in each dim vision, in every sound of their voices, whenever I began geography with them, – and there was no answer to that sad question 'Why?' (TSYP, 333)

Tolstoy recognizes the importance of teaching 'how mankind lives' in relation to the 'laws of natural phenomena all over the globe and the distribution of the human race upon it' but he claims that the subject of geography does not do this, but merely creates a set of facts for examination purposes. In his teaching of geography, Tolstoy considers learning from the present context advantageous, as this is a point of reference for pupils. Geography should begin with the schoolroom and the students' own village. However, when he tried this, it soon became a lesson not about geography, but a lesson about drawing. Tolstoy concludes his discussion of history and geography by stressing that '*Up to the university I not only see no need of the study of history and geography, but even a great injury in it*' (TSYP, 339; translator's italics). Tolstoy argues that facts and information not perceived by children to be relevant to their own development should be omitted from study. Otherwise how can schooling help the development of children's own thinking skills?

Tolstoy's dislike of geography can also be seen in his literature. In one of his last works, 'The Wisdom of Children' (WC, 1910), Tolstoy uses geography as an example of the worthlessness of modern education. Forty years earlier, in *War and Peace*, Tolstoy had also derided the subject. One of the commanders, Langeron, at the council of war at Kutuzov's quarters near Austerlitz, expresses his annoyance with the battle plans by dubbing the council meeting as 'a geography lesson!' (WP, 303). Later in his life, Tolstoy reflected that the medium of film, which he encountered in Moscow, could be of much educational worth in schools, particularly in geography, but the medium had only been used to ill-effect.

Despite his frustration with history and geography, Tolstoy explains that sacred history and Russian history were popular subjects at Yasnaya Polyana. The main method of instruction involved storytelling. First Tolstoy would tell the story to a group of children sitting around the teacher. Then he would ask questions to check the students' comprehension. Next the students would write down what they could remember. Tolstoy included a number of such passages of students' work in the *Yasnaya Polyana* journal, demonstrating his concern with students' own interpretations. This interest in students' responses resurfaces in Tolstoy's late work, 'The Teaching of Jesus' for which he used a class of children to select the most important elements of the Gospels.

In sacred history, Tolstoy made extensive use of the Bible. He believed that secondary histories, such as the *Russian Primary Chronicle*, could not equal the poetry and educational worth of the Bible. The stories of the Old Testament enchanted the children, Tolstoy thought, because the stories are both accessible and also complex. At this stage in his career Tolstoy had neither begun to openly promulgate, nor resolve his own view of religion. However, as with his discussions on the nature of art and his telling of stories that he would later use in his fiction, we can also see this period as formative in a religious sense. Tolstoy's experiences teaching the Bible were powerful and he therefore saw learning about the Bible as a foundation to a good relationship with his pupils, and a good introduction to the enterprise of learning itself:

> I tried to read the Bible to them, and I completely took possession of them. The edge of the curtain was lifted, and they surrendered themselves to me unconditionally. They fell in love with the book, with the study, and with me. All I had now to do was to guide them on. (TSYP, 310)

Following his success teaching the Old Testament, Tolstoy felt the next natural step was to teach about other ancient civilizations. However, as he found that students were not interested in learning about the Egyptians and Phoenicians, he gave up teaching about world history and moved on to teach Russian history. Tolstoy believed the children responded better to Russian history because it was something that concerned them and roused national sentiments. Tolstoy suggests that history is most easily taught by relating to the present and then working backwards so children can put the past into perspective and see how it is relevant to them. He recognizes that appealing to the nationalism of the children cannot make all of history exciting, but goes on to retell at length his experience teaching about the Napoleonic invasion of 1812 to an enthralled class. He concludes of his experiments teaching history and geography by stating the only elements that rouse interest in these subjects are poetry and patriotism – the key ingredients for Tolstoy's next venture, the creation of *War and Peace*.

The arts

Tolstoy's desire to support children's investigation into subjects that were naturally interesting to them is demonstrated by his account of teaching singing. Tolstoy claims that singing first found its way onto the curriculum after the children were excited after swimming one summer, when they spontaneously began to sing. Using this enthusiasm, he began to teach harmonies, which he believed children could learn easily and naturally. He decided to work on this and practiced choral singing by having the students sing chords, then scales. The theory behind music had interested Tolstoy since his late adolescence but his description of teaching it in the *Yasnaya Polyana* journal focuses on the children's excitement as they discovered the effect of harmonies and minor chords. Some of the unmusical children dropped out of these classes but Tolstoy tells of how the other students could practice for up to four hours at a time. He writes that he unwittingly began to use a method similar to that of French music pedagogue Chevet, whom he had seen in Paris. Tolstoy claims that in Paris he saw many workmen singing as a result of Chevet's methods, which he saw as ideal for making music popular and accessible to the working classes. He wished to pioneer a similar method for Russian peasants.

Tolstoy's approach to music involved using figures for notes rather than conventional tablature, teaching the timing and melody separately, then bringing them together to form the completed piece. Tolstoy claims that in Chevet's methods there are many exercises, but it is unnecessary to use them as any teacher can devise suitable exercises on the spot for the needs of that particular lesson. According to Tolstoy's principle of independent learning, the teacher must tailor his lesson for the pupil and therefore no pedagogical rule can be considered absolute, which is 'always a source of error in methods' (PVM, 180).

Tolstoy describes how, as the music became more advanced, the musical children who had not dropped out of the lessons began to teach themselves intuitively. He aided this with diagrams which illustrated the major, minor and chromatic scales. However, Tolstoy notes how this free and self-motivated learning was soon spoilt by 'vainglory' as the teachers decided to arrange a performance of the children's singing at the local church. Although this was apparently successful with the church congregation, music lessons were made compulsory in order to prepare for it and the spontaneity and enthusiasm of the pupils were lost.

Tolstoy believed that to create, enjoy and find benefit in art was an important human aspiration, equal across social classes. Teaching the arts was therefore not only educationally valid, but necessary. In 'The School at Yasnaya Polyana' Tolstoy claims the arts can lead children to 'that region of the better enjoyments, toward which his being strives with all the powers of his soul' (TSYP, 340). It is absurd to deny children the enjoyment of the arts. Attempts to confine the teaching of singing and drawing to subjects that can be considered useful for later life, such as technical drawing and church singing, are also ill-founded. Tolstoy argues children are naturally drawn to the arts as part of their innate desire to make sense of their lives and the world around them, therefore the arts should be part of the curriculum.

In the teaching of literature, Tolstoy rarely found any book suitable for such noble goals. He tried Gogol, Defoe, Pushkin and a translation of Homer's *Iliad* but the students found these books immensely difficult and boring. He notes that a number of books designed to be popular and accessible seemed artificial and condescending. He concludes of his experiences that the only books suitable for the peasantry, that were genuinely popular, are those written by the people themselves, such as books of Russian proverbs, songs and legends. The origins of Tolstoy's interest in the genre of folk tales, and in a straightforward, honest literature of the people, which he pursued in later life, can be seen in his experiences at the school. In the *Yasnaya Polyana* journal Tolstoy laments the futility of the literature of the upper classes and makes a plea for a kind of 'transitional literature' to be developed. This preempts his own disillusionment with the decadence and worthlessness of the novel after writing *Anna Karenina*.

In his writings on teaching literature, Tolstoy claims that it is not that students do not understand the words, or how to read, but that most often the peasant children do not understand the concepts in literature. He says that forcefully explaining literary language by use of repetition and didactic exposition in the classroom is therefore useless. It was a form of cultural colonization, a problem that Tolstoy wished to solve with the Yasnaya Polyana experiment by attempting to educate the peasantry while preserving their own culture.

In 'Should We Teach the Peasant Children to Write, or Should They Teach Us?' Tolstoy discusses his experiences setting compositions and suggests that the 'gap' between the social classes, and student and teacher, can be solved by artistic collaboration, and through such a process create a 'literature of the people.' The article focuses on the writing of 'He Feeds You with a Spoon and Pokes You in the Eye with the Handle,' a collaboration between Tolstoy, Morozov (Fyedka) and his friend Makarov (Syomka). He also describes Morozov's own story, 'The Life of a Soldier's Wife.' Both of these stories were printed in the *Yasnaya Polyana* journal. In 'Should We Teach the Peasant Children to Write, or Should They Teach Us?' Tolstoy reflects on the process of writing these stories, to what extent he aided the students, and what pedagogical methods could be extrapolated from them.

Tolstoy writes that the main task of the teacher is to give students a choice of suitable subjects for writing compositions. In the case of these two stories, he had provided proverbs for this purpose. Tolstoy believed these could be a suitable starting point because a number of different narratives could fulfill the suggested meaning of the proverb. Tolstoy's use of proverbs is connected with his interest in spiritual and moral truths and their expression through narrative and in this exercise we can see the seeds of Tolstoy's belief in practical moral knowledge, which he elucidates later in his fiction and essays, and most of all in his last major work *A Calendar of Wisdom*, which consists entirely of aphorisms.

In his description of the writing of the compositions, Tolstoy claims that his successful collaborations with Fyedka and Syomka are evidence for the innate goodness of the child and the worth of heuristic learning. He argues that the child's instincts for truth, beauty and goodness are not related to any teacher's measure of a child's 'development' but that these concepts can only be understood in harmony with each other. Tolstoy suggests that at each stage of development, when we educate a child we should be aiming to harmonize beauty, truth and goodness. This is based upon his view that children naturally develop of their own accord, as it is part of their nature. The mistake of pedagogues is to seek development rather than harmony of development. Rousseau is correct, man is born perfect, Tolstoy claims, and this condition of perfection at birth, is because the child is in a perfect harmony of truth, goodness and beauty. It follows that this harmony can be corrupted by experience.

Educators often overlook the original harmonious state of childhood and corrupt the child through an imbalanced curriculum.

Tolstoy argues that educators should not try and force development but should allow children to rediscover their natural, true and beautiful selves. He likens this to the art of sculpting. A good sculptor will add and take away from his clay to make a balanced, beautiful statue. A bad sculptor will always add more and more material. Tolstoy claims that a teacher should do the same, not aggressively promoting development but moderating it, allowing harmony to resume in the child. He declares that educators are often misguided in their false notion of a child's development and 'do not understand the value of the primitive beauty of the child' (SWTP, 246). Tolstoy suggests that like a bad sculptor, teachers often want to plaster over the imperfections of the child, yet he claims the more educators try and do this, the more they are moving away from 'balancing' the child and will only make the child corrupt:

> To train and teach a child is impossible and senseless for the simple reason that the child stands nearer than I do, nearer than any adult does, to the ideal of harmony, of truth, beauty and goodness. (SWTP, 246)

Tolstoy adds that the teacher's role is merely to provide the material with which the child can intuitively 'balance' themselves. He asserts that as soon as he gave Fyedka complete freedom, he created an unequaled work of literature. He concludes, therefore, that it is not possible to teach children composition, but only to suggest how to begin to write.

Given his rather abstract argument so far, which Tolstoy hesitates in describing as a method or theory, Tolstoy offers more practical advice for creative writing. As in other subjects, Tolstoy suggests that to encourage success teachers must give a wide choice of subjects and allow students to read each other's work as examples. Vitally, the teacher must never suggest corrections regarding handwriting or spelling, but rather assist by encouraging students to choose words judiciously, while keeping in mind the location and the general structure of the narrative. Tolstoy recommends beginning the writing and then allowing the student to 'manipulate' what has been written. The children then choose which words and images to use and this allows them to start writing themselves.

Tolstoy's interest in children's compositions goes to the heart of his concern with social class and the arts. He claims that if the people do not consider high art forms as art, it should not merely be deduced that they are uneducated, but that the art forms of the aristocracy are corrupt, decadent and meaningless. Tolstoy uses an analogy of 'a well-known physiological fact' to illustrate his point. A man who is used to fresh, healthy air walks into a polluted factory and faints on account of the pollution. But hundreds of people continue to work and breathe in the poisonous air. After observation, the physiologist will claim that the person who lives in the fresh air is the healthiest. The same relationship, Tolstoy argues, exists between the common people and the arts. The foul room houses the art of the educated classes, the common people stand outside it in fresh air. It would be possible to educate a peasant to understand classical art but when he did, he would only be breathing the stale air with the full depth of his lungs. This is Tolstoy's explanation of the revulsion of ordinary people when they are introduced to the stagnant and contrived world of the arts of 'educated people.'

Tolstoy considers the need for a new art form or 'new knowledge' that is acceptable to all people – common and 'educated.' His experiment at Yasnaya Polyana can be seen as dialogue between social classes to see what literature they could create. Tolstoy understands this as a symbiotic process: the sentiment and creativity of the people could 'educate' the upper classes as well as *vice versa*. He observes that the music and poetry of the common people can be more beautiful than the works of Pushkin and Beethoven. Indeed, Pushkin and Beethoven only please the upper classes because they are as corrupt as their audience. It follows, therefore, that to argue training is necessary to understand beauty is ridiculous. The natural beauty of the sun, someone's face and 'an act of love and self-sacrifice' are universal and do not require any instruction. Tolstoy argues that he can make such claims because the experience of 'free pedagogy' is able to shed light on many problems. The process of interacting with the children had aided his understanding of such issues. He notes that for years he has been trying to teach the worth of Pushkin, but that 'the chief effect of developing the poetical feeling has been to kill it, that the highly poetical natures have shown the greatest loathing for such explanations' (TSYP, 346).

Literacy

Tolstoy's school was not only a vehicle for arts education, however. He was also deeply interested in the issue of teaching basic literacy. In the article 'On Methods of Teaching the Rudiments' (OTR, February 1862), Tolstoy first discusses this problem, which he later takes up in earnest in the most tangible product of his pedagogical laboratory, his primers for Russian, the *Azbuka* and *New Azbuka*. Tolstoy begins the article 'On Methods of Teaching the Rudiments' by stating his skepticism concerning the contemporary obsession for developing new pedagogical strategies to teach literacy. Tolstoy asserts that education and literacy should not be equated. There are many illiterate people who are intelligent and skilled in the fields of the military, agriculture, craftsmanship and commerce. Conversely, there are many literate people who seem to have no more skills or knowledge as a result of being able to read and write. Tolstoy speculates as to whether the written word is an aristocratic pastime, irrelevant to those who are constantly occupied by manual labor. After all, he writes, the masses have educated themselves in knowledge essential to life without schools or the need to write. Tolstoy argues that the historical origins of the education system explain this because the education system has been constructed from the highest level down. Primary schools were not introduced first, but monastic and secondary schools. Primary schools were eventually conceived to prepare students for the next level and, therefore, basic literacy became their main purpose. But, Tolstoy argues, very few students progress from the primary school to the highest level. Thus he feels the purpose of primary schools should not be to help the people attend the next institution.

Tolstoy considers that there are three methods of teaching basic reading. The first consists in teaching the names of letters, then the sounds of combinations of letters and then learning one book off by heart. The second differs in that it teaches the sound of vowels attached to consonants. The third is the phonetic method where each letter is learnt by its sound, not by its name. He comments that the first two methods can be used to good effect in moderation. The first method, learning the names of letters, makes them easy to remember, but makes spelling harder. The second method helps spelling but can confuse the student about the letters themselves and the pronunciation of Russian vowels. But Tolstoy is scathing about the pure phonetic method, which he claims is 'one of the most comical monstrosities of the German mind' (OTR, 43). This is because it necessitates teachers and students attempting to produce the sounds of consonants without a vowel.

'On Methods of Teaching the Rudiments' also sets out Tolstoy's views on the practice and purpose of educational research underlying the Yasnaya Polyana experiment. He levels criticism at the work of leading pedagogues, arguing that the inventors of new methods like to suggest that their method is much better than the old. But in reality good, experienced teachers should use their judgment to select a combination of methods suitable for the task at hand: 'Experience has convinced us that there is not one bad and not one good method; that the failure of a method consists in the exclusive adherence of one method' (OTR, 44). Tolstoy gives an example of a peasant teacher who uses the traditional method of teaching the names of the letters. In doing so, the peasant will always explain that the consonants really do not have vowels attached. In addition, when learning words, the peasants will in any case also naturally resort to splitting them up into syllables where necessary. Hence good teachers using traditional methods will also unconsciously use elements of the newer phonetic method as part of their search to use what is convenient to the pupil. Tolstoy claims that he knows hundreds of cases where students have learnt well using the old method of learning the letters' names first, and he knows hundreds of cases where the new methods have failed. He claims this is because the old method uses the new method within it whereas the new method merely limits potentially useful methods which could be freely used by teacher or students.

A further problem with educational fads concerns research and new ideas. Tolstoy argues that any new pedagogical method runs the risk of not being accurately assimilated by teachers and pupils. He describes how his own methods proved unsuccessful when adopted by a teacher who had studied at the Yasnaya Polyana school. Tolstoy was dismayed that this teacher, who purported to use his methods, had actually departed from them in a number of ways. For example, the teacher used the phonetic method. When Tolstoy arrived to observe the school he was disappointed to find that the students who could already read according to the old method felt the need to relearn the alphabet according to the phonetic method. Furthermore, the 'unfortunate' students who could read were occupying themselves learning passages off by heart from what Tolstoy considered an 'abominable' edition of fairy tales. Similarly, the students had been taught sacred history not by the Bible, as Tolstoy strongly believed they should, but through a secondary source, without the chance to recount what they could remember. Tolstoy harshly comments that the peasants could teach themselves better by traditional methods than the university educated teacher who had avoided their use.

Tolstoy's conclusion to 'On Methods of Teaching the Rudiments' represents some of the key principles of his educational thought. He suggests that the best method to teach Russian is not the new or the old method, but the method which is most familiar to the teacher. From this foundation the teacher can then add new methods, perhaps of his own invention, to aid learning as he or she sees fit. With regard to literacy, Tolstoy found that teaching the names of the letters, then combining them to make syllables, worked the best, but like all methods this was imperfect and was capable of being improved. For Tolstoy, as different methods suit different pupils, it was obvious that an educator should help each pupil select the most suitable method for his or her own learning. He writes the best teacher acts as a facilitator 'who has at his tongue's end the explanation of what it is that is bothering the pupil' (OTR, 58).

Tolstoy believed that blind adherence to any method is harmful, and teachers should focus on the individual needs of pupils. Teachers should therefore occupy themselves with understanding and testing as many methods as they can by experience. Tolstoy uses the metaphor of a step to explain this. A teacher must regard a new method as a step from which they can progress, but no more: 'as teaching is an art, completeness and perfection are not obtainable, while development and perfectibility are endless' (OTR, 59). Furthermore, the teacher's craft must not be dictated by the results of experiments that have taken place elsewhere.

Good practice must be based upon each teacher's own experience and artisanship, and educators should constantly strive for a more engaging, fairer and more child-centered approach. Indeed, perhaps the most important result of Tolstoy's pedagogical laboratory was its affirmation of his belief in the value of ongoing educational experimentation itself.

With regards to his conclusions on the teaching of literacy, Tolstoy argues that students who had previously been taught how to read in conventional schools had been hampered in their learning. He attributes this to the meaninglessness of the reading material commonly used and the reliance on rote learning. Tolstoy claims schools should be responsive to the needs of their students and that, although the focus on literacy may be pleasing to the school's founders, it is usually seen as a force of repression by the people. For this reason, Tolstoy believed the discussion concerning new methods of teaching literacy was in some ways futile, and unnecessarily expended energy that could be diverted to more important aspects of education. He argues that, afterall, it is clearly possible for a father or brother to teach a child the alphabet in less than three months – an unmethodological approach similar to that enshrined in Tolstoy's later textbook, the *Azbuka*.

The *Azbuka*, *New Azbuka* and *Russian Books for Reading*

Tolstoy's *Azbuka* consists of four parts: the first three are concerned with learning, reading and writing and the fourth is given over to numeracy. The first part begins with the Russian alphabet printed in large type. Then there are pages with pictures of words beginning with each letter, the words and pictures chosen from objects of everyday rural life: a cart, a harness and mushrooms, for example. The pictures were drawn with the help of Tolstoy's own children and each comes with a variety of forms of each letter, including different fonts and cursive forms. After these pictures, come groups of syllables with no meanings, first two letters, then three, four and five. Tolstoy's intention was to encourage students to read familiar words. Once they had understood and practiced common syllables, from these words and from the syllabic exercises, students could then use their knowledge to read new words. Following the groups of syllables, therefore, there are simple sentences.

It is interesting that these sentences are aphorisms and common sayings used by the peasants with a practical or moral element, such as 'While you were sleeping, we were weaving' or 'Dawn gives you money' (AZ, 29). Tolstoy's belief in the value of a sense of humor in school, which is evident in his earlier pedagogical articles, is also obvious. One of the first sentences reads: 'To learn Azbuka makes you scream so the entire house can hear' (AZ, 30). The riddles and proverbs get progressively longer and consist of the kind of material that Tolstoy suggests is the best impetus to begin creative writing.

Part II of the book contains short stories written in simple language for beginners, starting with a number of very short renditions of Aesop's fables. It also includes one of the stories written earlier in 1862, 'The Life of a Soldier's Wife' by Tolstoy's student Morozov (Fedyka). Some stories are Tolstoy's own compositions, later to be regarded as some of his best short stories, such as 'God Sees the Truth, but Waits'; 'A Prisoner in the Caucasus' and 'The Bear-Hunt' (1872). A number of these stories are autobiographic and many are ingeniously short and simple, while still being entertaining or having a moral value.

Tolstoy's son Sergei tells of how Tolstoy would test the stories on his own children, asking them to retell them in his own words. One amusing story, demonstrating Tolstoy's mastery of simple repetition to create a meaningful tale, is 'The Peasant and the Cucumbers' (1872), a story of fewer than 200 words. A peasant goes to a garden to steal some cucumbers. As he creeps into the garden he thinks to himself that with the money he makes from his theft, he will buy a hen. His thinking continues, with the hen he will raise chicks, which he will sell to buy a sow. With the sow, the peasant dreams, he will breed pigs to sell. After selling them, he will buy a mare and raise colts. With the proceeds from the horses he will buy a house and grow cucumbers himself, but around his crops he would supervise the watchmen placed to guard them by shouting 'Oi there! Keep a sharp lookout!' As the peasant shouts this aloud, he raises the alarm to his own crime and is caught and beaten by the watchmen. In this story we see a narrative twist and moral theme similar to those in Tolstoy's later great short stories, such as 'How Much Land Does a Man Need?' (1886), in which a man bargains with the Bashkirs of the Steppes for land, and dies trying to greedily obtain more land than is necessary.

As the *Azbuka* progresses, the texts become longer and more complex. Tolstoy selected stories that he felt were beautiful and clear. He used material that he had gathered from talking to the peasantry and from translations of folk stories from around the world. The stories are obviously intended to have educational value over and above that of basic literacy and, true to Tolstoy's heuristic pedagogy, the moral of each is inductive, rather than didactic.

Part III of the *Azbuka* is comprised entirely of religious material. In the same way that the stories of part II parallel Tolstoy's literary genres of later years, this religious component foreshadows Tolstoy's later religious works. It begins with stories from a standard Russian Orthodox history, the *Russian Primary Chronicle*, printed in columns with vernacular Russian placed alongside the Old Slavonic. Particularly significant, however, is Tolstoy's short excerpt from the Gospel of Matthew reproduced only in the vernacular. Tolstoy devotes one page to the Gospel, but only includes Matthew chapter 22, verses 34–40. In this passage the Sadducees and Pharisees question Jesus and ask him which is the greatest of all the commandments. Jesus replies with the two commandments of love which form the cornerstone of Christianity and later became the foundation to Tolstoy's own simple religious creed: 'Love God with all your heart and soul, and love your neighbor as you love yourself.' Tolstoy had liked this passage since his youth. Its inclusion in the *Azbuka* is clearly meant to have more purpose than to promote literacy, and it reflects Tolstoy's belief in the importance of using genuine biblical text in the classroom. In the *Azbuka* Tolstoy also includes the Lord's Prayer, the Orthodox creed and the Decalogue, but these are only given in Old Slavonic, the liturgical language of the Orthodox Church. Part IV of the *Azbuka* comprises solely of arithmetic; it begins with charts showing the Russian, Roman and Arabic numerals with their Russian pronunciation, along with their position on an abacus. It then moves on to examples of sums and exercises.

The *New Azbuka* is a condensed, simplified version of the first. Unlike the *Azbuka*, the *New Azbuka* has no pictures, and although it uses similar sentences and vocabulary, it is less idiosyncratic. However, it does not depart from the rationale and structure of the original and includes some of the same materials. The *New Azbuka* is designed, like its predecessor, to enable someone who cannot read or write to be able to do so by the end of the book. It is not based on any particular method and moves from the simple to the complex, beginning with the alphabet and syllables, progressing to sentences and stories with the same elements of twist, humor and amusement found in the original. Similar to the first *Azbuka*, its third section contains common prayers in Slavonic and Russian, although it omits the passage from Matthew included in the earlier textbook. The final section again is comprised of basic arithmetic. The *New Azbuka* was supplemented by four *Russian Books for Reading*. These books contain a number of stories suitable for early readers, including some of those previously published in the *Azbuka*. Some are narratives based on the phenomena of the natural world, told as fables, others famous stories from around the world.

Tolstoy's textbooks, the *Azbuka*, *New Azbuka* and *Russian Books for Reading*, are more than just simple introductions to the written Russian language. Much of the content of the textbooks enshrines the Tolstoyan values of Christian forgiveness, the worth of manual labor and the importance of living a good, simple life. In the use of narrative as a device for moral instruction, the inclusion of the wisdom of the ordinary people and that of the Gospel, we see Tolstoy's artistic, educational and religious interests drawn together.

The textbooks partially fulfilled Tolstoy's desire to use folk tales to create a genre both for, and inspired by, the people, and his inclusion of pithy aphorisms can be seen as a precursor to *A Calendar of Wisdom*. Methodologically, the textbooks also draw together a number of concepts and themes prevalent in Tolstoy's pedagogical articles. Like the peasant school itself, they have little theoretical basis, but are shot through with humor, goodwill and religious and moral content. Most importantly, the textbooks can be seen as the fruit of a long and sincere collaboration between student and teacher, peasant and noble, to try to determine how the learning process should proceed.

Tolstoy's restatement on popular education

Tolstoy's second essay titled 'On Popular Education' was published 13 years after his initial statement of the same title. The 1875 essay cannot be considered as a final statement of Tolstoy's views on education but it does give an indication of how Tolstoy's educational views were beginning to set, as a result of his educational experiments. In this essay we can also see Tolstoy's emerging religious ideals contributing to his educational ideas as he describes education as a 'spiritual food' (PE, 323).

The essay was published in the context of Tolstoy's 'great debate' with the pedagogues and the failure of the *Azbuka*. It begins with a critique of two leading Russian pedagogues of the 'German school' Bunakov and Evtushevski, and their methods of teaching basic literacy. Tolstoy again criticizes the imposition of theoretically determined arguments for pedagogical methods. He argues, as he did earlier, that philosophy can provide no basis for pedagogy because there is no resolution to the great philosophical questions, only conjecture: 'a thing [philosophy] which is not clear cannot be the basis of anything, least of all of such an important and simple thing as popular education' (PE, 255).

Tolstoy repeats many arguments from the *Yasnaya Polyana* journal, and also preempts his later prophetic assertions. Education was 'one of the most important affairs of life' but pedagogues, particularly of the German school, rather than focusing on the important aspects of education, have advanced 'monstrous' pedantry in the place of genuine educational inquiry. In opposition to the pedagogues, Tolstoy restates his view of the 1860s. The questions to be asked should not be concerned with the 'science' of how to teach, but rather how teachers and pupils should form the best relationship for learning. Understanding the lives of the peasantry and developing a good teacher-pupil relationship is much more important than abstract methodology. He recounts his experiences abroad and contrasts them with the school at Yasnaya Polyana:

> Nearly everything which the pedagogical world had written about school was separated by an immeasurable abyss from reality [at Yasnaya Polyana] we began to look for those contents and methods which were readily taken up by the pupils [I wanted to know] what I taught was neither injurious nor useless. (PE, 287)

Tolstoy realizes in retrospect another important ramification of the granting of freedom of choice to the learners as he had done in the past. He reflects that in his schools, the teachers had been 'above all learning something all the time' (PE, 295). He again stresses that education should be constantly thought of as an experiment that evolves with the needs of students: 'a teacher never permitted himself to think that in cases of failure it was the pupil's fault ... for every failure of a pupil or of all the pupils he tried to find a remedy' (PE, 295). Pedagogical innovation and improvement was therefore not the job of theoreticians but of each and every teacher, which led to ongoing education of the teachers: 'Every teacher, in advancing his pupils, feels the need of learning himself, which was constantly the case with all the teachers I had' (PE, 297).

As he does in his earlier articles, Tolstoy considers the relationship between learner and teacher as the most fundamental part of the learning process. He stresses the importance of teaching in a way that raises the children's interest and establishes friendly and natural relationships with students. In addition to this it was essential that teachers were enthusiastic and knowledgeable about their subject: 'the more the teacher knows and loves his subject, the more natural and easy his instruction will be' (PE, 293). In the conclusion to 'On Popular Education' and to his educational experiment at Yasnaya Polyana, Tolstoy repeats the same maxim that he first used in his essay of the same title, published 13 years previously: 'the only criterion of pedagogy is freedom, the only method – experience' (PE, 288).

Chapter 6

The Devil of False Education

Tolstoy was alarmed at the prospect of political and ideological manipulation of young minds in schools. In the *Yasnaya Polyana* journal, he passionately argues against a centralized, state-funded national education system and then extends his criticism to the universities. Tolstoy's critique derives from his understanding of the term 'education.' For Tolstoy, the process of learning should consist in allowing the learner freedom to form concepts themselves; the school should broker such an education by promoting a natural investigation of the world through a continuing collaboration between teacher and students. Given Tolstoy's convictions expressed in his pedagogical articles, it is no surprise he also criticizes conventional forms of education in his literature. In his later writings, he goes on to condemn the education systems of modern nation-states as cogs in the machine of a corrupt, deceptive and evil social order.

In 'Training and Education,' included in the July 1862 edition of the *Yasnaya Polyana* journal, Tolstoy outlines his definition of 'education' and how it differs from the terms 'training' and 'instruction.' Tolstoy believed that the pedagogues of his time had confused training and instruction with education to the detriment of learners. Instruction and training are based upon the idea that the pupil is subordinate to the teacher: the only learning that takes place is that which is directly controlled and imparted by the teacher. Tolstoy claims that such an approach blocks learners off from the natural educational opportunities of life. In their place, it erroneously places the narrow beliefs of the instructor as those solely deemed worthy of study.

Tolstoy defines education in 'Training and Education' as 'the sum of all the influences which develop a human being, and give him or her a broader outlook on the world and new information' (TE, 294). A true education goes far beyond instruction and training: it is intrinsically unpredictable, free and heuristic in nature. Tolstoy lists games, suffering, parental discipline, work, independent study, the arts, science and the experience of life itself all as contributing to a genuine education. Training and instruction, on the other hand, can only be considered the passing of limited information from one person to another and are therefore 'sterile, illegitimate and impossible' (TE, 296).

Tolstoy considers how such a narrow concept as 'training' could have come about. He claims that it has its origins in the family, religion, the state and high society. All of these social structures foster in people the desire to make children the same as themselves. This is natural for parents, and the basis of training in religion is also understandable, given that religions claim to be the exclusive route to salvation. Tolstoy sees the government and high society's agenda in training people to perform the tasks necessary for their survival, however, as deeply problematic.

Tolstoy observes that all educational institutions in society are run by the upper classes and, because of this, it is no surprise that the students, who also include those from the lower classes, complain that they are being trained in useless and foreign ideas. Tolstoy cites the example of a schoolmistress who complains that no matter how she tries to train girls to be ladies, she can never obliterate the influence of the family home. Tolstoy argues that this is perfectly understandable. The nurture of the home in providing food, warmth and care is far more powerful than the experience of learning to speak French or learning about Alexander the Great. It is only natural that girls would learn more at home than at school. Tolstoy applies this analogy to all educational institutions, identifying the underlying problem with such forms of training: 'one person or a small collection of people are admitted to have the right to make other people into what they want them to be' (TE, 301).

In contrast to these criticisms, Tolstoy justifies the possibility of the Yasnaya Polyana school educating in a 'free' way, rather than coercing students into a predetermined mold. Tolstoy argues that a school is not a building or even an organization. It is instead, 'the conscious action of the educator upon the persons who are educating themselves' (TE, 320). By this Tolstoy means that although schools should provide a service, the school should not deliberately form the character, beliefs or formation of knowledge of the pupils. Rather the pupils should be given the freedom to understand the order of things in the way they feel they should. At the Yasnaya Polyana school, therefore, Tolstoy claims, the students are more independent, fresher, and have a better sense of justice than those who have merely been trained.

In the last article of the *Yasnaya Polyana* journal, 'Progress and the Definition of Education' (PDE, December 1862), Tolstoy further clarifies his definition of education as emancipatory by arguing that education is conceptually related to the notion of equality. For Tolstoy 'education is the activity of man which has for its base the need of equality.' Tolstoy stresses that this definition is derived from observation, and he means the term 'education' in its most general sense. The tendency of pupils toward an equalization of knowledge with their teacher is an important part in the educational process and can be the only true cause of education. Other 'causes' such as motivation for financial gain, or to help society in an instrumental sense, only cloud the fundamental aim of every educator.

Education and progress

In 'Progress and the Definition of Education' Tolstoy discusses the relation of education to the then widely held Hegelian view of historical progress. The argument for a historical basis for education – that one generation has the right to educate the next because they have the necessary knowledge and experience according to the law of progress in human history – is flawed, Tolstoy argues. We cannot make judgments about the worth of something solely based on its position in history. Instead, we should think by 'direct consciousness' about what is true, not merely allow our intellectual judgments to be dictated by time and place. Tolstoy asserts that in his educational experiment he is searching for eternal and immutable laws governing education: 'that common mental law which ... could be a criterion for the correct human activity in education' (PDE, 159). The historical view cannot find such absolutes and cannot help decide what is necessary to teach.

Tolstoy continues his argument by attacking the very idea of progress. Unlike many of his time, Tolstoy did not agree with the natural progression of history. He argues in 'Progress and the Definition of Education' that the examples given by historians of the universal progress of humankind are limited. They ignore the fact that the majority of humankind does not live in Western Europe, and those who do live outside Europe often think it is less civilized or 'advanced' than their own country. This is because people's ideas of improvement in well-being differ: some think it is material comfort, others the progress of love and equality. Tolstoy argues that if society progresses in one aspect of well-being, another may well deteriorate. To prove his point, he cites examples of great thinkers and artists in history, such as Homer and Raphael, who have not been equaled in the modern era.

In 'Progress and the Definition of Education' Tolstoy also raises a number of concerns about the negative side-effects of the so-called progress of his age. He articulates his concern that industrialization will exploit the poor rather than bring them wealth and criticizes the decadence of the aristocratic literary classes. Tolstoy's lack of faith in science and technology to deliver social amelioration, without a similar spiritual revolution, key to his mature religious views, is evident in this early article: 'the progress of well-being, according to our conviction, not only does not spring from the progress of civilisation, but for the most part is opposed to it' (PDE, 179). In opposition to so-called progress, Tolstoy champions the rural workers who 'in the absence of city temptations' do not require manufactured goods or railways that require the destruction of the forests (PDE, 176).

The problem of a national education system

In 'A Project of a Plan for the Establishment of Popular Schools' (PES, March 1862) Tolstoy critiques a government proposal for the instigation of compulsory state-funded education for all of Russia. The article foreshadows Tolstoy's later criticism of education as a corrupting factor in society and also illustrates a number of Tolstoy's views on the organization and management of schools. The government plan, which was not enacted, was first postulated by the Minister for Education, E. P. Kovalevski, and then his replacement, A. V. Golovin. It outlines a plan for levying a tax which would pay for 50,000 schools to be established across Russia – as had been instituted in America.

Tolstoy argues that a foreign model such as that suggested by the government proposal would not work in Russia. The people would see the tax as an unnecessary burden and the responsibility for encouraging the students to attend the school would fall with the Justice of the Peace and the police. He claims that the forced instigation of schools would only enrage the population, rather than encourage them to become educated. He is skeptical that it is possible to centrally determine a course of study for all of Russia and believes that public officials would not be able to administer such a large task while being responsive to the needs of each locality.

The biggest problem with the plan was that schools would not be under the control of local peasants, but would be dictated to by the government. Tolstoy claims that the officials in charge would have no experience of dealing with the peasantry and would not be able to coordinate and evaluate schools remotely. Measuring the success of a school is problematic, Tolstoy argues, in terms of inspections and by the examination of pupils' knowledge and progress. For example, a conscientious teacher would not wish to show off his pupils to an inspector, whereas a less scrupulous teacher would only work for the inspection. Tolstoy, therefore, argues that a higher administrative authority would only do harm to the pupils because a bureaucrat with no real working knowledge of the school would appoint and dismiss teachers, the most important part of the job, by hearsay rather than a genuine understanding of their ability.

Tolstoy is equally skeptical about the provision in the plan for training teachers. He claims that attempts to train teachers in France, Germany, England and Russia have all met with failure. Tolstoy is convinced that training teachers is as impossible as it is 'to train artists and poets' because teachers have to learn through their own experience. In addition, a course of study set up by the government would be too narrow. Such centralized prescription of the curriculum is highly problematic, writes Tolstoy:

> [A centralized curriculum] excludes the possibility of all lively interest of the teacher in his work; [and] it gives rise to endless abuses (the writer of the text book need only make one mistake, and that mistake becomes obligatory all over Russia). (PES, 78)

Tolstoy also thinks that such centralized courses are unlikely to actually be followed by teachers who are responsible to the needs of the community and the children. For a higher institution it may be possible to separate courses of study but in the primary school all subjects become one. Tolstoy illustrates this by giving the example of teaching of literacy, noting that once students can read they need to understand a whole range of subjects, which cannot be limited.

The proposal to have an annual public exam also concerns Tolstoy. He claims that exams have no educational worth and they lead to deceit and forgery by officials. Furthermore, it is wrong to make children of 8 compete with each other. He asserts that it is impossible to determine the knowledge of an 8-year-old child or the teacher's worth in a 2-hour examination. The resulting diploma that would be given to children would be worthless in enticing the peasant children to school.

Tolstoy then goes on to discuss a part of the project that would legalize private independent schools. Apparently, a law of 1828 forbade these schools, but in reality no one acted as though this law existed, and thousands of schools had been founded without permission. Tolstoy asks whether there is an existent law that prescribes text books and the appointment of teachers, because he is unsure if some of the circulars of the committee are requests or laws. Tolstoy laments any attempt to tighten this regulation, claiming that many people would still not wish to register their schools or would still be ignorant of the need to do so.

Part of Tolstoy's argument against such legislation is that the distinction between home education and school is impossible to define, thus pre-empting the closing remarks of his last statement on education 'On Upbringing' (OU, 1909). He cites an example of an Innkeeper hiring a teacher for his two children but three others come for instruction, he asks if this would count as a school. Here Tolstoy again stresses his opposition to government interference in education: 'There are relations of man to man, which cannot be defined by laws, such as domestic relations, the relations of him who educates to him who is being educated, and so forth' (PES, 87). Tolstoy is also skeptical of the inclusion of articles in the proposal that state the education provided by each school should be supervised by the clergy in the spirit of the Orthodox faith.

In the second part 'A Project of a Plan for the Establishment of Popular Schools,' Tolstoy explains his concern of the lack of consultation with the public over the plan. Had so-called experts been consulted it would have made no difference. What is important is the people themselves are consulted, but that the Ministry of Public Instruction ruled this out before the committee was formed to discuss the details. Tolstoy claims that the project was limited to its main conclusions from the outset: the government would have to raise funds for it themselves; it would be controlled by the government; the clergy would have power; schools would be treated uniformly across Russia. Tolstoy again asserts, as he does elsewhere in the *Yasnaya Polyana* journal, that in order to invent a Russian system of education, it would have to grow out of the will of the people and this could not happen by government diktat.

Tolstoy argues the project, if implemented as planned, would have much more negative results than the government intended. Before any education could take place, the peasants would be informed of a tax for the setting up of schools and then another levy for the building of the school. The money would be collected with difficulty, and would necessitate the use of force and compulsion. The curator would most likely be a member of the landed gentry and so education, 'the most serious business in the world will become his plaything' (PES, 99). The peasants would resent giving up land for the teacher's use. The curator would most likely give jobs to prospective teachers who had finished their courses at university or seminaries and these would not necessarily be the best people for the job.

Tolstoy claims that in recent years people had become more interested in education and a number of 'free' schools had been set up, but this free movement of the masses would be hampered by the government initiative imposing its own system of education. He concludes 'A Project of a Plan for the Establishment of Popular Schools' by stating that the proposal would only enrage the people who would then turn away from education because the government had hurried to instigate an ill-considered plan.

The problem with universities

In the article 'Training and Education' Tolstoy criticizes the education offered by universities. Eikhenbaum (1982b) believes that much of this scathing criticism is leveled against Chernyshevsky, the editor of *The Contemporary*. As well as exposing Tolstoy's exasperation with the intelligentsia, the article also coincided with the suspension of *The Contemporary* and the arrest of Chernyshevsky, during a time of civil unrest in the universities. According to Eikhenbaum, Tolstoy, fearing arrest deliberately attacked them. Armstrong and Pinch (1982) argue that the uncensored document may have criticized schools as well as universities but the Minister of Education censored this, feeling that academics would probably attempt to defend themselves but schools would not. Regardless of the issues surrounding the circumstances of Tolstoy's writing, it is not surprising that Tolstoy criticizes universities in the *Yasnaya Polyana* journal given his dissatisfaction with his own time at university, clearly documented in *Youth*.

In 'Training and Education' Tolstoy accuses the universities as being the source of the decadence, false pride and arrogance of the upper classes. The academic subjects taught are wholly inapplicable to life, whereas the student, taken from home, is encouraged to lead a life of sloth and to pick up bad habits such as smoking and drinking. The only methods of study are memorization of materials for exams so students do not take part in any real investigation but merely have to ingratiate themselves with the professors by agreeing with their views on a given subject. Tolstoy criticizes lectures as being an 'amusing ritual, devoid of significance' (TE, 307). He claims that the reason the lectures are not published is because they are not of sufficient quality, and thinks that their justification as 'oral communication' would be valid if only they allowed for true debate.

Tolstoy observes that of fifty students at a lecture, ten people take notes. Six of these are doing so just to please the professor. Four are writing down notes sincerely but only two of them will complete the notes on the whole lecture course. This is similar to the description given in *Youth*, where Nicholas finds the lectures useless and makes sketches of the people around him. Because of the insufficiency of the lectures, students fall back on the textbooks anyway. Naturally the students need to interrupt to ask questions but this is not possible as the lecturer goes on at his own speed. The lectures are therefore only attended by students in order to please the lecturer, and to pass the oral exams conducted by the professors.

Tolstoy considers that as the basic idea of the university is to be a 'gathering of people for the purpose of mutual education' there must be many unofficial universities in Russia (TE, 308). However, the official universities which are supposed to be liberal in nature are little more than women's colleges or military academies set up with the sole purpose of training the upper classes. Tolstoy explains that the problem with universities is that they neither endorse the important principle of freedom in education nor that of coercion. Better, he says, would be to form universities on the basis of the people's needs, but this is impossible because no one has yet considered what they may be.

Tolstoy levels particular criticism at the examinations in universities, which he argues serve not as a measure of knowledge, but merely as an opportunity for the professors to exercise their power over students. The examinations are preceded by the frenetic activity of students swotting up and cramming the syllabus, with the hope of impressing the professors. Tolstoy claims that students who do well at university could study just as well on their own and only need the use of a library. The so-called educative influence of institutions like Oxford is not proven empirically, and universities have a corrupting influence on students who mostly live away from the good influence of their families. There is clearly no benefit in the university system because students have no contact with the professors and consequently there is 'no trust and love' between the educator and learner (TE, 314).

Tolstoy argues that the maleducative and corrupting influence of the university can be contrasted with the positive influence of the family which naturally prepares young people for life and work. University merely places an immature young man in a world of temptation, without moral guidance or support. Tolstoy notes that the university student may return home after his course arrogant and in disagreement with the commonsense of his family but he will not have the important skills Russia needs. Qualified university graduates cannot earn what a peasant manager of railway labourers earns because they ultimately do not have any useful skills. Likewise in schools, graduates and non-graduate teachers get paid the same because a university education does not mean the teacher will be any better. In short, Tolstoy asserts, 'the university does not prepare the sort of people that mankind needs, but the sort of people that corrupt society needs' (TE, 315). Those graduates who do find themselves in employment in the civil service do so through nepotism, not because of their knowledge acquired at university. Furthermore, Tolstoy continues, there are, after all, many fair and good people without a university education.

Tolstoy considers one objection to his critique of universities – that other European societies find universities beneficial. In response Tolstoy argues, it is not clear European countries have developed in the best way and furthermore it is not certain that Russia needs to follow European countries – humanity may not necessarily develop universally in the same manner. He looks east to Asia, claiming that those societies are quite often educated but in a different way from the West.

In 1903 over 40 years after writing 'Training and Education' Tolstoy remained critical of universities. Tolstoy's friend Goldenweiser recounts how Tolstoy advised one young visitor at Yasnaya Polyana that it would be better for him to study what he wished in a public library, rather than to enter a university. According to Goldenweiser, Tolstoy then spoke about his own experience at Kazan noting that he could pursue his intellectual interests, in particular the study of Rousseau, better outside of university than as a student. Goldenweiser also records the following comments Tolstoy made about secondary schools, also echoing his views of 40 years earlier:

> Everyman is a perfectly individual being, who has never existed before and will never happen again. It is just the individuality, the singularity of him, which is valuable; but school tries to efface all this and to make a man after its own pattern. The pupils of the Tula secondary school came to me lately and asked what they should do. I said to them: above all, try to forget everything you have been taught. (GW, 121–122)

Criticism of formal education in Tolstoy's novels

Criticism of formal education is evident throughout Tolstoy's literature after 1862 and reflects many of the themes set out in the pedagogical articles and his earlier writings.

The romanticization of the simple or natural, in contrast to the imposed rules of 'educated' society, as presented in the experience of the child in *Childhood*, *Boyhood* and *Youth* is continued in a slightly different form in *The Cossacks*. The novella, began in the Caucasus and finished ten years later while Tolstoy taught at his school, champions the exotic and free lives of the Cossacks. The earthy wisdom of the natural folk is personified in the character of 'Daddy' Eroshka, based on Tolstoy's friend Yepishka, a skilled, if not often drunk, hunter. Eroshka is a simple bachelor who is both friendly, a source of amusement to the children of the village, and an important repository of knowledge and confidant of the young Olenin and his Cossack rival, Lukashka. Eroshka, an experienced huntsman, wonders why 'Russians were all "simple" and so rich, and why they knew nothing and yet were educated' (TC, 93). Tolstoy juxtaposes the naturalness of Daddy Eroshka's practical knowledge and affable, generous nature with the pretentious and self-aggrandized teacher, Elias Vasilich, who attempts to use French and classical allusions to show off his superior class:

> The Teacher, Elias Vasilich, was an *educated* Cossack. He had been to Russia proper, was a regimental school teacher, and above all, he was noble. He wished to appear noble, but one could not help feeling that beneath his grotesque pretence of polish, his affectation, his self-confidence, and his absurd way of speaking, he was just the same as Daddy Eroshka. (TC, 106; translator's italics)

Similar themes are reaffirmed in *War and Peace*. In the opening scene, Prince Vasili Kuragin laments that despite providing the best education for his son, the rake Anatole, has turned out an 'imbecile' (WP, 7). At the debacle of the proposal of Anatole to Maria Bolkonsky, Prince Vasili stresses to the old Prince Bolkonsky that he did what he could in sending him abroad to be educated. Again, when the exploits of Dolohov, Anatole and Pierre are lamented in society, it is blamed on Pierre's education abroad and the effects of a 'modern education' (WP, 41). The worthlessness of rational education is also suggested in the eccentric old Prince Bolkonsky's attempts to educate his daughter. He aims to develop the two virtues of 'energy' and 'intelligence' through lessons in algebra and geometry until Maria is 20. But his attempt to combat 'superstition' and 'idleness' in such a way is partly counterproductive as Maria becomes increasingly interested in religion and invites superstitious pilgrims into her home.

In another episode in *War and Peace* that questions the worth of education, Pierre gives money for schools, which ends up in embezzlement, and in a sham village school. Pierre discusses this with Andrei, and not knowing that the school was a front, claims setting up schools for the peasantry is a good thing. Andrei denies the use of education as he believes it to be a way of making people think beyond the 'animal existence' of avoiding physical and mental suffering. Why lift the peasants out of their animal existence and 'awaken spiritual needs' when 'animal happiness is the only happiness possible' (WP, 450)?

Such discussions on education also occur in *Anna Karenina*. When Levin visits the Sviazhskys, the topic of schools and education becomes part of a detailed debate between Levin and Sviazhsky. Sviazhsky argues that for the improvement of Russian society, Russia needs to educate the people and for this 'three things are needed: schools, schools, schools!' (AK, 361). Levin, like Andrei, makes the argument that schools will not help the people. What they need is economic development, after which schools and education will naturally follow with greater prosperity and more leisure time. For Levin, to educate the people before an improvement in economic conditions would only give them knowledge of things which they are yet unable to obtain: 'you say schools, education, will give them fresh wants. So much the worse, since they won't be able to satisfy them. And in what way knowledge of addition and subtraction and the catechism is going to better their material position, I never could make out' (AK, 361).

In another similar discussion, Levin and his brother discuss the merits of the *Zemstva*, and Levin states his indecision regarding the provision of education for the peasantry:

> why should I bother myself about establishing ... schools to which I should never send my children, to which the peasants would not want to send theirs either – and to which I am not at all sure they ought to send them? (AK, 264)

Pushed further by his brother, Levin argues that he cannot see education as being 'good or practical' (AK, 265). The irritation that bothered Levin throughout the discussion coincides with his desire to leave his visitor in the house and go and mow with the peasants.

Levin's epiphanies after observing peasant life demonstrate Tolstoy's distrust of education in comparison with a simple life consisting of physical labor. As Levin lies under the stars on a freshly stacked haycock reflecting on the 'consecrated' nature of physical labor, he thinks about what he is to do with his life, wishing to renounce his old decadent life and live an honest simple one, part of which involves renouncing 'his utterly useless education' (AK, 298).

The uselessness and unnatural nature of formal and traditional forms of education is also reflected in Levin's view of his sister-in-law's insistence on speaking French to her children. Levin thinks to himself that speaking French to the children is 'affected and unnatural' and that through this the children only learn pretence – 'Learning French and unlearning sincerity'. He further reflects that over-educating is not necessary for a child's development: 'All one has to do is not spoil children, not contort them, and they're sure to be delightful' (AK, 293). On another occasion, Levin agrees to help Dolly with the education of Oblonsky's son, only reluctantly following the textbook rather than using his own preferred methods. Levin's distaste for textbooks is again restated in a conversation with Lvov, Kitty's sister's husband, where he plays down the importance of grammar in favor of 'moral training.'

An example of a poor form of education is given by the unemotional and methodical bureaucrat Karenin. Karenin takes particular interest in the education of his son, Seriozha, when Anna leaves him. He reads books on pedagogy, and devises a program of study, only to be dissatisfied with his son; 'he displays a certain indifference towards the essential questions which ought to touch the heart of every man and every child' reports Karenin to Countess Lydia Ivanova (AK, 545).

The inadequacy of Karenin's rational curriculum of instruction is demonstrated by Tolstoy's depiction of the dreamy psychology of Seriozha's learning: 'He felt he was not to blame for not having learned the lesson: try as he would, he positively could not manage it. While the teacher was explaining, he believed he understood, but as soon as he was left alone he positively could not remember or understand' (AK, 551). The disappointment of not being able to please the teacher leads Seriozha to ask the teacher when his birthday is, to which he receives the cold answer 'Birthdays are of no importance to a rational being' (AK, 551). Here we see Tolstoy comparing the intuitive kindness of the child with the imposed rationalistic and irrelevant regime of adults, the same regime that reasons it is better to tell Seriozha that his mother is dead than tell him that she has left his father. Just as Levin wishes to leave the decadent, false life of high society for the goodly, earthly life of the peasants, the goodness of the child and his natural desire for his mother is juxtaposed with the false morality of keeping up appearances. In another memorable vignette, Karenin punishes his son for not understanding the lessons 'necessary' for him to become Christian, yet as Tolstoy explains, although Seriozha learnt his lessons badly, he was 'far cleverer than the boys his teacher held up as examples' as his 'soul was full of other more urgent claims than those his father and teacher made upon him' (AK, 554).

False education as the work of the devil

Tolstoy's denunciation of formal education is strongly linked to his condemnation of modern society itself. The famous short-story 'The Death of Ivan Ilych' confirms Tolstoy's critique of the education of his time. In it Tolstoy suggests education is just another part of the machinery of a society that fails to promote true moral action, in favor of spiritless materialism. Tolstoy places the education of Ivan Ilych's son along with the empty, decadent paraphernalia of Ivan Ilych's middle-class aspirations, such as the furniture and bronze statues. These pretentious, pointless articles are obtained because they are the 'done thing'; not because they are right. It is telling that Tolstoy's brief description of Ivan Ilych's son is that of one who is morally corrupted, a boy who has eyes that give 'the look of boys of thirteen or fourteen who are not pure-minded' (DII, 119).

Although Tolstoy makes no reference to the teaching profession other than with regards to Ivan Ilych's son going through the motions and 'duly learning what is taught at High Schools' (DII, 134), it is important to note Tolstoy's criticism of the professions, and indeed the sham theatre of dry professionalism itself. Tolstoy's dislike and disbelief of doctors is well known and documented. In the short story Tolstoy compares Ivan Ilych's own abilities as a lawyer with those of the doctor. This criticism resounds with Tolstoy's view of the role of the teacher.

Although both Ivan Ilych and his doctor can deftly apply the powers of rational thought to provide a concise summary of the facts, it is not this kind of professionalism which is needed. The doctor's rationalism is ultimately useless, providing an empty hope, and his visits become a form of mere artful deception. This is similar to Tolstoy's view of the work of the teacher as essentially intuitive. As argued in his pedagogical articles, education, like medicine and law should not be based upon deductive reasoning or the application of theory alone, but on the forming of a warm nurturing relationship that recognizes the experience of individuals.

Tolstoy's condemnation of formal education and its place in the corrupt social order comes to its ultimate and poetic conclusion in the late religious fable, 'The Restoration of Hell' (1903). To begin the tale, Tolstoy vividly describes Beelzebub and his devils in hell at the point of Jesus' crucifixion. The devils realize that they have lost the battle and that Christ's message has been victorious. However, Tolstoy narrates, slowly in the hundreds of years after the crucifixion, the devils succeed in restoring hell through the corruption of the teachings of Jesus.

One devil, 'a shiny black one, naked except for a cape thrown over his shoulders' hatches an ingenious plan by creating the Church (ROH, 311). With this invention the devil intends that the people would not believe in the teaching of Jesus but in the Church, which corrupted by its power, would promulgate the distractions of schism, rituals, pointless doctrine and legitimized institutionalized violence and theft. To make doubly sure that men do not turn to the simple, self-evident truth of Jesus' teaching, to treat others as we would like to be treated, another devil 'with a flat receding forehead, protruding ears, and feeble limbs' (ROH, 324) tells of another great deception, science, which like the Church, also stops men of thinking about how they should live. Around these two arch-devils of science and the Church clamor and snarl a number of devils, all in charge of deceptions that aid and promote the disunity of humankind: the devil of technology, the devil of intoxication, and so forth. In among these is the 'devil of education' that has a crucial part in upholding the rest of the great lies. He states that he has been successful in encouraging humankind to keep up the hypocritical sham of mass education, by having persuaded 'men that while living badly and not even knowing what a right life consists, they teach children the right way of living' (ROH, 329). The story ends with the two arch-devils of the Church and science joining paws and encircling Beelzebub in a dance, snorting and snapping their tails.

This fable demonstrates Tolstoy's view that education played a vital role in supporting the Tsarist social order, bolstering the political ends of the Church, science and the government in the profusion of evil and deceit. However, it is not just the political nature of the ideological battle between the scientists and the Church that is to blame for ensnaring individuals, the process of studying and the forms of knowledge favored by intellectuals also form a barrier against the simple, good life of loving God and neighbor. The devil of science explains how he had managed to deceive men by the power of rational thought itself, the natural sciences being a decoy to encourage the most intelligent people to search for wealth or alleviation from inevitable death and disease. On the other hand, theology has become an enterprise with which to 'absorb' men so they would not 'think about how to live' and philosophy was just the study of 'everything written by a man called Aristotle' (ROH, 325).

This fable can be seen as an extreme polemic advocating an extreme point of view: the Tolstoyan denial of modern civilization. It is written in a hyperbolic style, and its form must be considered as one intended for amusement, as well as political satire and spiritual revelation. However, there is no doubt that Tolstoy passionately believed in the message it espoused. It draws upon views long held by Tolstoy concerning education, its related forms of knowledge and the undesirability of state or Church control of a national education system. According to Tolstoy, if it is not free and true, education, by enslaving and deceiving, could become the work of the Devil himself.

Chapter 7
The Spiritual Nature of a Genuine Education

An examination of Tolstoy's later correspondence and diary entries provides proof of his continuing, passionate interest in education into old age. Following his so-called spiritual conversion, perhaps unsurprisingly, Tolstoy's educational writings became more overtly spiritual and religious. As no copyright existed on his works after 1881, many of his letters were distributed all over the world as pamphlets and in compilations. In one such letter, translated and distributed as the 'Letter to Liberals' written on 31 August 1896, Tolstoy maintains his criticism of the 'pseudo-educational institutions' which advanced not education, but the deception and ignorance of the people.

Tolstoy's diary entry of 11 May 1901 gives some further insight into his reasoning. The corrupt status quo was due to nothing other than false religious education, which could be seen as the source of contemporary Russia's woes:

> In my search for the cause of evil in the world I've been delving deeper and deeper. At first, I imagined the cause of evil to be evil people, then the rotten structure of society, then the violence which upholds this rotten structure, then the participation in violence of the people who suffer from it (the army), then the lack of religion in these people, and finally I became convinced that the root of it all is religious education. And therefore, in order to eliminate evil, there is no need to replace people, to dissuade people from participating in violence or even to refute false and expand true religion, but only to educate children in the true religion. (TD, 495)

Tolstoy's mature view that education should be based on the 'true religion,' is partly due to his belief that 'genuine' knowledge could not be gleaned from the decadent and illusory rational discourse of the academy.

As Tolstoy observes elsewhere in his diary, people who can't read and write are 'more sensible than scholars' because 'in their consciousness the natural and sensible order of importance of objects and questions has not been disturbed' by scientific, rational enquiry (TD, 573). Traditional forms of education neglect the central moral questions that face all human beings. As Tolstoy writes: 'Man doesn't know what is good and what is bad, but he writes a research paper on a fallen aerolite or the origin of the word "cowl"' (TD, 573).

Despite Tolstoy's plea that children should be brought up as servants of God in the true religion, he never rejected the tenets of a heuristic and individual pedagogy expounded in his earlier works. He felt that as well as having a moral duty to be truthful to their students, teachers should also avoid imposing their own convictions on children. The pamphlet *The Religious Education of Young* (c.1901), published by Chertkov drawing on material from Tolstoy's notebooks, reaffirms Tolstoy's belief that false religious education was one of the key contributors to the immoral social order. To initiate a better form of education, teachers should communicate moral values through the curriculum, but above all, through their own actions. An essential part of this was honesty – the teacher must admit their ignorance if question arises that cannot be answered – such as the origin of the universe. This is far better than promulgating the fraudulent myths of Orthodox Christianity, the 'religious lie' which maims the souls of children. After all, the child is already aware of God, and this implicit knowledge should be nurtured rather than usurped.

All Tolstoy's late writings on education stress its spiritual basis. This is not so much a change in his thinking as a natural conclusion to his own spiritual and intellectual journey, in which his experience of teaching played its part. His educational ideas reflect his theological and aesthetic views. Tolstoy's interest in religious education and his insight into the moral and spiritual development of children dates from his earliest works of literature. In both *Boyhood* and *Youth*, the onset of new stages of Nicholas' development is heralded by his moral and spiritual awakening. A key part of this growth is Nicholas' discovery of the feeling of remorse and the voice of conscience in a journey of self-awareness which takes on deeply spiritual overtones:

> The blacker the circle of my recollections of the past, the clearer and brighter stood out the clear, bright point of the present and fairer

streamed the rainbow colours of the future. That voice of repentance and passionate desire for perfection was the main new sensation of my soul at this period of my development, and it was this that laid a new foundation for my views of myself, or mankind, and of God's universe. (YO, 231)

As in all Tolstoy's fiction, nevertheless, religious conversion and spiritual development is tempered by disillusion and imperfection. Nicholas is annoyed that his newly found virtues are unnoticed by the rest of the household, and the application of his 'Rules of Life' seem 'misshapen on paper and in life in general'(YO, 236). The moral arrogance of Nicholas is humorously retold by Tolstoy as he brags to his cab driver, beaming with spiritual pride about his candid confession to a monk, even though he uses the man's services without paying for them. The embarrassment of this leads his new found purity to disperse 'like smoke' (YO, 245).

Tolstoy's experiences teaching the Bible at the Yasnaya Polyana school can also be seen as contributing to his later religious conception of education. Even in the 1860s, for Tolstoy the natural impetus to learn is existential not instrumental. During the *Yasnaya Polyana* experiment, he describes how the fundamental task of the educator is to inspire children to learn for themselves, and to do this it is necessary to show the student that there may be aspects to the world and human existence that they may not yet understand. No one, child or adult, would wish to learn if it were merely to be able to read, write and count. The teacher must have a higher vision of the world and introduce students to it by lifting 'one side of the shroud which has been concealing from him [the pupil] all the charm of that world of thought, knowledge, and poetry, to which instruction was to introduce him' (TSYP, 309–310). Tolstoy found in his experimental school that there was no book as good as the Bible to begin the learning process and establish the role of the teacher in performing this task.

Later writings on education

An important collection of Tolstoy's mature educational thought can be found in Volume 23 of Harvard Slavonic scholar Leo Wiener's translation of Tolstoy's complete works. 'Miscellaneous Letters and Essays' includes a compendium of three essays on education, taken from Tolstoy's letters and diaries between 1887 and 1901. Like many of Tolstoy's religious essays, which were edited and published from his correspondence, these writings give much insight into Tolstoy's mature worldview and the conclusion to his long spiritual struggles. But, along with Tolstoy's other educational writings written after 1862, they have been almost entirely overlooked by educationists who have taken an interest in Tolstoy. Given the public nature of all of Tolstoy's writings at this time, they can be considered more than casual, private musings: they are, as with his religious essays of the time, intended for the benefit of all who seek the truth.

The first essay Wiener includes is a translation of a letter Tolstoy sent to his biographer Biryukov in 1901 (TOEI, 359–368). Tolstoy begins it by explaining the necessary connection between religion and education. Given that religion consists of the very basis of a person's life – and for Tolstoy there could be no escaping religion since he defined it as a man's attitude to his own existence – it follows that education, the 'preparation of men for life,' should have its foundation in religion. However, in modern times, religion has become regarded as a subject that is taught in schools out of convention rather than belief; its survival in schools is a superficial token to a different age.

The true basis of education should be 'justified by reason, by the sincere striving and experience of every man' (TOEI, 360). Tolstoy considered that this 'true basis' of education is best conceived as what was most simply and rationally expressed in the teachings of Jesus, but not in the sense that any mainstream denomination had received them. Essential to this Christian message was that everyone should consider themselves part of the fulfillment of the work of God, and that the first step in fulfilling this will is in our actions toward our fellow human beings. Thus, education should be based upon everything and anything that can contribute to the fraternity of the human race. Those things which do not contribute should be omitted, those things which easily and freely contribute to the uniting of people should be taught first, and those with a less obvious relationship to general well-being should come later.

Tolstoy goes on to discuss how such an education should take place. This is done through the psychological action of one human on another, either consciously or unconsciously. He claims that the stronger, older person is less easily influenced, whereas younger people are more sensitive to the actions of others. Therefore, the teacher has a moral responsibility to ensure that impressionable and vulnerable students are 'subjected' to good and true 'suggestions,' rather than what is false or bad. It is for this reason that Tolstoy claims hypocrisy is the greatest threat to genuine education.

Tolstoy criticizes artificial institutions, such as military schools, where students learn prepackaged, prescribed moral rules. These 'conscious' messages, which are advocated by adults, merely support the unjust social order of Tsarist Russia. Tolstoy claims this superficial arrangement has led to the imbalanced development of society: while it has progressed in some aspects, its citizens are not genuinely enlightened. Moral enlightenment is the most important thing for the education of individuals and society as a whole but because of the corrupt nature of the education system, it is the uneducated laborers who are more likely to live a genuine, moral life.

Tolstoy contends that education is bound to fail because of the double standards of any middle- or upper-class family intending to morally educate its children. For the bourgeois can only sustain their place in society through the immoral exploitation of the under-classes, and although this may not be noticeable to adults, it is clearly obvious to children. The children inherit this hypocrisy from their parents because at one moment they are taught to respect others, but at another, they learn to treat a whole section of society with contempt. Tolstoy continues to assert that no moral lesson or sermon will ever have effect while children's parents live off the labor of others; they will just learn to lie to themselves and to others. Thus it follows that one of the most important conditions of a genuine education is that the lives of the educators themselves should be good, not just superficially, but down to the very foundations of their lives. Tolstoy argues that if teachers follow one important condition, 'the striving after perfection in love,' and the children understand this intention, then the education 'will be good' (TOEI, 364).

Tolstoy continues his musings with an important line of thinking evident throughout his works on education, that teachers must continually try to improve their craft. 'For the education of children to be successful,' Tolstoy asserts, 'the educators must continue to educate themselves' (TOEI, 364). Tolstoy claims that there are many ways in which a teacher can achieve this aim, but most importantly a teacher must develop self-understanding, self-control, 'the labour of every man over his own soul.' Tolstoy suggests that an individual's moral efficacy can be improved by helping out unfortunate people or attempting to make peace with enemies. But these are only off-the-cuff suggestions, Tolstoy re-affirms. His main point is that if more attention were paid to the moral and spiritual enlightenment of educators, then our understanding of education and its implementation would increase exponentially. Once we have established a just moral basis for education, it is then possible to begin to determine what practical measures are necessary to perfect educators. This then becomes the 'science' of the development of education.

Tolstoy also discusses what the content of the curriculum should be. He suggests that learning is nothing other than the 'transmission of what the wisest and best men have thought and expressed in the various branches of knowledge' (TOEI, 365). Tolstoy considers that knowledge belongs to three groups, all of which aspire to different 'directions' of human thought, a concept he first argues for in his essay *On Life*. The first group is the 'philosophico-religious direction.' This is humankind's pursuit of the meaning of life. The second is the experimental sciences that seek knowledge of the world through the verification of hypotheses based on empirical tests. The third 'direction' is the direction of logic, which draws conclusions from a priori truths, primarily mathematics. According to Tolstoy these three kinds of human inquiry all legitimately pursue the universal brotherhood of man and are sciences in the sense that their truth claims are readily accessible to everyone and can ostensibly be verified. Sciences which consist of truth claims that are not capable of being readily confirmed should be avoided.

Tolstoy also claims that there are three essential modes of 'transmission' that contribute to the fraternity of the human race. The first is language, so languages become a science worthy of study as they contribute to the good of humanity. Tolstoy also stressed the importance of learning languages in a conversation with his friend, Goldenweiser, quipping that mathematics and languages were 'the only positive knowledge that one can give a pupil' as in both cases one could either know or not know any given information (GW, 64). In his writing, however, Tolstoy does not make such flippant remarks. He argues that the second mode should be that of drawing – how to transmit knowledge visually, and the third music – the 'science' of communicating mood and emotion through sound. To the three branches of knowledge, the modes of communication, Tolstoy adds the art of handicraft, the ability to make useful objects for the important business of learning to look after oneself, such as cleaning and cooking with which all children should be involved on a daily basis.

Despite this theoretical view of the curriculum, Tolstoy maintains that the amount of curriculum time devoted to each of the subjects should be decided by the student. Teachers can organize a suitable program of study but the pupils should then only attend the sessions that they wish to. Tolstoy reaffirms his belief that study should be noncompulsory, stating that this may seem strange to those educated by the corrupt traditional method, but the results of coercion in education have long-lasting spiritual effects. One important result of the freedom of each student to decide their own individual program of study is that they can learn at their own rate and ability. Only freedom can allow students to progress according to their needs. Any other system, Tolstoy argues, results in a hypocritical paradox where the teacher would be 'telling the pupil that violence must not be used in life' while 'exerting most grievous mental violence against him' (TOEI, 366). Yet Tolstoy's educational regimen would not be easy: of the sixteen waking hours, half should be devoted to carrying out the necessary chores and recreation and the other half should consist of study of the subjects which, out of the seven offered, interest him or her the most. Tolstoy also stresses the tentative nature of this statement of his educational ideas, echoing the conclusions of his pedagogical experiment of the early 1860s. No predetermined theoretical positions should be assumed; the school should progress according to the needs of its students and its own development.

As a hasty end to his thoughts, Tolstoy suggests a few ideas concerning drawing, music and languages. In drawing, children should be given the freedom to draw what they see around them with crayons. Similarly, pupils should begin music by using their voices. Piano lessons are considered to be an example of a false, imposed education. If students develop outstanding talents in the arts they should move on to more advanced instruments and instruction as their ability dictates. With regard to languages, Tolstoy suggests that French, German, English and Esperanto should be taught by giving the students a book that they already know in Russian and then, after assisting their comprehension, deconstructing the grammar and vocabulary of the language.

The second part of Wiener's compendium brings together more thoughts on education given in Tolstoy's letters and diaries (TOEI, 369–379). These snippets contain essential conclusions and admissions from Tolstoy regarding his long interest in educational matters. They corroborate much of what we can learn from his other writings, and they help clarify exactly what Tolstoy's views were, separating his most strongly held views from those less important themes and arguments present among his conjectural, polemical and experimental educational writings: 'I have thought a great deal about education' states Tolstoy, 'there are questions as to which one arrives at doubtful conclusions, and others as to which the conclusions arrived at are final' (TOEI, 369). Again he asserts that the fundamental basis of education is the striving of the teacher for self-perfection, a feature at the heart of his earlier pedagogical experimentation. He argues as soon as an adult realizes that the education of others begins with his or her own education, the seemingly insoluble problems of educational inquiry disappear. For education, like Levin's epiphany in *Anna Karenina*, rests on the question of 'how should someone live their life?' Thus the beginning of educational enquiry for a prospective teacher should be attempting to answer the question 'how should I live my life?'

Tolstoy gives two immutable educational laws for the teacher in this task: to strive for self-perfection and to avoid hypocrisy. Education takes place by the influence of 'the heart' on students and as part of this transaction, pupils are most sensitive to the example of their educators, by whose own actions they are most likely to be 'infected.' Thus a teacher's faults of vanity, greed and irritability are bound to make a negative impact, even if that teacher uses the most artful methods of instruction. For Tolstoy the most important 'tool' given to educators is 'the consciousness of our own errors and in our mending of them' (TOEI, 371).

Tolstoy then repeats his criticism of the education system of Tsarist Russia. Because of the hypocritical nature of a system that attempts to instill moral values through coercion and manipulation, children are subjected to a 'corruption of the mind' by the educational authorities. The natural purpose of every man's life to 'manifest his individuality' is 'wiped out' by the present form of education (TOEI, 373). Tolstoy describes the hypocrisy of expelling a boy from a school because of violence, when the teacher himself used violence to 'educate' the children. He also criticizes the 'senseless memorizing' which he considers to be the heart of the university and school system and affirms the importance of teaching by example; otherwise education becomes nothing other than a form of deception.

Tolstoy also considers teaching the two opposing world views of science and religion as another form of deception in education. He saw that the insistence of teaching the critical reasoning skills of science in one lesson and then the dogma of the Church, with no rational explanation in another, as something that would 'mix-up' a man from his childhood (TOEI, 376). Because of this, public education, as Tolstoy saw it, was 'very artfully organized for the moral corruption' of children (TOEI, 376). Educated parents could teach their children much better than schools. He urges parents to ensure that their children learn what is good from them, as one human life that has absorbed everything from his or her parents, is more abiding and valuable a legacy than the writing of books. Tolstoy admits that he does not know how to promote these good things completely, but the importance of a moral vision of education is paramount. He stresses this in a paragraph which shows the unity of his artistic, educational and religious endeavors:

> Education, the transmission of knowledge, is real when it transmits the important, necessary contents (moral instruction) in a clear, rational, comprehensible form (science), and so that it charms, infects, attracts by its sincerity to whom it is transmitted (art). (TOEI, 378)

In comparison with Tolstoy's ideals, therefore, the system of education in Tsarist Russia was dysfunctional: the moral instruction was not reasonable; the science education had no moral content, and the methods of instruction were not artful. Moreover, the preference for rote learning favored those who had no ideas of their own. As Tolstoy concluded from his tour of European schools during the 1860s: in a corrupt education system, 'somnambulists learn best of all' (TOEI, 378).

Tolstoy continues his condemnation of the education system in Tsarist Russia. Education must proceed by the 'demands of the learner' and with 'the aid of God' (TOEI, 378–379). Yet these principles were consistently omitted in the schools of the time. Particularly disturbing, Tolstoy argues, were the military academies where the 'souls of all adolescent young men are ruined' (TOEI, 379). On the topic of female universities Tolstoy considers that the education of women is a good thing, but not in the form of universities. He claims that the lecture system indoctrinates and stupefies its students.

The third section of Wiener's compilation is a letter dated 13 December 1899 (TOEI, 380–383). In this letter Tolstoy affirms his belief that the cause of evil in the world is not the economic structure or the use of violence by the government, but 'false religious doctrine, which is inculcated by means of education' (TOEI, 380). He describes how when a young child asks his educators what life is and how it should be lived, instead of attempting to answer the question, it is put to one side. In its place is given a cruel myth in which an odd character called God sent his son to redeem us. Tolstoy claims that this may seem entirely normal, but in reality a 'terrible transformation' is taking place and corrupting the child. This is because the child is not a blank page when it comes to its educators:

> The child has a dim conception of what is the beginning of everything, that cause of his existence, that force, in whose power he is, and he has the same high, indefinite, and inexpressible conception, cognized by his whole being, of the beginning, which is proper for all rational men. (TOEI, 381)

Tolstoy argues that children are aware of the complex moral questions concerning life, yet they are told that morality consists in certain prayers and rituals. According to false religious education, children are told that the 'law of God' consists of superstitions, miracles and blind faith. Tolstoy claims the government needs this deception in order to 'hypnotize' children with such lies to maintain the social order. Thus Tolstoy considers a secular education preferable to one which attempts to inculcate or indoctrinate with the dogma of the established church.

Tolstoy's last essay on education

Tolstoy's final systematic statement on education, 'On Upbringing,' is found in a letter to Valentin Bulgakov, written in April 1909. Tolstoy took a number of days to write this, pondering over it, and asking his secretary, Gusev, to comment on it. Bulgakov, a student at the University of Moscow, was attempting to write a book giving a coherent account of Tolstoy's worldview and philosophy. Bulgakov's book was later approved by Tolstoy and he wrote a foreword for it. On the strength of his understanding of Tolstoy's thought, Bulgakov was offered a job as Tolstoy's personal secretary. The position was vacant as Gusev had been arrested and exiled for distributing Tolstoy's banned writings.

Bulgakov had found that, although many of Tolstoy's views on specific issues were addressed in his many essays, he needed to clarify, among other things, Tolstoy's position on education (VB, xxii). In response to Bulgakov's queries, Tolstoy wrote at length on the subject, explaining that as he could not remember exactly what his opinion was in previous works, and as it may well have changed since, he would offer a restatement of his educational vision for Bulgakov's systematic exposition his philosophy.

Tolstoy begins the essay by explaining that there is no distinction to be made between education and upbringing. We cannot bring up a child without educating or transferring our knowledge; similarly, we cannot educate or pass on our knowledge to a child without inducing them to a way of life. In short, educating a child facilitates their upbringing and vice versa. For education to be fruitful, however, it must move humankind to the good and this is best made possible by allowing students to choose what they should study. The learning should take place between students and educators on a 'shared platform' from which students and teachers choose the most topical issues of study for the 'sensible life' of people.

Tolstoy then goes on to criticize the education of the time. True education, he argues is balanced, holistic and centered on the individual student's needs, yet contemporary education exists only to satisfy the needs of the authorities. To illustrate this point, Tolstoy asks the reader to imagine a diagram of a sphere with lines intersecting it, like rays, going to its center and then emanating from it. The sphere represents the individual and knowledge, or that which is to be learnt, is represented as rays emanating to and from the person. According to Tolstoy each ray, representing a different form of knowledge, should be equally spaced around the perimeter of the sphere, and of equal length. However, this balance is distorted and contorted by the authorities' control of education. This reflects Tolstoy's earlier view of the equilibrium of the child given in 'Should We Teach the Peasant Children to Write, or Should They Teach Us?' In this essay he also stresses the harmful consequences of interfering in the natural learning process of children.

As a result of the interference of the government and the Church, Tolstoy writes, students learn 'a lot of nonsense.' The pedantic details of the tenets of the Russian Orthodox religion and pointless facts about science and history serve as a diversion from the key task of true education: to encourage an 'understanding of the meaning of life as understood by billions of people, two thirds of whom are non-Christian' (OU, 65). The problem is exacerbated by the ignorance of 'the educated' who arrogantly assume that they have no more to learn. Furthermore, the false and irrelevant knowledge chosen by such ignorant people can only be promulgated by educational methods that rely on the use of force and coercion.

Tolstoy then turns his attention to the 'life of people.' After a suitable moral basis for education has been established, rather than learning about the wars and conquests of kings and empires, 'ethnography' should be studied. Tolstoy uses the term 'ethnography' to mean a study of how ordinary people of all classes live in both Russia and abroad. This practical knowledge of work, family and domestic affairs – nothing other than knowledge of life itself, is far more useful than the irrelevancies of literature, history and science. That is not to say that science education is not important, but it should be part of a balanced, ethical curriculum which has the important affairs of human existence at its heart: how people should live.

Tolstoy is particularly concerned with the negative effects of contemporary religious education which he believes clouds the moral and spiritual judgment of the young. He describes the religious education provided by the Church as 'a collection of the crude superstitions and tasteless sophisms that is now called God's law' (OU, 66). This form of religious education fails because it does not begin with an investigation into the purpose and nature of human existence. A true education must proceed from existential and experiential roots: the realization of one's own position in the order of the physical and moral universe, by asking such questions as 'What am I?,' 'How does my individual life relate to eternity?' and 'What should my attitude to the world and the people in it be?' The foundations of education should thus be based on a consideration of the purpose and goodness of existence: it is only from such a consideration that a negotiation over the content and methods of schooling can be discussed. Tolstoy argues that these questions are religious questions and until they are asked, no individual can freely choose what is good for themselves and others, or understand how the objective moral law of good and evil can be applied in every circumstance. Tolstoy stresses this religious view is universal and is at the heart of the best thinkers throughout time. To demonstrate this, he cites many of the same major religious figures as he does in *A Calendar of Wisdom*.

The educational vision of Tolstoy's last major works

Tolstoy was especially pleased with his last major works – a series of compilations of wise thoughts and aphorisms from around the world. He created and published a number of editions based on this concept, under a variety of different titles. For the purposes of the analysis below, I refer to this collection in its only popular English translation – *A Calendar of Wisdom* as translated and edited by Peter Sekirin. Sekirin's English translation only appeared in 1997. Consequently, Western educationalists have seldom included its contents in their evaluation of Tolstoy's educational thought, although Tolstoy clearly meant his compilations of wisdom to be educational resources. He told his friend Goldenweiser that he wished to express the wisdom of great thinkers in a way that could be understood by children – something which, according to Tolstoy, all good art should allow.

On each page of the *Calendar* several quotations on a common theme are arranged to be read on a daily basis. The quotations are abbreviated and paraphrased by Tolstoy and come from a variety of sources from around the world and throughout history. He cites Moses, Jesus, Krishna and Buddha along with now less well-known thinkers such as the Unitarian Harriet Martineau, sister of the Principal of Manchester College, now Harris Manchester College, Oxford – James Martineau. The themes are not stated but implicit and every page has at least one aphorism by Tolstoy himself. For example, 19 May has six quotations in total, one each from 'Chinese wisdom,' Cicero and Kant, and three from Tolstoy. All of them enshrine the principle that there is a 'true and unchanging law, the law which gives us true direction and forbids us to commit sin' (CW, 140). Or as Tolstoy puts it himself on the same page, 'the foundation of all faiths is the same' (CW, 140).

In *A Calendar of Wisdom* we can see the merging of the genres of educational writing, religious essays and literature that becomes the apogee of Tolstoy's life's work. He wished to cover all aspects of human existence in an all-encompassing vision, just as he had done in his novels; but here the same universalism is engendered through another biblical genre, not of the epic narrative or parable, but the proverb. We can also make another comparison with Tolstoy's experiments with pedagogy in the 1860s, after which he concluded that proverbs can provide a suitable genesis for creative writing in the classroom. In *A Calendar of Wisdom*, Tolstoy has worked in reverse: narrative is stripped bare; readers are to slowly digest five or six pure, powerful and unadulterated moral truths per day, on which they can then build the narratives of their own lives in reflection.

As well as documenting the scope of Tolstoy's extensive journey of thinking and art, these proverbs make obvious the conclusion of Tolstoy's thought on education and its place in his belief system. They resonate with key themes expounded in his earlier pedagogical articles and literature. It is interesting that Tolstoy, who eschewed a rigid didactic pedagogical approach in his earlier years, came to conclude his literary works in this way. Gone are the delicate narratives and psychological analyses. They are replaced with assertive aphorisms, distilled from the wisdom of the centuries and prepared for all across the divides of class and religion. Rather than bringing the wisdom of the peasants and common folklore to the attention of the literary classes as Tolstoy had attempted in his pedagogical articles and moral fairy tales, in *A Calendar of Wisdom* he attempts to bring the wisdom of the classical and oriental worlds to all sections of society in an overarching synthesis.

One anecdote told by Tolstoy's daughter, Alexandra, confirms this. She relates how one of the peasants of Yasnaya Polyana who helped her do the housework, once asked her why she was unhappy. The peasant said that she never felt down, even when her husband was drunk, because she would read the thoughts of Marcus Aurelius from a copy of the *Calendar* that Tolstoy had given her. Astonished by this, Alexandra told her father, who suggested that the woman understood true wisdom and the peasant was 'the person from whom one could learn' (AT, 505).

Espoused in a number of the aphorisms, included in the *Calendar*, and inextricably linked to his view of education and central to his overall philosophy, is Tolstoy's conception of the nature of such genuine or worthwhile knowledge. For Tolstoy, the essential knowledge to be attained was *how* to live. As he argues in *On Life*, science teaches facts that are not useful for human beings' development as moral actors, and religion builds up a false system that obfuscates the obvious natural truths intuitively accessible to all. He celebrates Socrates' belief that the most fundamental and significant human pursuit is morality. Since Socrates' time, however, people have not progressed as they have misinterpreted the real purpose of knowledge:

> People know little, because they try to understand those things which are not open to them for understanding: God, eternity, spirit; or those which are not worth thinking about: how water becomes frozen, or the theory of numbers, or how viruses can transmit different illnesses. The only real knowledge is how to live your life. (CW, 209)

Many of Tolstoy's aphorisms reaffirm these ideas; God defies rational knowledge but has been universally accessible through intuition throughout the ages. All we have to do is strip back our false knowledge and the genuine knowledge will shine through. People have often confused knowledge with wisdom or virtue, and this is particularly true of the modern predicament. Even if science increases our knowledge of the material world, we are still left with the need to live out our lives in a morally acceptable way, as Tolstoy sums up: 'No matter how great our knowledge may be, it cannot help us to fulfil the major purpose of our life – our moral perfection' (CW, 253).

In the *Calendar* the purpose of education, literature and art is perceived as the passing on of the divine wisdom of the millennia. In this respect Tolstoy endorses the use of the intellect 'The intellect liberates a person. Therefore the less intellectual life one has, the less liberated one is' (CW, 214). For Tolstoy, the fundamental truths of human existence are emancipatory and man can be freed by the intellectual consideration of the moral imperative, which is encouraged by the study of how people have lived their lives. But as we have already seen, a fundamental component of Tolstoy's understanding of worthwhile knowledge – of how to live – is anti-intellectual. It is the responsibility of the individual to self-perfect through the consideration of 'essential' moral knowledge. This cannot be taught; virtue can only be achieved independently:

> It would be nice if wisdom could flow from one man who is full of it to another who has none, in the same way that in two connected vessels water flows from one to the other until the level is the same in both of them. But the problem is that to achieve wisdom you have to make an independent, serious effort on your own. (CW, 17)

The independent nature of Tolstoy's pedagogy evident since the 1860s now takes on an absolute spiritual quality. As we all crave the good and have an innate capacity for truth, we should focus on what we feel and how we respond to what we study. Tolstoy therefore urges students to:

> Read less, study less, but think more. Learn, both from your teachers and from the books which you read, only those things which you really need and really want to know. (CW, 9)

Given the natural ability of humankind to educate itself by listening to its own shared and individual experience, it is not surprising that in the *Calendar* Tolstoy again emphasizes the spiritual intuition of the child to self-educate and be a model of morality for adults to aspire to emulate. Tolstoy suggests that part of the child's ability to understand the meaning of life is in recognizing the inability of humans to fathom the meaning of the universe and to focus on the morally binding present:

> It is not possible to embrace the meaning of life if you are looking for its universal significance. At the same time, at the level of the individual it is so simple that it can be explained to fools and infants. (CW, 293)

Given the pedagogic aims of the *Calendar*, it is not surprising that some of it is devoted to how we should relate to those whom we may be hoping to educate. Here, Tolstoy again condemns hypocrisy as the worst trait of teachers. More harm is done by attempting to teach children things of which adults are unsure, particularly in the realm of religion, than admitting that adults may not know all the answers. For Tolstoy the most important element of teaching children is to lead by example. Despite their spiritually intuitive nature, children are capable of being corrupted, and the Tolstoyan values of simplicity and labor are to be encouraged in them.

The wisdom of children

Another late work that draws together Tolstoy's interests in art, education and religion is 'The Teaching of Jesus.' This affirms Tolstoy's views and also demonstrates the final intersection of the different strands of Tolstoy's lifelong pursuits. It is an historical account of the life and teaching of Jesus. However, crucially, in line with Tolstoy's religious views, it ends before the resurrection and excludes any reference to the incarnation or miracles. In Tolstoy's version of events, God does not act in the world by supernatural action but by the action of spiritually inspired humans: 'God does not establish the Kingdom of Heaven by His own power, but leaves people to establish it themselves' (TOJ, 355). Tolstoy's Jesus is an exemplary human, a moral and talented teacher who denies his body for the good of the spirit and of others, and who explicates the eternal truths of human existence, to pursue the spiritual condition of holiness and moral perfection. It is interesting that in the story Jesus becomes an increasingly talented pedagogue and storyteller, illustrating Tolstoy's view of the role of the teacher and storyteller: teachers should be artists, and artists should only communicate the truth.

Tolstoy's preface to the story explains its origin. In 1907 he had formed a class of village children and sought to explain the teaching of

Jesus in the most simple way. Tolstoy claims that he was guided by their questions, and by what they understood most easily. Thus in 'The Teaching of Jesus,' the long combination of Tolstoy's experiments in education, religion and storytelling come to their resolution, reflecting Tolstoy's view of the child in the story. Children need to understand the 'eternal truths' of the law of God, but children also have a special religious receptivity that can inform adults. Tolstoy affirms this view of education and his conception of the child. When some children are brought to Jesus, he paraphrases Matthew 19.13: 'You should not turn the children away. Children should not be sent away, but we should learn from them, for they are nearer to the Kingdom of God than grown-up people' (TOJ, 368).

Similar views are expounded in Tolstoy's last work, 'The Wisdom of Children' which presents yet another conclusion to Tolstoy's lifelong interest in religion and education. 'The Wisdom of Children' consists of 20 short dialogues between children and adults. Each dialogue has a title based on a social or moral issue, such as 'Prison,' 'War,' 'Capital Punishment,' 'Repentance' or 'Private Property.' This new genre with which Tolstoy experimented at the end of his life was the result of the culmination of a number of influences and ideals: the natural goodness of the child, the destructive tendency of society to obscure the innate goodness of all humans and the worth of studying the innocent, but penetrating, insight of children's reasoning. It is obvious from Tolstoy's diary entries of the time that he was not pleased with the dialogues. He writes on 20 February 1909, 'I have no enthusiasm . . . for *The Wisdom of Children*' (TD, 604) and again on 26 March 'Yesterday I wrote a rather bad dialogue for *The Wisdom of Children*' (TD, 608).

In all the dialogues, which seem simplistic and aesthetically unsophisticated, the dramatic irony consists of the supposed wisdom of the child's questioning being ignored by the folly of adults and their ill thought-out, immoral, words and deeds. However, this irony only works if we assume Tolstoy's moral and political sentiments. Less subtle in the majority of dialogues, children are verbally insulted in order to justify the existing social order or are simply wronged by the adults around them. For example, in 'Drunkenness' a drunken father beats his daughter. This results in the daughter discussing with her peers the wish that the 'Tsar would stop selling vodka,' reasoning that as the Tsar collects taxes from the sale of alcohol, he is 'dealing' in the substance that brought about the violence. In school the next day, the children ask their teacher at the beginning of a lesson why the Tsar sells vodka. The teacher replies that the Tsar needs the money for the upkeep of schools and the army. The children then ask why vodka must be sold to this end, to which they receive a reply designed to get them quickly onto their prepared, but irrelevant, lesson: 'Because that's the law! Well, children, now you're here, take your places' (WC, 459).

The concept behind these dialogues continues the essence of Tolstoy's mature educational thought: we are still to learn from the child and adults can have a corrupt, negative influence on their accurate moral inquisitiveness. Indeed, the final dialogue titled 'Education' restates Tolstoy's views on education in particular (WC, 490–492). In it Katya, aged 7, and her 15-year-old brother Nikolai discuss with their mother their desires not to study. It begins with Nikolai returning home from school, throwing his school books down in disgust at his low grade in geography echoing Tolstoy's disillusionment with the subject over 40 years earlier. He asks 'Where is Clifornia [*sic*]?' his mispronunciation giving away his annoyance with the futility of studying, and the time he has already wasted: 'much good their damned Geography is to me' (WC, 490). The family porter, overhearing the boy's protests, asserts that he should try to learn geography, even though he does not know why. In response to the porter's assumption of the purpose of geography, Nikolai responds, 'There's no "why" about it – it's just the custom. They think people can't get along without it' (WC, 491). Nikolai then inquires about how he can become a porter, favoring the manual task of chopping wood early in the morning over studying. His mother complains that it is his interest in country life that stops him learning about the 'necessary things.' The intended irony here is that in Tolstoy's view, of course, the truly necessary things are those that Nikolai is interested in: making the fire and the chickens. After Nikolai storms off, thinking about running away, asking only to be 'set free from this horrible studying,' the dialogue ends with Katya pursuing his line of argument. She states to her mother, 'I won't learn on any account what I don't want to.' Her mother responds, 'then you'll be a fool.' Katya closes the dialogue: 'God needs fools.'

Part 3

The Legacy of an Overlooked Educator

Chapter 8

The Reception and Influence of Tolstoy's Educational Thought

Today, Tolstoy is first and foremost thought of as a great writer and in the field of education many are unaware of his pedagogical works. In Slavonic studies, on the other hand, Tolstoy scholars have often overlooked his educational thought in order to concentrate on other aspects of his varied interests. Thematic studies, although superb works of scholarship, such as the definitive *Leo Tolstoy: Resident and Stranger* (Gustafson, 1986), pay little heed to Tolstoy's educational writings. In addition, biographical information in popular translations of Tolstoy's fiction often ignore, or mischaracterize, Tolstoy's works in the field of education and their connection to his religious views. Yet in-depth chronological studies of Tolstoy, such as Eikhenbaum's *Tolstoi in the Sixties* and *Tolstoi in the Seventies*, and the biographies written by those close to him, give much of their content over to education – an endeavor which Tolstoy himself admitted took a great deal of his time; but from the 1860s onwards, never received the acclaim, influence or impact that he envisaged.

Tolstoy was disappointed with the reception of the *Yasnaya Polyana* journal. In the Yasnaya Polyana school's short life span, those who had come into personal contact with Tolstoy seemed to be supportive of it, but the wider public, particularly the government and national press, were not supportive of his ideas, and within five years of its last issue, the *Yasnaya Polyana* journal had become extremely rare. Tolstoy felt that his pedagogical writings were unduly ignored. He wrote at the time that 'no cookery book is received with such silence' (TL, 156). Later, in 1868 reflecting on the response of educationists to the school, he told Eugene Schuyler:

> I must admit that I was annoyed – being younger then – not so much at the fact that my ideas were not accepted, as that those who

officially devoted themselves to educational interests did not think it worthwhile to refute them; but treated them with complete indifference. (SL, 284–285)

On the indifferent reception of the journal, Tolstoy wrote to Chernyshevsky, the editor of *The Contemporary* in February 1862 asking for the journal to be reviewed, stating that the 'journal and the cause mean everything to me' (TL, 154). Chernyshevsky subsequently reviewed the *Yasnaya Polyana* in the January 1863 edition of *The Contemporary* – one of only two articles to be written in the press about the journal during the journal's existence. The article was not wholly favorable. It concluded that before Tolstoy recommended his educational ideas to the rest of Russia, it would be better if he could formulate some substantial educational theories instead of espousing romantic sentiment. An article by Markov in *The Russian Messenger* levied even harsher criticism of Tolstoy's educational views, claiming that the methods expounded by Tolstoy in his description of the school did not match his own aims; that his idea of a free education was not only impossible but harmful to children; and that modern society had the right to institute compulsory education using modern methods. Biryukov sums up the reception of Tolstoy's ideas astutely, commenting 'Offended science did not even deign to take such ideas seriously' (BK, 330).

In addition to the negative reaction of the academic and educational community, Tolstoy's educational ideas were also suppressed by the government. The Tsarist establishment did not approve of the underlying political motivation of Tolstoy's pedagogical initiatives. In 1862 the school was raided by the authorities and Tolstoy's student teachers were arrested. Even though the printing press rumored to be installed at Yasnaya Polyana was never found, as a result of the raid the *Yasnaya Polyana* journal, to Tolstoy's frustration, was subjected to an even more lengthy censorship process than usual. After examining the journal in the autumn of 1862, the Minister of the Interior wrote to the Minister of Education arguing for the end of the journal, commenting that the journal would lead educators astray:

The continuation of the review [the *Yasnaya Polyana* journal] in the same spirit must, in my opinion, be considered the more dangerous as its editor is a man of remarkable talent, who cannot be suspected to be a criminal or an unprincipled man. The evil lies in the sophistry and eccentricity of his convictions, which, being expounded with extraordinary eloquence, may carry away inexperienced teachers in this direction, and thus give a wrong turn to popular education. (BK, 353)

The Minister of Education conducted a thorough review on this request, only to consider the journal innocuous and so implausible in its position that it would only receive derision among the 'scientific' educational community. The Minister concluded his report predicting Tolstoy would soon give up his efforts in education of his own accord.

Tolstoy did give up his work in education but for no more than a few years, and when he again became involved in education in the 1870s, not only did his underlying pedagogic principles remain the same, but so did their reception. The *Azbuka* and *New Azbuka*, although passing the censor, failed to gain government endorsement for use in schools. Resultantly they did not sell many copies. The *Russian Books for Reading* were recommended as supplementary texts and received more favorable reviews. Leading pedagogues, however, were annoyed by Tolstoy's insistence on proving his approach better than the phonetic methods, and Tolstoy's views were met with intense disapproval. As Eikhenbaum documents in his study of the period, reviewers concluded that Tolstoy was a reactionary, repudiating all the progress modern educational theory had made. By and large, his *Azbuka* was regarded as 'a step back, not forward' (Eikhenbaum, 1982a, 26).

After writing *Anna Karenina*, when his emerging religious beliefs had crystallized and set, Tolstoy concentrated on expounding his worldview. With this, the harassment and censorship of the Tsarist regime intensified. Tolstoy was excommunicated and his religious works were banned, while his supporters and advocates were often jailed or banished as a result of distributing them. The government sent a number of spies to Yasnaya Polyana. One, posing as a schoolmaster, came to ask for a copy of *On Life*, then banned. But as a result of his conversation with Tolstoy, instead of returning to the authorities with the evidence, converted to Tolstoy's views and was subsequently exiled to Siberia (JA, 272–273). In 1891, the Tula governor put a stop to a school at Yasnaya

Polyana for the peasantry, started by Tolstoy's daughters, Tatyana and Marya. Alexandra suggests that the authorities wished to counteract the influence of Tolstoy on the local population and in its place deliberately opened several poor-quality Church schools in the area (CAT, 105).

Despite his vocal protests and clashes with the authorities – or rather because of them – Tolstoy became more and more famous. Alexandra tells of one incident in Moscow, where thousands of people gathered to see Tolstoy and show their respect, so much so that the family was crushed as they attempted to get to the railway station. Newspaper photographers hid in the bushes at Yasnaya Polyana to try and photograph the family and people from all over Russia, and the world, came to ask Tolstoy's advice on many matters – including education.

During the late nineteenth and early twentieth century, Tolstoy's most ardent supporters, the Tolstoyans, printed many leaflets, pamphlets and books both by, and about, Tolstoy. Exiled in England, Tolstoy's close friend and publicist, Chertkov, popularized Tolstoy's thought by producing leaflets and pamphlets printed at the Free Age Press, located on a Tolstoyan commune, first in London and then in Hampshire. One of these leaflets, *The Religious Education of the Young* (c.1901) dealt with Tolstoy's views on education. With no copyright on his works, other fringe publishers representing Tolstoyan groups, such as the Simple Life Press, later known by its manager's name Arthur C. Fifield, also published works by Tolstoy and other figures that influenced the Tolstoyan movement, such as Emerson, Morris and Thoreau.

Although he had a close friendship with Chertkov, the Tolstoyans were unpopular with Tolstoy himself. His family and friends all note his concern at such a movement. He felt that people wishing to follow his religious beliefs should expend spiritual energy on self-perfection rather than attempting to live as part of a utopian commune. Such views were shared by Aylmer Maude, who although a lifelong advocate of Tolstoy, soon became disillusioned with the movement. He lived for 23 years in Russia and left his job as director of the Russian Carpet Company in 1897 partly as a result of the influence of Tolstoy's views on the conditions of the working poor. He and his wife Louise translated many of Tolstoy's works. Based on his experiences at the Purleigh colony and his part in the emigration of the Doukhobors from Russia to Canada, Maude became convinced of the impossibility of the Tolstoyan communes. He writes in his book *A peculiar People: The Doukhobors* that 'Tolstoyan principles when treated as axioms become unreasonable' (Maude, 1904, 69). He also notes many of the Tolstoyans 'insist most strenuously on just those parts of Tolstoy's teaching which are most questionable' (1904, 280). Nevertheless, long after Tolstoy's death Maude advanced Tolstoy's cause, literature and non-fiction writings. Only part of his extensive translation of Tolstoy's works is given over to Tolstoy's educational works. In his various compilations of Tolstoy's texts he includes some tales from Tolstoy's *Russian Books for Reading* and a brief extract of 'The School at Yasnaya Polyana.' In his revised biography, published to mark the centenary of Tolstoy's birth, however, Maude evaluates Tolstoy's educational endeavors, stating:

> Tolstoy does not stand before the world primarily as a schoolmaster ... but he certainly possessed, as he claims in one of his articles, 'a certain pedagogical tact' and is right in his belief that rigid discipline in schools, lack of freedom and initiative, continual demand for silence and obedience and refusal to allow pupils to criticise the lessons they receive, have a stupefying effect. (1929, 277)

Maude tempers this endorsement of Tolstoy's views with caution; he suspects that Tolstoy's methods should not be used with large classes, and people who lack Tolstoy's enthusiasm, influence and genius would not be able to command the authority that he did among children.

The reception of Tolstoy's educational thought in the twentieth century

Another advocate of Tolstoy's was Ernest Howard Crosby, an American who gave up his legal career to follow Tolstoy's philosophy of life. Crosby published two books on Tolstoy in English both published by the Simple Life Press, including the first book to be written in English about Tolstoy's educational ideas. In *Tolstoy and His Message* (1903), Crosby gives an overview of Tolstoy's life and religious views. In it he notes that 'it is to be hoped that Tolstoy will still write a book on education on the model of "What is Art?" It could not fail to be one of his most interesting and suggestive of his works' (1903, 15). Perhaps in the absence of this work, and in the desire to describe his experiences at Yasnaya Polyana, Crosby subsequently published *Tolstoy as Schoolmaster* (1904). This book, based mainly on a French translation of Tolstoy's early pedagogical journals – with some added reflections and reminisces – was then translated into Russian. Tolstoy commented that the fact that it had been translated into Russian was 'proof that it is good' (TL, 658). Yet Crosby's treatment of Tolstoy's educational ideas is hagiographic and simplistic. The first nine chapters give a description of the experimental school of 1861–1862 as given in the *Yasnaya Polyana* journals. Crosby then inserts a chapter on Tolstoy's later views, his own reflections on education and a description of a 'Mrs F-' who set up an experimental kindergarten in Brooklyn, New York, based on Tolstoyan principles. Crosby's own reflections on education do not develop Tolstoy's ideas further but do mention the work of Dewey favorably, considering him someone who could continue the reform of the educational practice and thought first initiated by Tolstoy.

Crosby's book was not the only book on the topic of Tolstoy and education published in the early twentieth century. *Tolstoi: The Teacher* (1923) written by the French critic Charles Baudouin is a more thorough study of Tolstoy's development as an educator, with some astute observations. Baudouin begins his treatment of Tolstoy by pointing out that above all Tolstoy was a realist, interested in testing his educational ideas in practice, and proficient in sensitively observing the minutiae of a child's psychology. In this regard he likens Tolstoy's great skill as a novelist – of understanding human nature – with his flair as a great educator. He immediately recognizes Tolstoy's religious ideas as essential to understanding Tolstoy's conception of education and locates Tolstoy within the tradition of Rousseau, Pestalozzi and Froebel while recognizing his strong distaste of the dogmatism caused by 'pedantic' theories.

Baudouin gives an accurate chronological description of Tolstoy's activities, which he sees as 'evolution' from teacher to thinker; splitting Tolstoy's engagement with education into three distinct parts, as Mossman (1993) also does later: the first period is that of the experimental school, the second of the *Azbuka* and the third Tolstoy's emphasis on spiritual education. In his treatment of the third period, Baudouin refers to important texts written by Tolstoy, overlooked by most subsequent commentators: 'On Upbringing' and the letters and diary entries recorded in 'Thoughts on Education and Instruction' (1887–1901). Baudouin concludes his analysis by claiming that Tolstoy's later philosophical and social ideas are nothing but the views he had of children and education, transposed to all human affairs. Baudouin describes these principles as:

> freedom, non-resistance and inviolence, an organic moral order emanating from external anarchy, the superiority of life over intellect, the necessity of living human relationships above the dual barrier of artificial hierarchies and cold abstractions, the unconcern for theoretical knowledge at the cost of knowledge of the concrete, the living and the useful. (1923, 213)

In the next decade, the British popular intellectual Bertrand Russell gave a much less favorable evaluation of Tolstoy's views. In *Education for Democracy* (1937), Russell dismisses Tolstoy's school, claiming that students only learnt when Tolstoy was teaching, and in this he was only successful because of his rage. Such an unkind, unsubstantiated treatment of Tolstoy is sustained in *History of Western Philosophy* (1961) where Russell passes over Tolstoy, as most philosophers have done, by declaring him 'intellectually inferior.'

Isaiah Berlin, on the other hand, gives more credence to Tolstoy's views. His essay *Tolstoy and Enlightenment* (1979, first published 1961) is one of the most comprehensive and astute treatments of Tolstoy's educational ideas. Berlin analyzes Tolstoy's educational writings in an attempt to evaluate Tolstoy's status as a thinker; his purpose is not to consider Tolstoy's views on strictly educational terms. Of Tolstoy's pedagogical thought, Berlin maintains a thesis which he also articulates in his more famous essay on Tolstoy's philosophy of history, *The Hedgehog and the Fox* (1988, first published 1953). In this essay Berlin gives two models of great thinkers: the hedgehogs and the foxes. This observation is based on Archilochus' image of a cunning fox trying various strategies to eat a hedgehog that has one unyielding defense. Berlin sees the hedgehogs as those thinkers who relate everything to one great vision, and the foxes as those who pursue many unconnected and conflicting ends. In the first group, who like the hedgehog have one main asset, are included Pascal, Plato and Marx. In the second, the foxes that have many clever but diffuse ways, are Shakespeare and Aristotle. Berlin argues that with regard to his philosophy of history, Tolstoy was really a fox, but tried to be a hedgehog: there was a paradox between the multifarious and complex nature of things he observed and the singular vision in which he wished to unite these observations. Berlin applies a similar evaluation to Tolstoy's educational thought: there was a contradiction between the truths he was seeking in his educational exploits and his awareness of the complex nature of the problem. For Berlin, such a recurrent, irresolvable tension made Tolstoy's efforts heroic but also tragically flawed.

Tolstoy's ideas and Anglophone educationists

The first extensive English translation of Tolstoy's educational writings appeared in volumes 4, 12 and 23 of Harvard scholar Leo Wiener's 1904 24 volume *The Complete Works of Count Tolstoy*. It was not until the 1960s that a discrete book of Tolstoy's original educational writings was published in English. It is telling of the attention paid to Tolstoy's educational ideas in the West, that to this day Wiener's 1904 translations – although themselves incomplete – still comprise the most comprehensive collection of Tolstoy's educational writings in English. The Chicago University anthology, edited by Archambault (1967), is a verbatim reissue of Wiener's translations included in Volume 4 of his compilation. Archambault's volume omitted Tolstoy's later educational writings including those in Volumes 12 and 23 of Wiener's original, such as materials from the *Azbuka* and *Russian Books for Reading* and extracts from Tolstoy's correspondence and notebooks. This oversight may explain Archambault's misrepresentation of Tolstoy's views, which has perhaps led to the often incomplete understanding of his ideas within the field of educational studies since that time.

The two subsequent English translations of Tolstoy's educational works, Armstrong and Pinch (1982) and Blaisdell and Edgar (2000), follow the pattern set by Archambault's selection and exclude his later educational writings, and with them Tolstoy's declaration of the religious nature of a genuine education. There still exists no publication which includes Tolstoy's writings on education after 1862, such as the *Azbuka*; his restatement of his views after the 'great debate,' 'On Popular Education'; or Tolstoy's last essay on education, 'On Upbringing.' Not only are these important writings excluded from the modern translations, but the analysis of the editors of recent volumes often excludes their religious content, leading to a mischaracterization of Tolstoy's views.

Archambault begins his introduction to Tolstoy's writings by comparing the need for a fresh examination of pedagogical theory and practice in the early 1860s, to that of the late 1960s. Although eloquently written, Archambault overlooks the spiritual motivation of Tolstoy's pedagogy and its relatedness to his artistic and literary endeavors. Like many of the subsequent commentators on Tolstoy's educational thought, Archambault sees the pedagogical articles of the 1860s in isolation, and crucially as though they were Tolstoy's lasting, final statements on the subject – which they were not. An examination of Tolstoy's treatment of education in *Childhood*, or his understanding of the role and legitimacy of philosophical argument in his later worldview, are crucial in understanding Tolstoy's educational thought. Many themes of interest to Tolstoy in later life are only latent in the early pedagogical articles and with a complete analysis of all his writings, Tolstoy's treatment of education can be seen to be a cohesive one – even if one that was skeptical of predetermined theory. Archambault, however, based on his limited understanding of Tolstoy, declares that he has no unified doctrine of education, and identifies Tolstoy's thought as a precursor to that of A. S. Neill, something that a closer examination of Tolstoy's educational writings in their entirety would seem to contradict.

Pinch and Armstrong's (1982) volume again focuses on Tolstoy's educational writings from 1860–1862, but with updated and clearer English than Wiener's translation. Nevertheless, they also seem to play down Tolstoy's deeply religious conception of education, stating that Tolstoy was at his 'least religious' during his phase of teaching and that there is no reason to think that Tolstoy 'was going through a fundamentalist phase' (1982, 329). This is misleading on two counts. Not only do the *Yasnaya Polyana* essays concerning the teaching of the Bible suggest that Tolstoy was at this time fascinated with religion, as his correspondence of the time corroborates, but Tolstoy never became fundamentalist, in the sense that he believed in the prime authority of religious scripture. The volume, as others, also omits Tolstoy's later educational writings.

Blaisdell and Edgar (2000) released another selection of Tolstoy's educational writings, *Tolstoy as Teacher*, but this contains less material than either of the previous two translations, with only extracts of some of Tolstoy's major educational writings appearing. It focuses on the obvious worth of Tolstoy's educational experiments to those interested in the teaching of creative writing. It is therefore of worth to teachers but does not aim to give a thorough exposition of Tolstoy's educational thought. The texts chosen are those concerned with writing compositions and the stories written by Tolstoy's students. Blaisdell's analysis, a chapter on using Tolstoy's fiction to teach creative writing, recommends some of Tolstoy's methods, such as using proverbs as the starting place for writing short stories. The commentary is precise and informative but, like the other books, ignores the importance of Tolstoy's religious views and their relation to his educational vision. The translation of 'The School at Yasnaya Polyana' omits the passages of students' work regarding Bible stories, and Blaisdell advises readers not to be 'put off' by the biblical quotations in his short stories.

Murphy (1992) gives the most thorough and accurate treatment of Tolstoy as an educator to date and is the only book on the topic that does not consist of translations of Tolstoy's original texts. Unlike the compilations of translations of Tolstoy's pedagogical works, Murphy recognizes the religious nature of Tolstoy's educational vision. He argues that Tolstoy is misrepresented solely as a progressive, in the tradition of Rousseau, Dewey and A. S. Neill. Although Tolstoy did share their dislike for coercion and authoritarianism, it was on the permanence and objective nature of moral and spiritual truths that Tolstoy's view of education was ultimately based. For Tolstoy, Murphy astutely recognizes, truth is fundamental to his work as an artist and educator.

Alongside the three translations of Tolstoy's educational works and Murphy's book, synopses of Tolstoy's educational thought appear sporadically in journal articles. The recurrence of mainly superficial treatments in journals at intervals of four or five years – most of which are largely given over to retelling the narrative of Tolstoy's concern with education in the 1860s – indicates the novelty of the subject matter to those in the field of educational studies and the lack of any thorough treatment of the subject.

Cohen (1981), in an article whose very title – 'The Educational Philosophy of Tolstoy,' belies much of Tolstoy's views, concurs with Archambault's analysis. Like Archambault and others, although acknowledging Tolstoy's attempt to conceive of education as an ongoing dynamic process, Cohen represents Tolstoy's pedagogical articles of the 1860s as definitive. Such a view contradicts the Yasnaya Polyana school's purpose and that of its eponymous journal: Tolstoy wished to instigate a dialogue with the pupils and the public and used the journal to express his thoughts as the experiment continued. In Cohen's case, such a misunderstanding of the articles' remit leads to a gross representation of Tolstoy's thought as whole: that Tolstoy's view of education was an amoral one, rejecting the right of the teacher to morally educate pupils. This was something that Tolstoy would later vehemently argue against. Cohen concludes by defining Tolstoy's 'philosophy' as an anti-theory. Tolstoy certainly rallied against the pedagogical theory of his day but to describe his views in this way does not adequately explain the relationship of Tolstoy's educational views to philosophy or theory. Tolstoy's views are as anti-philosophical as they are as anti-theoretical. Despite this, Tolstoy's vision for education, as explained in the earlier chapters of this book, when seen from the perspective of his entire life's work, does seem to have some conceptual unity.

The familiar story of Tolstoy the educator is told again in an article by Wagner and Sobotka (1986). They make an accurate assessment of Tolstoy's repudiation of educational theory: it is a natural conclusion of a teacher's genuine engagement with children. They discourage the comparison with A. S. Neill, and present Tolstoy as someone who was able to achieve intellectual rigor in the classroom without resorting to the dry methods of pedagogical theorists. Tolstoy was a great teacher who found the 'middle-ground' between the progressives and the traditionalists – a position which they argue would have been of much benefit in the West during the 1960s. Tolstoy appreciated the disadvantaged position of the peasantry and was sensitive to their cultural differences, but nevertheless he regarded intellectual development as essential for them. Wagner and Sobotka, unlike many commentators, link Tolstoy's pedagogical views to his literature, albeit briefly, and conclude with Tolstoy's influence on Wittgenstein – although perhaps mistakenly describing Wittgenstein as a 'successful' teacher.

Berthoff (1978) does not aim to give an overview of Tolstoy's educational thought or career in favor of making a more detailed analysis of Tolstoy's psychology of learning. By making reference to Tolstoy's method of writing compositions by using proverbs, she compares Tolstoy's understanding of 'meaning making' with that of Vygotsky. She sees this episode of the Yasnaya Polyana school as an illustration of a fundamental principle of learning – to promote 'the form-finding and form-creating powers of the human mind' (1978, 249). The proverbs acted as a prompt for the students themselves to explore, discover and make the proverb meaningful by relating it to their own experience. Berthoff argues that such a conception of learning is not only congruent with Vygotskyian psychology but is common in those methods of education endorsed by well-known educationists Montessori and Freire. Like these great educationists, Tolstoy was correct in identifying the role of the teacher as that of guide rather than instructor, as children have the innate ability to form meaning themselves. She concludes by stating that to promote this in the classroom is a key aspect of a humane form of education.

The essays of historians of education Mossman (1993) and Bantock (1984) provide summaries of Tolstoy's views and involvement with education. Mossman and Bantock rightly locate Tolstoy's educational views as a separate part of a wider reactionary movement against the industrialization and modernization of their age. Bantock evaluates Tolstoy's educational views in the context of his wider literature and their place in the educational landscape of the era – although again without stressing the religious nature of Tolstoy's later views. Mossman, on the other hand, identifies Tolstoy's religious views and sees them as the final part of the evolution of his educational ideas. Tolstoy has three distinct phases as an educator: the champion of freedom and student liberty in the 1860s, the promoter of literacy in the 1870s and the religious view of his later life. The last phase, Mossman argues, results from the earlier: Tolstoy's interaction with the peasantry helped forge his religious views. Like Levin, Tolstoy was impressed by the peasants' knowledge of 'how to live' and this then became the 'cornerstone' of his religious view. Mossman is undoubtedly right in asserting that Tolstoy's personal evolution is indebted to his experience teaching. However, the 'three periods' of Tolstoy's involvement in education should not perhaps be considered so distinct. For example, the *Azbuka* was not just a project concerned with literacy but also with aesthetic and spiritual education, while the *Yasnaya Polyana* journal itself concerned itself much with religion, even if not as overtly as Tolstoy's later writings.

Tolstoy and the progressives

In secondary literature, Tolstoy's educational thought is often compared with the educational 'progressives' or founders of alternative movements, such as Maria Montessori, John Dewey, Rudolph Steiner, Paulo Freire and A. S. Neill. Tolstoy certainly strikes upon some of the same issues that become significant in the thought of these educational thinkers – but there appears to be no causal connection whatsoever between Tolstoy and any of these later writers – let alone a significant influence. It should also be stressed that Tolstoy's views differ extensively from the varied thought of these educationists.

A fundamental component of Tolstoy's rationale, particularly in earlier years, was to repudiate any predetermined theoretical treatment of education in order to allow the teacher to be entirely free and unlimited in pedagogical innovation. It is unlikely Tolstoy would ever endorse a systematized 'method' of education; similarly he never wanted to initiate an 'alternative' approach to education but rather to ensure that the education of ordinary people was universally humane. There are, however, with the exception of Paulo Freire, some interesting connections between Tolstoy and more famous educationists, even if these links only serve to highlight the isolation of each thinker from Tolstoy.

Steiner never cites or refers to Tolstoy in his writings on education, which are far more esoteric, philosophical and theoretical than Tolstoy's views. The two are only vaguely connected by the support of the Theosophist movement. Steiner had close ties with this group and Tolstoy was considered a Theosophist by the movement's founder, Madame Blavatsky. Despite this identification, it should be noted that Tolstoy never felt the need to endorse, or be constrained by, any religious faction, and was indeed wary of the fringe movements of his time – not least his own followers, the Tolstoyans.

There is even less of an association between A. S. Neill and Tolstoy. In the setting up of Summerhill, Neill was certainly not influenced by Tolstoy and it remains to be demonstrated that Neill was even aware of Tolstoy's educational views before the 1960s. In his autobiography Neill explains that he became interested in 'free education' not by progressive educators, whom he lists excluding Tolstoy, as Rousseau, Froebel, Pestalozzi, Montessori and Dewey, but through psychology and psychoanalysis (Neill, 1973, 163). Such emphasis on abstract theories, and indeed Neill's disinclination to promote intellectual rigor or moral instruction to students would be strongly abhorrent to Tolstoy, who in his later years was fully committed to the need for moral education, even if through heuristic means.

Although some similarities can be seen between them, Montessori also developed her system of education in complete independence of Tolstoy. However, Montessori is linked with Tolstoy both through the acquaintance of one of his greatest admirers, Mahatma Gandhi, and the advocacy of Tolstoy's daughter, Tatyana. According to Kramer (1976), Tatyana read about Montessori's school in a Russian educational journal in 1912 and later presented a paper about her system in Moscow. Tatyana was so enthusiastic about Montessori's ideas that she also visited Montessori's school in Rome and returned to Russia with a number of her textbooks where she utilized her method (TT, 250). Coincidentally, another one of Montessori's visitors during the same period was a previous guest at Yasnaya Polyana, the American social activist Jane Addams.

Tolstoy and John Dewey

Edwards (1992) argues that there are similarities between Dewey's philosophy of psychology, pragmatism, and the way Tolstoy's characters develop and understand their world, in particular on how the mind works and the individual interacts with society. He suggests that Tolstoy's and Dewey's work in education may have led to the development of similar philosophical views. He argues that Dewey's understanding of intellectual processes can be successfully compared with the psychology of Tolstoy's characters in *War and Peace* in that they 'experience frequent ruptures in the patterns of experience which they expect, and in making continuing adjustments to an ever newly perceived reality, are continually receiving an education' (Edwards, 1992, 31).

Tolstoy and Dewey's thought is similar in many other ways. Both believed that education could ameliorate social problems; that education should be centered on the child; and that educational research could be instigated by the setting up of a 'pedagogical laboratory.' They both criticized the traditional forms of education of their time for being removed from the actual experience of the child, and saw the problems of forms of education in which knowledge is viewed as something 'fixed' that should be merely transmitted to the child.

A less obvious comparison can also be made between Tolstoy and Dewey's conception of religion. In an early essay 'My Pedagogic Creed' (1897) – an astonishingly brash document drawn out in the language of a religious creed – Dewey claims that a 'teacher is the prophet of the true God and the usherer in of the true kingdom of God' (1897, 95). Dewey explains what he means by this in his later essay, 'A Common Faith' (1934). For Dewey, there is a difference between 'religion' and the 'religious.' Religions are static, outmoded systems of superstitious beliefs. The religious instinct, however, is an experiential condition of humankind that can be considered separately from social and cultural institutions.

It is interesting to note that Dewey's essay, like Tolstoy's *On Life*, starts with the discussion of two rival camps in society, the scientific materialists and the institutionalized religions. Both Tolstoy and Dewey attempt to beat a path between the two that is based on the experience of the individual and the necessity to create a moral social order. Indeed, like Tolstoy's definition of religion as the relation of man to the universe or its source, Dewey's conception and argument is based on a critique of the Church, but a realization that an individual's personal transformation can contribute to the creation of a Kingdom of God on earth. Dewey's conception, however, differs from Tolstoy's anarcho-agriculturalism, in that such a 'religious' transformation for the common good is necessarily linked to democracy. Indeed, as self-renunciation and pacifism can create God's plan on earth for Tolstoy, for Dewey Christ's message is realized on earth by the function of a democratic society. Thus it is no surprise that in Dewey's treatment of religious education, 'Religion and Our Schools' (1908) Dewey claims that schools are performing a religious function in ensuring the development of citizens able to unite for the common good. But like Tolstoy, Dewey sees the teaching of religion, as in the catechesis of Christianity, as counterproductive in promoting the true religious transformation of individual.

The comparisons do end, however. Dewey's view of God is far removed from Tolstoy's. Tolstoy clearly sees the values of the traditional teachings of the world religions and, although at times Tolstoy stresses that understanding God is impossible, and he is therefore prepared to accept forms of agnostic spirituality, he is most definitely a theist and describes himself as Christian. Dewey, on the other hand, although he also stresses the importance of personal experience and the development of our ideals through a reflective negotiation of our interaction with reality, which is similar to Tolstoy's view, is prepared to dispense with the notion of God entirely, depending on the individual.

John Dewey himself never recognized any similarities between his educational thought and Tolstoy's – let alone acknowledged any influence. But he was certainly acquainted with Tolstoy's non-fictional works by the time of Tolstoy's death, when he wrote the unpublished essay 'Tolstoi's Art' (1910). Later he also wrote a foreword to a book comparing the moral psychology of Tolstoy and Nietzsche (1929a). With regard to Tolstoy's educational works specifically, however, it would seem that Dewey only briefly refers to them once in his entire corpus, at an address delivered on the Russian school system at the University of Chicago, on 21 February 1929 (1929b: 51).

Nevertheless, it would seem that there was some contact between Dewey and the Tolstoyans. Dewey would have probably come into close contact with the Tolstoyan movement as a result of his friendship with the American social activist Jane Addams, founder of the Hull House settlement in Chicago. Dewey was a trustee of the settlement and one of the teachers at his school lived there. Addams had visited Tolstoy with Maude in the 1890s and later hosted Maude on his visit to North

America in 1898. She was later to write, on the invitation of Maude, the introduction to the Tolstoy Centenary edition of *What Then Must We Do?* (1934). Through Addams' link with Maude, there is an interesting connection between Tolstoy and Dewey. Half the money remaining from the *Resurrection* book fund, primarily used to settle the Doukhobors, was given to Hull House (JA, 280). Furthermore, Dewey's connection with Addams and other social activists probably led him, somehow, into contact with the Tolstoyan Ernest Crosby. Columbia University Butler Library's copy of Crosby's book, *Tolstoy as Schoolmaster* (1904) appears to be a gift given to Dewey in 1905. As the New Yorker Blaisdell discovered when researching Tolstoy, it is inscribed 'Professor Dewey/ with the compliments of the author. [Signed] Ernest H. Crosby, March 27, 1905' (2000, 241).

Tolstoy's influence

Even if Tolstoy did not influence some of the great progressive educators of the twentieth century, he did leave a considerable legacy. The examples given below are by no means exhaustive – they exclude the influence Tolstoy had in Spain and Japan, for instance, not to mention the convoluted reception Tolstoy's educational thought has had in his native country – but the following examples do illustrate the magnitude and diverse impact Tolstoy has had on individual schools and teachers.

Toward the end of his life Tolstoy was extremely famous and received many visitors at Yasnaya Polyana and engaged in correspondence with people all over the world. Among these sympathizers were teachers and community leaders who would seek advice on education. Kupersmith and Nolan (2006) document how, as a result of one such meeting, an American Rabbi founded a school – Delaware Valley College in Pennsylvania. Rabbi Krauskopf visited Tolstoy in the summer of 1894. He had intended to visit the Tsar to discuss the persecution of the Jewish population of Russia that had been suffering from the pogroms, wishing to create a safe Jewish homeland within Russia. As it transpired, Krauskopf did not meet the Tsar, but he did visit Yasnaya Polyana.

Kupersmith and Nolan relate two interesting anecdotes about this trip. First, Krauskopf and a fellow American traveler on arriving at Yasnaya Polyana asked a laborer where Tolstoy lived, only to find that laborer to be Tolstoy himself – not an uncommon story told by visitors to Yasnaya Polyana. Secondly, they recount how the Rabbi felt so in awe of Tolstoy that he described his meeting as though he had met a modern-day Moses or Isaiah. According to Krauskopf, Tolstoy argued that the plans to create a Jewish homeland within Russia would not come to fruition and that American society did not live up to its own principles – including in its public education system. Tolstoy suggested that Krauskopf attempt the plan he had intended for Russia but in America, by setting up an agricultural school to bring back the ghettoized Jewish youth to farming. Returning to America, Krauskopf procured some land, enrolled six students, and the school he created eventually became Delaware Valley College.

Another school set up under the influence of Tolstoy was by his daughter Alexandra. Her elder sisters had attempted setting up a school in Yasnaya Polyana in the early 1890s and she also tried to teach during her father's lifetime. After her father's death she wished to continue his work, of which she considered education an important part. The story of her work in the early Soviet era illustrates much of the new regime's antipathy toward Tolstoy's thought. In *I Worked for the Soviet* (1935) she explains how after being incarcerated as a political prisoner, she worked tirelessly to pursue her father's ideals, even meeting Stalin himself in the process. In 1918 she founded the Yasnaya Polyana Society to protect the estate and organize educational provision for the peasants. She tells how the first attempts to build a school in Tolstoy's memory were stalled in the confusion of the early Bolshevik era, as the timber mysteriously disappeared, probably embezzled. After a period of imprisonment, during which she organized some lessons for illiterate prisoners, Alexandra was appointed by the People's Commissariat of Education as the 'Director of the Yasnaya Polyana Schools Educational Experimental Station.' By 1929 there were four primary schools and three high schools comprising a memorial school, an agricultural school and an industrial school. These were partly funded by foreign charities that were still in contact with Yasnaya Polyana. Alexandra notes at this time that as soon as a school was opened, it was full of pupils, and that true to her father's beliefs, students enjoyed good relationships with their teachers and took part in activities such as tree planting and running a dairy.

Alexandra tried to run the schools in keeping with Tolstoy's ideals and not to let them succumb to the Communist propaganda being enforced at that time. This caused problems with local Communist groups who attempted to undermine her efforts and reported her to the authorities. The school was subject to frequent checks from the Central Executive Committee and a 'political grammar' teacher was sent from Moscow to ensure the school was conforming to the propaganda measures, such as the 'godless corners' that were being ordered in schools. She tells of an interesting episode where a professor from Moscow suggested a research project that involved asking the children questions such as, 'Who does the Red Army defend?' and 'Who are the enemies of the people?'

The tension between the demands of the new state and the educational vision of her father troubled her. She describes how on one occasion she was walking past a classroom when she heard a child ask a teacher, 'Does God exist?' Alexandra went in the classroom as the teacher did not know how to answer the question and said, 'Yes, of course he does children.' She reasoned that there was no point in forbidding the propaganda posters of drunken clergy but not daring to tell children about the teaching of Christ:

> The children were ignorant in religion and moral matters and the teachers were afraid to instruct them. If a child happened to have an interest in such subjects, the teacher would either have to not answer his questions or would try to avoid giving a clear answer. I thought of my father. I knew what he would have said: it's better to let all of those children be illiterate than to darken their minds as you are doing. (1935, 218)

Alexandra wished to use the 1928 Jubilee of Tolstoy's birth to safeguard the schools and museum of Yasnaya Polyana. However, this plan soon back-fired. Lunachasky, the Commissar for Education stated in his speech, 'We are not afraid that the students of Yasnaya Polyana will be educated in a Tolstoyan spirit foreign to our aims . . . we shall purge them of all Tolstoyanism' (1935, 224). Subsequently she noticed how more and more the schools were drawn into the promotion of Soviet policies, and at the same time museum workers were drifting further and further from Tolstoy's ideas. She resigned and was able to gain permission to give a series of lectures in Japan, after which she lived in exile in the United States of America.

Perhaps the most well-documented recent emulator of Tolstoy's educational ideas in the West is the American educationist and author, George Dennison. In *The Lives of Children* (1969), Dennison describes his experiences teaching at a small school set up in New York based on, what Dennison understands as, the 'libertarian values' of Neill and Tolstoy. In common with the other American commentators of Tolstoy in the 1960s and 1970s, Dennison misconstrues Tolstoy's religious views, seeing them as both extraneous to his educational vision and 'conventional' of his time. But the experiment, and indeed, the form of writing Dennison uses in the book, can be seen in some sense as a modern-day instigation of the Yasnaya Polyana school and the journal devoted to it. Dennison devotes one chapter of *The Lives of Children* to explaining Tolstoy's views and sees his school as a direct descendant of Tolstoy's experiment. He even ends the book – after a lengthy quotation from Maude's biography describing children climbing on Tolstoy – with the conclusion that the emblem for American primary schools 'should be a medallion without words, showing Tolstoy with the children on his back' (1969, 282).

Another teacher influenced by Tolstoy was Ludwig Wittgenstein – often regarded as the greatest philosopher of the twentieth century. Wittgenstein shares many attributes with Tolstoy. For example, he was extremely wealthy but wished to live a life of pious simplicity, in a search of truth equal to Tolstoy's. Intellectually there are also comparisons to be drawn. Greenwood (1995) argues that there are conceptual likenesses between Wittgenstein's *Tractatus* (1961) and Tolstoy's criticism of philosophy expounded in *Anna Karenina*. Tolstoy's religious views and Wittgenstein's later writings on religion also share similarities: both men eschewed the metaphysical claims and official hierarchies of religious convention; but attempted to fully embrace the ethical injunction commanded by religious conviction.

Wittgenstein admired Tolstoy's fiction, particularly his short stories, but it was Tolstoy's translation of the Gospels – which he read ardently in the trenches of the First World War – that had the greatest impact. Wittgenstein learnt passages of Tolstoy's text off by heart and was so entranced with them that he became known among the other soldiers as 'the man with the gospels' (Monk, 1991, 116).

Tolstoy and Wittgenstein shared a mutual interest in the love of physical labor. In one of his restless periodic breaks from philosophy, Wittgenstein visited Russia with the Tolstoyan desire of becoming a farm laborer – only to give up the idea when the Soviet authorities would only allow him to become a professor. In another Tolstoyan episode, resonating with Auerbach's Eugen, Wittgenstein attempted elementary school teaching in the Austrian countryside. As a teacher, Wittgenstein seems to have shared some qualities with Tolstoy: at times he engaged in creative, experimental lessons; he read Tolstoy's fables with his classes and even followed Tolstoy's example in writing a basic literacy textbook – a spelling dictionary for primary schools. The textbook, unlike Tolstoy's *Azbuka* was endorsed by the authorities and was published quickly, according to Monk, with some success. Like Tolstoy's *Azbuka* the book was based on Wittgenstein's practical experience teaching and was designed for the rural poor, concentrating on using the everyday language of the people. Yet in the classroom, as Monk documents, Wittgenstein displayed some undesirable attributes. He was strict, often violent, and would spend a disproportionate amount of time teaching mathematics – hitting children if they gave incorrect answers. It was the result of such practices that led to Wittgenstein resigning his teaching post. On one occasion, by no means out of the ordinary, he hit one of his students so hard that the boy fell down. At the subsequent disciplinary hearing, Wittgenstein was not found guilty of misconduct but the case had caused a scandal in the local area, in which Wittgenstein was already unpopular.

The influence of Tolstoy on Wittgenstein's life does not end with his ill-fated attempt at teaching. As Monk recounts at the end of his biography, Wittgenstein's burial at St Giles Church, Cambridge bears testament to his lifelong admiration of Tolstoy. When he died, despite not being a practicing Christian in any orthodox sense, those around Wittgenstein decided that he should be given a Catholic funeral. This was because of a conversation he had had with his friend Drury concerning the burial of Tolstoy's brother. Wittgenstein had commended

Tolstoy's view that a religious funeral was appropriate for his brother, even though Tolstoy himself did not agree with the teachings of the Church.

An even greater twentieth-century figure that Tolstoy influenced was the great pacifist Indian leader Mohandas Karamchand Gandhi, often known by the honorific 'Mahatma.' Gandhi's spiritual autobiography, *The Story of My Experiments with Truth* (1982) follows the form of Tolstoy's *A Confession*. In it Gandhi describes how Tolstoy's views on Christianity, pacifism and simplicity influenced him, leading to his establishment of the commune 'Tolstoy Farm' in South Africa. The two great men corresponded in Tolstoy's old age, and their letters demonstrate their common aspirations and mutual admiration. Tolstoy's essay *The Kingdom of God is within You* was particularly important in influencing Gandhi's doctrine of Satyagraha.

In his letters to Gandhi, Tolstoy continued his familiar critique of modern society and the denouncement of the horrors of so-called Christian civilization. In his letter of 7 September 1910 he explains that the cause of society's problems was the prevalence of violence and absence of love. In his following attempt to explain what love is, Tolstoy could not help but invoke his view of children and education:

> Love, i.e. the striving of human souls towards unity and the activity resulting from such striving, is the highest and only law of human life is felt and known by every person in the depth of his soul (as we see most clearly of all with children) – known by him until he is snared by the false teachings of the world. (TL, 706)

By way of proving this, Tolstoy goes on to describe how in a scripture examination in a Moscow school, a girl successfully argued with the examiner – a bishop. In her response to a question regarding the sixth commandment, rather than giving the answer drilled into her by her formal education – that killing was morally permissible in the eyes of the established church in the case of war and capital punishment, the girl insisted that taking a human life must always be wrong. To this, the Bishop eventually had to concede defeat as the girl 'went away victorious.'

Gandhi shared Tolstoy's interest in education, yet it is unlikely that Gandhi read Tolstoy's pedagogical articles. There are similarities between the two men's views on education, however, as Kumar (1997) explains. Gandhi, like Tolstoy in the 1860s, was concerned about the negative effects of industrialization and the importation of Western methods of education. Part of his fear of modern systems of education was the lack of autonomy given to the teacher and, also mirroring Tolstoy, the intrusion of the government in education. He saw the possibility of a distinctly Indian system of education, closely related to his economic and social vision of small, self-sufficient village communes. His 'basic education' program therefore stressed the importance of learning handicrafts and practical skills and knowledge – something that later in life Tolstoy had also suggested for Russia.

Both Tolstoy and Gandhi stressed the importance of the moral example of the teacher, and for Gandhi this alleviated the need for formal religious education as such. Religion, as it was conceived by wider Indian society at that time, was divisive. But the common truth at the core of all religions, which both Tolstoy and Gandhi believed, would have a unifying effect if demonstrated through the actions and intention of the teacher.

Chapter 9

Tolstoy's Relevance for Today's Educators

Tolstoy was horrified at the effects of nineteenth-century educational institutions on their pupils. Of the schools of continental Europe, he noted that ironically the teacher's job was done when the student had suspended their natural intelligence and curiosity and replaced it with fear, silence and the preoccupation with meaningless learning by rote. Not only were students harmed by schooling they received, but they were divorced from the natural, nurturing environments of the home or farm, and oppressed under the yoke of religion or government. Tolstoy concluded from his tour of European schools during the 1860s that the education system corrupts children, making those who are 'somnambulists learn best of all.'

Many of the ills of nineteenth-century educational institutions that Tolstoy wished to eradicate, such as corporal punishment and rote learning have, in many countries, been abolished. But the questions Tolstoy asked – 'how do I know what to teach, and how do I teach it?' are, of course, still pertinent to educators. Given Tolstoy's originality and unique position, his educational thought can be seen as more than just the product of a particular era or reaction to the specific practices of the nineteenth century. Tolstoy was, in his educational experimentation, as he remarks himself, both looking toward the future and, in part, attempting to establish some immutable laws that govern the educational process across time and culture.

Tolstoy's biographer and friend, Maude, reflected that people were inclined either to accept Tolstoy's thought uncritically or reject it completely, without considering that aspects of it may be true and others erroneous. In noting the relevance of Tolstoy's views, I do not wish to advocate them as such. Instead, while acknowledging some of their deficiencies, I would like to recognize the freshness of some of Tolstoy's insights, and to highlight elements of his thought that are not only relevant today, but are likely to continue to be relevant to those who, like Tolstoy, wish to provide a humane, ethical and inspiring education.

There is little doubt that Tolstoy would be concerned about some aspects of schools today, such as the centralized control of the curriculum, use of assessment and consequent disengagement of the young, documented – among some more positive findings, in the recent *Nuffield Review of 14–19 Education and Training in England and Wales* (Pring et al., 2009). However, in suggesting Tolstoy's relevance to educators, although I am sure there are endless apt comparisons, I do not wish to relate Tolstoy's views to any particular time, place or educational tradition, but to point to areas of Tolstoy's thinking which have something positive to offer today's educators and those of the future.

Knowledge, curriculum and indoctrination

At the heart of Tolstoy's wrangling with education was knowing 'what to teach?' According to Tolstoy, answering this question had previously been considered a philosophical problem, but in fact, it was not one that philosophy could solve. The schools of the past had been based on the 'truths' of philosophies that have since been proved false. The existence of rival philosophies also made devising the curriculum by philosophical methods problematic. Furthermore, an attempt to create a 'free' pedagogy determined by a conceptual argument would only yield a new kind of dogma. Tolstoy believed that the curriculum is best constructed in collaboration with students and society itself. Through the *Yasnaya Polyana* journal, Tolstoy sought to initiate a process of dialogue and consultation to mediate between social classes and generations. As then current forms of education failed children, even the theories of progressive educational thinkers, he felt children, teachers and society at large should all play a part in determining what kind of education should be provided.

Tolstoy always maintained that students should have a choice in what they study and there should be no coercion in this. As well as endorsing his view of the natural development of the child, it could be said that Tolstoy's view also rests on the principle of uncertainty – something that he champions as typically Russian in *War and Peace* in opposition to the theoretical views of the Germans. According to Tolstoy, given that there can be no philosophically derived epistemic guarantees in the construction of the curriculum, it is better to admit uncertainty than it is to construct a curriculum based on error. When the epistemic uncertainty of the educator is to be passed onto the students, then the curriculum can be constructed in accordance with the younger generation's needs.

In his later writings, Tolstoy again stresses that it is important students study what they wish, but he also adds to his earlier views. Education should proceed on a 'shared platform' between teachers and students, from which students choose what they wish to study. The curriculum offered on the platform can be constructed from the three branches of human knowledge that consist of demonstrable propositions. Because their truth claims can be, according to Tolstoy, verified, they are therefore legitimate to be passed on to the next generation. The first of these branches is philosophical and religious knowledge, the second, the findings and methods of empirical sciences and the third, deducible logical truths, such as mathematics.

For Tolstoy, of most importance is the first branch. Students should be able to contemplate and discuss questions of an existential nature. Until such questions are discussed, the student can only have a limited understanding of what is good. Tolstoy believed that establishing core values and attitudes was essential for education to take place and the individual to develop. This is an important and relevant strand in Tolstoy's thinking about curriculum – education must answer the 'questions posed to man' as he puts it in the *Yasnaya Polyana* journal or 'establish a relationship to the world' as he later asserts in his religious essays. Such an existential approach to education has much to commend educators today who wish to challenge and motivate pupils by posing the pressing questions facing humanity.

Tolstoy believed that any education based on an ideological agenda or which did not meet students' immediate needs, was wrong. The best way to remedy this was for student and teacher to investigate phenomena together, to start off by asking questions and then allow students to form their own views based on the evidence available. The progressives Dewey and Freire make similar observations. Traditional forms of education present facts to the student, rather than demonstrating that human knowledge grows through revision, collaboration and investigation. This view of the relationship between knowledge and the curriculum has much to offer educators today. If questions of import are tackled together from a 'shared platform' in a search for truth, many areas of the curriculum will be more interesting and relevant to students' lives and the problem of indoctrination is kept at bay.

Related to his belief in the 'shared platform' is Tolstoy's prophecy of publicly accessible, voluntary educational institutions. Tolstoy believed that in the future wholly free institutions would be founded that allowed students to study what they wished. He first discusses this in the essay 'Training and Education' in the *Yasnaya Polyana* journal, where he states that education should be 'an extremely varied conscious action of one human being upon another for the purpose of communicating knowledge without forcing the pupils either by direct force or diplomacy' (TE, 324). Tolstoy accepts that a school based on this definition would be very different from that traditionally conceived. It could be a library, museum, theater or discussion group. But these informal education institutions would be adept at constantly evolving according to the needs of the pupils and the abilities of the teachers.

Later in life, Tolstoy commented to his friend Goldenweiser that he believed such an institution already existed – the Kensington Museum in London. However, it is possible that Tolstoy mistakenly remembered a similar method of 'query-boxes' used at public lectures in Berlin (BK, 273). According to Tolstoy's description, the Museum had a large public library and employed specialists in various subjects. The public could place in boxes questions that interested them. Experts would then organize lectures around these topics to the public's demand. Such an arrangement, Goldenweiser notes, was 'in keeping with the true object of teaching – to answer the questions which arise in the minds of the students' (GW, 122).

Tolstoy's vision of high-quality public institutions which provide services for those interested in learning is still relevant today. Part of this vision was Tolstoy's wish for an education system that was based on the questions pertinent to people, not one that was instrumental in perpetuating social inequality. Education should be expanded to people of all social classes because of its intrinsic worth and as a public right, not an ideological imposition. It is possible that this vision will be easier to realize in the digital age, now that new means of information sharing and the desire for more flexible methods of study are revolutionizing the possibilities of continuing education and other forms of self-study.

Concern over indoctrination and coercion, one of Tolstoy's main preoccupations, also remains germane to educators. His critique of the modern notion of progress and his claim that technological advancement did not necessarily lead to an improvement of well-being but often to new forms of enslavement, including in the classroom, may seem less bizarre today than it did in previous decades. In the last century a number of countries, including his own, instituted systems of education that were particularly indoctrinatory and the prospect of indoctrinatory influences in education is an ever-present one, both in and outside state education systems.

Tolstoy and religious education

Tolstoy was vehemently opposed to a religious education based on Christian catechesis sponsored by an established church. His view of religious education is therefore particularly relevant to educational contexts, such as Great Britain, where the authority of religion has been challenged and the subject is often taught as 'non-confessional' – that is, it does not aim to induct the student into any particular religion. For Tolstoy, religious education should not be a form of indoctrination into a particular set of beliefs, but it should introduce children to the universal nature of human spirituality. Tolstoy was progressive in his use of materials from all the world's religions. The *Yasnaya Polyana* journal included an article on the Prophet Muhammad; his *Azbuka* contained extracts from the Bible and stories from many parts of the world. In later life, as he became more knowledgeable about Buddhism, Taoism and Hinduism, Tolstoy included aspects of their teachings and traditional fables in *A Calendar of Wisdom*. His approach to religious education, therefore, resonates with the modern multicultural society whose schools cater for children of many faiths and none.

Even though Tolstoy's own religious views were radical, because of his hatred of indoctrination, his concept of religious education, in which freedom of belief was central, can be seen to be relevant to religious educators today. Unlike the 'religious studies' approach, which is primarily based on an academic study of the world's religions, Tolstoy believed that religious education should not start from a neutral standpoint, but from child-centered evaluation and exploration. He believed that an objective, merely academic, study of religions would be pointless. In *On Life* Tolstoy paraphrases a secularist who after examining the world's traditions, comments: 'there are a thousand religions and they are all absurd, so why should we study them?' (OL, 25). Tolstoy's view was different because he did not see the existence of more than one faith a challenge to the validity of religious belief, nor their teachings contradictory. Considering the teachings of the worlds' religions could promote a common understanding of universal human values.

Tolstoy's approach to studying religion is exemplified by the way he used the Bible in the classroom. Tolstoy enthused at the educational value of the Bible, seeing it as indispensable. However, Tolstoy did not use the Bible as a vehicle for catechism or mere exposition of Christianity. He saw it rather as a heuristic device from which children could contemplate spiritual and moral truths, to enter what he describes as 'ever new perspectives of thought, knowledge and power.' The key to education for Tolstoy was rousing children's curiosity, the child should be provoked into the pursuit of knowledge by 'recognising the falseness and insufficiency of their view of things.' The stories and wisdom of the Bible were essential in this process of making students love knowledge and reflect on universal aspects of human experience.

Any approach to religious education will rest on certain assumptions about its subject matter, religion, and how people may grow in knowledge of it. For example, traditional confessionalism assumes that the tenets of Christianity are true in one sense or another and we can grow in knowledge of religion by learning about doctrine or religious narrative. The religious studies approach, on the other hand, often makes the assumption that religion can be understood in essentially cultural terms; to understand a religion is to understand its features: certain places of worship, festivals, customs and practices, all of which have certain underlying beliefs. Tolstoy's view of religion, however, is radically different and not concerned with doctrine, tradition or surface features.

As Tolstoy sets out in 'Religion and Morality', it is based on a response to universal existential questions of meaning and purpose:

> no reasonable man can help pausing to ask himself, 'what is the meaning of my momentary, uncertain, and unstable existence amid this eternal, firmly defined and unending universe?'... That question faces everyman, and in one way or another everyman answers it. And in the reply to that question lies the essence of every religion. (RM, 172–173)

This definition of religion is useful to religious educators because it identifies religion as something relevant to everyone, something of critical importance in the context of increasing secularization. Tolstoy's definition also brings the secular alternatives to religion within the boundaries of religious education, thus making it more inclusive and its universal relevance more immediate to all. For Tolstoy, it was the truth that mattered, particularly in religion. True religion is not a set of doctrines to be assented to on account of authority, but the ongoing search for truth. This allows for religious education to be dynamic and purposeful, but also allows students to make their own decisions with regard to religious matters. It is non-confessional, in this sense, provided that it does not seek to impose one viewpoint over another. Allowing students to evaluate and critique religion in this way can be seen as an attempt to make religion applicable to the contemporary world, particularly to rethink how religious values can be reconciled with a scientific worldview. Indeed, Tolstoy saw any religious education that did not try and accommodate religious and scientific worldviews as counterproductive.

Tolstoy's view of the relationship between theory and practice

Tolstoy advances a view of education that is essentially practical. In the *Yasnaya Polyana* journal Tolstoy argues that education is best conceived as a perpetual pedagogical laboratory, never abstracting rigid theories from observations, but ever responding to the needs of students and teachers – 'the only method of education is experiment, and its only criterion freedom' (TSYP, 31). Education should be atheoretical; a preconceived view of education cannot be enough to determine correct educational practice. Tolstoy's idea of a 'no-theory theory' could be seen as contradictory. In saying that there cannot be a theory of education, he is making a statement about a preconceived idea – but must Tolstoy advocate a 'theory' to level criticism against 'theoretical' views?

The approach to education Tolstoy expounds does not amount to a theory, but it is based on a particular understanding of human nature and an epistemological outlook that eschews the sole legitimacy of the scientific method. Tolstoy was not an educational nihilist, least of all a relativist. In his view, education can be subject to discussion and reason, but in so doing educationists should base their views on experience and on basic human truths. Tolstoy felt that human values never change, but that these values can only be understood as experience itself: there is a difference, as Ivan Ilych found, for example, between knowing *about* death and *being* a dying man. Such a view of experience stresses the primacy of intuition rather than rational thought, and runs throughout Tolstoy's writings. It is explained in his religious tracts, and artistically rendered in the unexpected spiritual revelations of his major characters in his fiction: Nicholas in the storm, Olenin in the forest, Levin at work with the peasants, Ivan lying in his bed. Such forms of personal, responsive, experiential knowledge in Tolstoy's fiction are often pitched against the forms of knowledge favored by conceited professionals – Ivan Ilych's doctor, the tutor St Jerome or the German general Pfuhl – the 'theoreticians who are so fond of their theory that they lose sight of that theory – its application in practice' (WP, 758).

A conceptual assumption of Tolstoy's views, although in a sense providing support for his atheoretical outlook, was the notion of 'natural development' – that learners innately possess the inclination, and means to learn. This view is strongly related to Tolstoy's belief in the innate goodness of the child. Teachers do not need to tell children what they need to learn; children are in a better position to know that themselves. Tolstoy claims that as there is a natural 'equilibrium' in each child between 'goodness, truth and beauty,' if children are coerced in their education it may distort their innate harmony. For education to be beneficial it must not mold children into a fixed pattern of development, rather it should allow them to progress freely.

Tolstoy considered his own development progressed by such free principles: as long as he studied what he felt was important, he was successful. He commented to his friend Goldenweiser in later life: 'I have been learning all my life and do not cease to learn, and this is what I have noticed: learning is only fruitful when it corresponds to one's needs' (GW, 84). Tolstoy's application of this view to his students, however may not be so apt. His insistence that a child will intuitively know what is good for them to learn, and is indeed the perfect paradigm of 'goodness, truth and beauty,' although laudable in its positivity, can also seem wonderfully naive. Children are capable of doing wrong; they may not always want to do what is good for them. Furthermore, in schools today as in Tolstoy's time, discipline is required to keep order to allow others to learn and to prevent 'mob' rule. Yet Tolstoy believed that it was the schools themselves that created the conditions for the corruption of children. According to him, any display of disaffection and disengagement in the pupil is due to the inadequacy of the school and its methods. To counter these problems, it must be remembered that Tolstoy realized the importance of small class sizes and, of course, the ability of the teacher to gauge what the students needed to know in the course of their natural development, and to inspire them to want to learn more. The *Azbuka* is indicative of Tolstoy's belief in 'natural development'; it begins with the simple and proceeds to the complex, but it does not rest on any particular theory of how students learn to read. It is replete with varied curiosities designed to stimulate interest and capture the imagination; to enhance children's knowledge and introduce them to new worlds beyond their own experience.

One important concern of Tolstoy's was that abstract theories may not work in practice. He recognized educators must be able to adapt to students' needs as and when necessary. Given the individuality of each child, and the differing requirements of distinct geographical districts, a general theory of learning could not account for the complexity of each individual student or even each individual school. This is not to say that teachers should not learn from each other, or from their experience, or learn new methods. The purpose of the *Yasnaya Polyana* journal was to enable teachers to further their thinking about practice, but ultimately they were free to exercise their judgment as to what kind of approach to use and when.

Tolstoy's anti-theoretical stance can be seen to capture something of relevance to educators to this day. Even if we dispute Tolstoy's criticism of theory and scientific forms of knowledge, there is a sense that education must be seen as a practical activity. In their interactions with students, educators make thousands of judgments per day and at the level of each teacher, such 'knowledge' must not be abstract, but practiced. Furthermore, Tolstoy recognized that aspects of a teacher's character such as the ability to inspire, make jokes or empathize are far more important to a lesson's success than the application of fixed pedagogical methods. Just as it did for Tolstoy in his day, being a successful educator today still involves developing skills, dispositions and attitudes as much as it does theoretical knowledge.

The autonomy of the teacher and Tolstoy's view of educational research

Tolstoy believed that the most important aspect of running a school was having good teachers. Such a simple observation is as true today as it has ever been. He felt that teachers should be free to react to emerging needs of students. In this sense, teachers should be at the helm of educational research, not bureaucrats and administrators outside the school, far away from the children. Tolstoy did not believe that a bureaucracy guided by supposedly 'scientific knowledge' could determine a suitable system of education. Tolstoy believed teachers themselves should continually strive to improve their practice in the classroom on a day-to-day basis.

There is a great emphasis in Tolstoy's thought on the autonomy and intelligence of teachers in their task. Like Auerbach's Eugen, Tolstoy embraced an approach to teaching that emphasized the teacher's duty to captivate pupils. Instructing, lecturing and memorizing all have their place as pedagogic strategies – but their use must not be based on a system of manipulation, reward or 'diplomacy,' it must be based on the response of the students. To be sensitive to the needs of the students, it is best if the teacher does as he or she feels naturally inclined. They should express their enthusiasm, thoughts and feelings freely, and in so doing use all their powers of imagination and insight; to teach, in Auerbach's words, from the 'pure drive of nature.'

Tolstoy's understanding of Auerbach's plea to eschew theory and in its place emphasize the 'drive of nature' is not anarchical. For Tolstoy, teaching is a morally binding and difficult task. The teacher is not free to do whatever they wish. Rather the teacher is compelled to do what is necessary for the good of the children, in the words of the motto of the *Yasnaya Polyana* journal – to be 'pushed' by the needs of students. In this sense, Tolstoy did not need theory – he was constantly seeking to improve his own practice.

Tolstoy certainly was an energetic teacher and his desire to teach to the 'convenience' of pupils rather than to that of the teacher may explain the burn-out that coincided with his short period of intense teaching. This is perhaps one flaw of his views – that his methods would be draining on teachers. He clearly felt exhausted by his efforts, retreating to the steppes of Samara to take the kumys cure when he tired. In 1905, when his daughter Alexandra had set up a school at Yasnaya Polyana, he asked her one morning in sympathy: 'Do you ever have mornings when you find it difficult to get up, when you don't feel like working and are tired of it?' (CAT, 106).

Another weakness of Tolstoy's position is, of course, that not all teachers may be so naturally gifted or dedicated to their work. Tolstoy himself was no doubt a charismatic, captivating presence in the classroom. However, for those teachers who lack the natural authority and storytelling abilities of Tolstoy, his approach may not be so plausible. Tolstoy's daughter Alexandra found this when teaching at her school. She tried making up her own methods as her father had done but was often met with boredom and disinterest. When her father appeared at the school, as he frequently did, however, the students soon became lively and engaged as he was quickly able to win their confidence and interest.

According to Tolstoy it was possible to educate teachers in his techniques. Or rather he felt that experience teaching in his schools helped teachers understand what they themselves 'needed' to know as educators. An important line of Tolstoy's thinking is that teachers must continually try to improve their craft. 'For the education of children to be successful,' Tolstoy asserts, 'the educators must continue to educate themselves.' The teacher should learn from the pupils which method is best, and what subject knowledge is necessary, in an ongoing exchange of ideas. Such a view of teacher education, and its relationship to practice and experience, is still relevant today. Similar views have been endorsed by teacher educators, encouraging teachers to conduct small-scale research projects with their students, and boost their knowledge and understanding as part of their career development.

Another important emphasis of Tolstoy's educational thought was his empirical view of educational research. At the experimental school at Yasnaya Polyana, Tolstoy wished to use empirical methods to find out what strategies worked well in the classroom. To ascertain this he observed students as they collaborated in groups, analyzed their work, consulted their opinions, transcribed dialogues of classroom interaction, and performed an 'experiment' between the abilities of his class and that of another school's. Little of this empirical investigation was objective or scientific but at the heart of Tolstoy's experimental approach was the desire that educational innovation should progress on evidence.

Tolstoy's observations were often focused on the experience of students, and in this sense he was opposed to the conventional methods of scientific investigation of his time. When visiting schools in Germany, he asked students about their schools. He mused that if the 'real' effects of schooling on students were considered and understood, rather than just statistical data, it would be obvious that there was a strong case against the methods employed. In his empirical observations, Tolstoy did not wish to test or establish a hypothesis, only to determine how a teacher must think and act. This was to be drawn from an investigation of what it was like to be a pupil in the class, and what it was like to be a teacher – both of which Tolstoy analyzed with incredible freshness and his accounts are therefore still of worth to teachers today. Tolstoy's experimental school can be seen as a precursor to traditions in educational research that seek to understand the experience of children and 'practitioner,' or 'action research,' where teachers are encouraged to change aspects of their teaching and research and research and evaluate the effects. These methods of research, true to the spirit of Tolstoy's experiments, also have much to offer educators today.

The relevance of a literary genius

Educationists have often only looked to the *Yasnaya Polyana* journal to examine Tolstoy's contribution to educational thought, but this represents only a part of Tolstoy's writings relevant to education. The *Azbuka* and *New Azbuka* were for Tolstoy much more important works and they demonstrate some key aspects of his views on education. Although textbooks, they are shot through with evidence of his humor, creativity and love of life's varied experiences – all of which he wished to share with his readers. Although clearly designed to be accessible for all learners and remaining simple in style, his textbooks and readers were intellectually rigorous, challenging and versatile resources. Such qualities in teaching resources are as equally important, and perhaps rare, today.

Tolstoy's fiction is also relevant to educators, partly because literature gives access to areas of human experience and understanding often excluded from the formal discourse of education. Educational themes are present throughout Tolstoy's oeuvre and across all his literary genres. His early novellas *Childhood*, *Boyhood* and *Youth* are concerned with the psychology of growing up and the first-person experience of learning. His didactic folk tales, which were first attempted in collaboration with his pupils, and the preparation of his textbooks, were designed with the purpose of educating all social classes through the medium of story. In his great novels, Tolstoy was concerned with understanding the way experience forms an individual's knowledge of, and relation to, the outside world – as an educationist he had a similar interest in how such development could be nurtured and encouraged naturally without undue interference. Tolstoy was an astute of observer of character and human interaction, and had an elephantine imagination. Such qualities are perhaps best demonstrated through the art of storytelling, and these attributes, particularly the way Tolstoy used them to inspire his students, are of much import for educators today. Given the relevance of Tolstoy's literary approach and understanding, it is perhaps no coincidence that his greatest educational inspiration, Berthold Auerbach, was also a writer. Likewise, perhaps the greatest relevance of Tolstoy's own story as an educator is its inspirational value *as a story*.

It is likely that Tolstoy's educational thought is of interest to educators because of his status as one of the world's greatest writers. The insights Tolstoy's literary powers yielded when he devoted them to education are inspiring. His skills as an author also give his educational thought a different perspective from other educationists – the perceptive powers of an artistic genius. And throughout all his works, one theme remains clear: educators should constantly have in mind the experience of the child. Teachers must be sensitive to what is actually going on with their students in the here and now. Tolstoy was concerned with the 'actual effect' of the school as opposed to what adults might claim about it – and such a voice in educational debates will always be relevant. Educators will continue to ask themselves, as Tolstoy did, 'How can things be better? And do things have to be the same?' But Tolstoy did not ask these questions just to improve children's experiences of education, but with the intent of changing society itself for the better.

Tolstoy believed that if we really want the world to be a better place and to improve on the present, we must pass the challenges on to the future generation to work out, rather than just attempting to 'fill up' young people with the inadequate knowledge of the past. He felt that all too often schools put children off learning rather than encouraging them. What schools should be teaching, he mused, is the love of learning, not knowledge itself. Such views will always remain fundamental to those who wish to promote a kind of education that has its recipients' autonomy at heart and the promotion of an open and equal society as its goal.

Committed educators are always seeking new ways to look at their craft, and Tolstoy's views can certainly do that. Some of his assertions were intended to be timeless and these often demonstrate the complexity of the educational process, if only by their vagueness. Nevertheless, within the concepts of 'experience,' 'experiment' and 'striving for perfection' all manner of educational virtues are encapsulated. These eternal ideas, if not specific, are perhaps as Tolstoy argues, more relevant than 'abstract theory.' They stress the more essential, human qualities that should underlie the educational process.

In the 1860s, Tolstoy asked the deceptively complex questions: how do I know what to teach and how should I teach it? These questions, typical of his frank approach to pressing problems, arose from both practical and political concerns. Tolstoy wanted to know how he should teach on a day-to-day basis in his school, but he was also seeking answers to the question of education within the political and social upheaval of nineteenth-century Russia. Tolstoy was writing at a time when the old order was being eroded and challenged. The need to construct a modern nation, and the emancipation of the serfs in particular, had precipitated discussion over popular education.

Tolstoy attempted to provide and develop education suitable for the rural working class, in the context of centuries of social inequality, and to reaffirm spiritual values in the face of growing materialism. His solutions to these issues may seem as extreme as some of the practices and problems that his time presented to him, but within his thoughts on the matter there are some core educational values which will always remain of relevance to educators.

Chapter 10

Conclusion

In this book, I have not so much intended to advocate Tolstoy's views as tell his story. And as education was in his time, and is likely to continue to be, susceptible to the diktat of governments and bureaucrats who are more preoccupied with measurement and prescription than creativity and inspiration, Tolstoy's is a heroic story – even if a tragically idealistic one, significant only because of his literary authority.

Tolstoy was profoundly affected by his experiences teaching and the students he taught. He remembered the students of his experimental school throughout his life. As late as 1908, Tolstoy helped Vasily Morozov, or 'Fyedka,' revise a story he had written for publication, and was at the same time still forming classes for the peasant children on his estate. On a number of occasions Tolstoy also received large numbers of school children from the surrounding district. He would try to guess the Yasnaya Polyana children's names by the resemblance they had to their grandparents – whom he had taught over 40 years ago. Maude, Biryukov and Goldenweiser all recount how Tolstoy told them, when reflecting on his long life, that his period of teaching in the 1860s was one of his happiest, exclaiming: 'What a happy time that was! How I loved that work!' (GW, 86–87).

From the creative impetus Tolstoy received during the Yasnaya Polyana experiment, Tolstoy wrote some of the world's greatest literature. The same experience launched him on a trajectory toward one of the most intense spiritual searches ever documented. His vision of education is inextricably linked to his religious beliefs, both in terms of his final conception of education as a means to promote the good of others and the fraternity of humankind, and also in the effect that his experience of teaching had on his own spiritual growth.

Tolstoy's spiritual 'conversion' was not a sudden one, but a slow maturation lyrically illustrated in the development of his fiction and aided by his educational exploits. Teaching religious education lessons at his school, and observing the children's enchantment with the stories of the Bible, confirmed Tolstoy's growing religious convictions. The conclusions Tolstoy came to as a result of his long search have often been perceived as contradictory. They do not, and did not, fit into neat categories. Tolstoy was against government but not a revolutionary; believed in God but not in the Church; was rich but wanted to be poor; and believed in absolute morals while upholding the sanctity of the individual conscience. In his views of education we can see the repercussions of such unique perspectives. He believed in a universal system of education for the people, but not one under state control; he saw religious education as fundamental, but not one that was constrained by Orthodox Christianity; he believed in the freedom of the child, but also in the inspirational authority of the teacher. His position straddles many conventional dichotomies and this has led to much misunderstanding of Tolstoy's educational views: he is often still cast as an advocate of 'progressive' education, rather than 'traditional.' Yet Tolstoy was conservative in some of his values and methods. He wished to preserve Russian culture and rural life against the onslaught of industrialization and, more than anything, he wished to promote a common understanding of Christian spiritual values.

The centrality of Tolstoy's religious vision within his educational thought has not been widely acknowledged nor understood. Tolstoy scholarship has been considered to be in the realm of Slavonic studies and Russian literature rather than education. Few books have been published about Tolstoy's educational ideas and little substantial research has been undertaken to understand Tolstoy's reception or lasting influence on education. Wiener's translations of 1904 remain the most comprehensive resource published in English; although they do not fully represent the contents of the *Yasnaya Polyana* journal, or include Tolstoy's writings on the subject between 1904 and 1910. Those books which have been published since Wiener's translations also overlook Tolstoy's later educational writings, thus excluding his more overtly spiritual postulations.

Of all Tolstoy's commentators, Murphy is the only Anglophone educationist who has stressed the significance of religion to Tolstoy's work as an educator. Perhaps this is because educationists have feared casting

Tolstoy as a religious thinker. After all, Tolstoy's views would fit neither a conventional secular nor conventional religious context. It may be that, if only in recent times, without the negative association of the 'Tolstoyans' and with increasing interest in spiritual development, even in state-sponsored education, that Tolstoy's views can be considered more than the grandiose delusions of a world-famous author.

Tolstoy's last major work, *A Calendar of Wisdom*, should not be overlooked when appraising his educational thought. The aphorisms contained in this work conclude Tolstoy's thoughts on education and their place within his belief system. Tolstoy often championed the wisdom of the peasants in opposition to the culture of the decadent classes, but *A Calendar of Wisdom* refers to many classical figures and philosophers. *A Calendar of Wisdom* can be seen as the 'bridge' between high culture and the people that Tolstoy first thought about during the days of the Yasnaya Polyana school, demonstrating his belief in the goodness and unity of humanity in general.

Tolstoy was especially pleased with *A Calendar of Wisdom* and the work can be seen to document the extensive scope of his lifelong spiritual and intellectual journey. Despite the lack of a scholarly approach in all his intellectual exploration, and his own failure in the formal education system, Tolstoy made a wide-ranging investigation into the world's cultures and languages, making him one of history's great autodidacts. It was the value of such personal investigation in his own quest for the truth that led Tolstoy to advocate a similar view of education for others – if people, adults and children could learn what they felt they 'needed' to know, and this learning was supported by suitable organizations and individuals, then the problem of education would be solved. *A Calendar of Wisdom* itself can be seen as an attempt to make such learning easier. It is nothing more than a collection of short, readily digested ideas, an accumulation of 'how people live' throughout the world, the kind of knowledge Tolstoy felt would be 'needed' by everyone – a daily lesson for people of all ages and classes.

It is telling that many of the aphorisms in *A Calendar of Wisdom* are written by Tolstoy himself. Tolstoy believed his knowledge had been earned by experience. He writes in *A Calendar of Wisdom* that to become wise one should be able to discern what is good from what is bad. He then states that to know this, one should first gain an understanding of what is not good: 'You should know what is not clever, what is not just, and what it is not necessary to do' (CW, 275). This would seem to fit the narrative of Tolstoy's lifelong moral development. It would also seem to fit his method of learning to teach. His experimentation in school led him up many blind alleys, such as labeling a child who stole, asking children to read together as a class and teaching geography by the Socratic method. But Tolstoy's forays into 'how-not-to-do-things,' both in his life, and educational thinking, led him to the same answer – like life, the secret of education is not so much in its content, but in the moral integrity of the process itself. Thus if teachers follow one important condition, 'the striving after perfection in love' and the children understand this intention, then the education will be good. It is for such reasons that Tolstoy claims hypocrisy to be the greatest threat to a genuine education.

Love, Tolstoy's ultimate solution to the world's problems, including education, should not be considered an overly simple answer to his lifelong questioning. For Tolstoy, love only defines the correct attitude and sentiment that should saturate a more complex approach to a problem. Love is the motivation for the practical striving by which one achieves goodness. Tolstoy's view is not that education is so simple that no theory is required, but rather that it is so complex and prone to ideology that only a dynamic, humanistic, personalized approach can account for the complexity of the process: a teacher should be able to use his or her intuition and understanding of individual children to provide a bespoke pedagogical approach for each child.

Tolstoy's concern with striving for goodness is reflected in his entire project with the experimental school, in which he attempted to help the most disadvantaged section of society – the peasants. Tolstoy is perhaps guilty of the romanticization of the peasants' lives, but his opposition to paternalism is at the center of his conception of education: the peasants themselves should be able to determine the kind of education provided for them, both in terms of curriculum content and pedagogical strategy.

In *A Calendar of Wisdom*, Tolstoy sums up his life's work as a writer and educator, the maxim becoming the very meaning of life: 'If you know the truth, or think you know the truth, pass it on to others as simply as you can, along with the feeling of love toward them'

(CW, 123). According to Tolstoy the purpose of life is the same as education, which in his terms, is the same as the purpose of literature. This concurs with the view he states 40 years earlier in the *Yasnaya Polyana* journal:

> Only that instruction has everywhere and in all ages been regarded as good, in which the pupil becomes completely equal to the teacher, – and the more so, the better, and the less the worse. Precisely the same phenomena may be observed in literature ... We regard only those books as good, in which the author, or educator, transmits all his knowledge to the reader or the learner. (PDE, 189)

From *Childhood* to the *Yasnaya Polyana* journal, *Anna Karenina* to 'The Wisdom of Children,' the themes of Tolstoy's educational, religious and literary writings overlap. Tolstoy the novelist is inseparable from his religious and educational beliefs. To reuse, in a different sense, Isaiah Berlin's famous analogy – the hedgehog using its one defense against the cunning fox that has many methods of attack – in my view, Tolstoy is like a hedgehog, he has one asset in his defense – a moral vision. It was on this moral vision that his religious, educational and literary works were centered. For him writing was teaching, teaching's essence was morality and morality's essence religion.

In his religious quest Tolstoy craved the knowledge of 'how to live' and this search is analogous to his educational pursuits: he wished to find practical understanding. For Tolstoy, religion is a moral injunction, not an ontological claim. This is comparable with his view of education: pedagogy is an ethical practice, not theoretical or scientific. It has a simple moral basis, but how it is manifested is not straightforward: it requires constant innovation which cannot be predicted or prescribed. Education must be based on consultation and experiment with pupils, and therefore it can only be defined as a dynamic, dialogic process between the generations. In proposing such a definition, Tolstoy, in one sense, wisely leaves the problems of education in our time, for us to solve. However, he also stresses the importance of some principles and qualities to which we should never forget – those of human intuition, care and nurture, freedom, and inspiration.

Epilogue

> You have hidden these things from the wise and the intelligent and have revealed them to infants
>
> Matthew 11.25

The Gospels were Tolstoy's greatest influence and the above verse can be seen to express the foundation of his spirituality. For Tolstoy, the moral law is present in the hearts of everyone. It is so simple that it is readily understood by children, even if it is often ignored by adults. Such views are explicit in Tolstoy's late essays and fables, and in much of the content of the *Yasnaya Polyana* journal, published decades earlier. Part 5, chapter 19 of *Anna Karenina* begins with the same verse. Levin thinks of it as he reflects on the intuitive, practical knowledge of his wife as she nurses his dying brother. Such love and care far surpass Levin's natural reaction to the situation – to 'wisely' contemplate abstract and philosophical questions concerning mortality.

Tolstoy's interpretation of Matthew 11.25 underpins his educational thought in two ways. First, pedagogy should be based on human values and feeling rather than on theoretical presuppositions. No cold, abstract theory can replace human intuition. Indeed, education should not even be defined in terms of pedagogy, but in terms of a positive relationship between teacher and learner. For Tolstoy, to create such a rapport was, as for Auerbach's Eugen, the sacred duty of every teacher.

Secondly, given their insight – and the importance of intuitive forms of knowledge easily available to them – children should have a part to play in deciding the content of the curriculum and the nature of the educational process itself. A corollary of this consultation between generations is that educators would be constantly educating themselves – resulting in a virtuous cycle of human development.

Tolstoy's views on education are certainly bold, and perhaps eccentric. Given their foundation in Tolstoy's unorthodox and radical religious views, it is unlikely that many readers today will agree with them wholly. Even Tolstoy admitted that his educational writings were never intended to be a final, conclusive answer to the problems of education. However, in his observations Tolstoy does strike upon some undeniable aspects of education as we all conceive it. At its core, Tolstoy's vision is a moral one. Education should aim for the good of the pupil and that of others. And to achieve this aim, schools should first recognize the good in their pupils. On a day-to-day basis, teachers, as many have found out through experience, cannot afford to give up on such ideals in their work, or such faith in their students.

In his diary of 6 May 1908, written two years before his death, Tolstoy reflects, as he did often in later years, on death and the prospect of an afterlife. He writes: 'to die means to go back to where you came from. What is there there? It must be something good, judging by the wonderful creatures, the children, who come from there' (TD, 582). This entry is indicative of Tolstoy's view of childhood, religion and life. He is comforted by the thought of returning to a natural, pure and undamaged childlike state. Given these views, exemplified in Tolstoy's reading of Matthew 11.25, it is fitting that Tolstoy's remains should lie at the 'place of the green stick,' in a grave dug and tended by his ex-pupil. Although a simple mound of turf bearing no monument, its very location – a place where Tolstoy played as a child and where the ideal of universal love and fraternity was first revealed to him, bears testament to his deeply held spirituality, his belief in the value and insights of childhood, and a lifetime's devotion to the pursuit of truth.

Bibliography

To avoid misrepresenting the chronology of Tolstoy's writings by referencing them by the year of publication of the English edition referred to, I have listed them according to the original publication date in Russian. When I have repeatedly quoted from Tolstoy's writings, I have also given them abbreviations; these are indicated below in bold print after the date of first publication. Similarly, when I have frequently cited biographical sources in the text, such as the diaries and memoirs, I have also abbreviated them by using the initials of their author. References to Christian's translations of *Tolstoy's Letters*, *Tolstoy's Diaries* and Edmond's translation of *War and Peace*, each of which consists of two volumes, abbreviated as TL, TD and WP, are referred to without indicating volume number, as the page numbers are continuous.

Tolstoy's writings

Tolstoy's Letters (vol. 1 1828–1879, vol. 2 1880–1910) **TL**. Selected, translated and edited by R. F. Christian. 1978. London: Athlone Press.
Tolstoy's Diaries (vol. 1 1847–1894, vol. 2 1895–1910) **TD**. Selected, translated and edited by R. F. Christian. 1985. London: Athlone Press.
'Temporary Method for Learning Music' (1850). In *Polnoe sobranie sochinenii*. [Complete Works] 1957. Moscow: Khudozhestvennaia literatura, pp. 241–245, vol. 1.
Childhood (1852) **CH**. In *Childhood, Boyhood and Youth*. Translated by L. and A. Maude. 1947. London: Oxford University Press, pp. 7–125.
Boyhood (1854) **BH**. In *Childhood, Boyhood and Youth*. Translated by L. and A. Maude. 1947. London: Oxford University Press, pp. 129–219.
'Sevastopol in December 1854, May 1855, and August 1855' (1855–1856). In *Collected Shorter Fiction*. Translated by A. and L. Maude. 2001. London: Everyman, pp. 81–204, vol. 1.
Youth (1857) **YO**. In *Childhood, Boyhood and Youth*. Translated by L. and A. Maude. 1947. London: Oxford University Press, pp. 223–404.
'On the Education of the People' (January 1862) **OEP**. In *Tolstoy on Education: Tolstoy's Educational Writings 1861–1862*. Selected and edited by A. Pinch

and M. Armstrong; translated by A. Pinch. 1982. London: Athlone Press, pp. 65–86.

'The School at Yasnaya Polyana' (January, March and April 1862) **TSYP**. In *Tolstoy on Education*. Translated by L. Wiener with an introduction by R. D. Archambault. 1967. Chicago: University of Chicago Press, pp. 227–360.

'On Methods of Teaching the Rudiments' (February 1862) **OTR**. In *Tolstoy on Education*. Translated by L. Wiener with an introduction by R. D. Archambault. 1967. Chicago: University of Chicago Press, pp. 32–59.

'A Project of a Plan for the Establishment of Popular Schools' (March 1862) **PES**. In *Tolstoy on Education*. Translated by L. Wiener with an introduction by R. D. Archambault. 1967. Chicago: University of Chicago Press, pp. 60–104.

'Training and Education' (July 1862) **TE**. In *Tolstoy on Education: Tolstoy's Educational Writings 1861–1862*. Selected and edited by A. Pinch and M. Armstrong; translated by A. Pinch. 1982. London: Athlone Press, pp. 291–325.

'Should We Teach the Peasant Children to Write, or Should They Teach Us?' (September 1862) **SWTP**. In *Tolstoy on Education: Tolstoy's Educational Writings 1861–1862*. Selected and edited by A. Pinch and M. Armstrong; translated by A. Pinch. 1982. London: Athlone Press, pp. 222–247.

'Progress and the Definition of Education' (December 1862) **PDE**. In *Tolstoy on Education*. Translated by L. Wiener with an introduction by R. D. Archambault. 1967. Chicago: University of Chicago Press, pp. 152–190.

The Cossacks (1863) **TC**. In *The Cossacks and Other Stories*. Translated by L. and A. Maude. 1929. London: Oxford University Press, pp. 1–234.

War and Peace (1863–1869) **WP**. Translated by R. Edmonds. 1957. Harmondsworth: Penguin.

Azbuka [four books] (1872) **AZ**. In *Polnoe sobranie sochinenii*. [Complete Works] 1957. Moscow: Khudozhestvennaia literatura, pp. 6–787, vol. 22.

'The Bear-Hunt' (1872). In *Collected Shorter Fiction*. Translated by A. and L. Maude. 2001. London: Everyman, pp. 744–753, vol. 1.

'God Sees the Truth, but Waits' (1872). In *Collected Shorter Fiction*. Translated by A. and L. Maude. 2001. London: Everyman, pp. 702–711, vol. 1.

'The Peasant and the Cucumbers' (1872). In *The Complete Works of Count Tolstoy*. Translated and edited by L. Wiener. 1904. London: J. M. Dent & Co., pp. 40, vol. 12.

'A Prisoner in the Caucasus' (1872). In *Collected Shorter Fiction*. Translated by A. and L. Maude. 2001. London: Everyman, pp. 715–742, vol. 1.

New Azbuka (1874–1875). In *Polnoe sobranie sochinenii*. [Complete Works] 1957. Moscow: Khudozhestvennaia literatura, pp. 2–100, vol. 21.

Russian Books for Reading [four books] (1874–1875). In *Polnoe sobranie sochinenii*. [Complete Works] 1957. Moscow: Khudozhestvennaia literatura, pp. 102–329, vol. 21.

'On Popular Education' (1875) **PE**. In *The Complete Works of Count Tolstoy*. Translated and edited by L. Wiener. 1904. London: J. M. Dent & Co., pp. 251–323, vol. 12.
Anna Karenina (1874–1876) **AK**. Translated by R. Edmonds. 1978. Harmondsworth: Penguin.
A Confession (1879) **AC**. In *A Confession and Other Religious Writings*. Translated by J. Kentish. 1987. Harmondsworth: Penguin, pp. 19–80.
'The Four Gospels Harmonised' (1881–1882) **FGH**. In *The Complete Works of Count Tolstoy*. Translated and edited by L. Wiener. 1904. London: J. M. Dent & Co., pp. 4–451, vol. 14.
'Little Girls Wiser than Men' (1885). In *Collected Shorter Fiction*. Translated by A. and L. Maude. 2001. London: Everyman, pp. 100–102, vol. 2.
'The Death of Ivan Ilych' (1886) **DII**. In *Collected Shorter Fiction*. Translated by A. and L. Maude. 2001. London: Everyman, pp. 110–171, vol. 2.
'How Much Land Does a Man Need?' (1886). In *Collected Shorter Fiction*. Translated by A. and L. Maude. 2001. London: Everyman, pp. 190–207, vol. 2.
'What Then Must We Do?' (1886). In *I Cannot Be Silent: Writings on Politics, Art and Religion by Leo Tolstoy*. Edited by W. G. Jones. 1989. Bristol: Bristol Press, pp. 80–98.
On Life (1887) **OL**. In *On Life and Essays on Religion*. Translated by A. Maude. 1934. London: Oxford University Press, pp. 1–167.
The Kingdom of God is within You (1893). In *The Kingdom of God is within You and Peace Essays*. Translated by A. Maude. 1946. London: Oxford University Press, pp. 1–460.
'Reason and Religion' (1894). In *On Life and Essays on Religion*. Translated by A. Maude. 1934. London: Oxford University Press, pp. 199–204.
'Religion and Morality' (1894) **RM**. In *On Life and Essays on Religion*. Translated by A. Maude. 1934. London: Oxford University Press, pp. 168–198.
'Hadji Murad' (1896–1904). In *Collected Shorter Fiction*. Translated by A. and L. Maude. 2001. London: Everyman, pp. 605–738, vol. 2.
What is Art? (1898). In *What is Art? and Essays on Art*. Translated by A. Maude. 1946. Oxford: Oxford University Press, pp. 64–312.
Resurrection (1899). Translated by L. Maude. 1928. London: Oxford University Press.
'Thoughts on Education and Instruction' (1887–1901) **TOEI**. In *The Complete Works of Count Tolstoy*. Translated and edited by L. Wiener. 1904. London: J. M. Dent & Co., pp. 358–383, vol. 23.
The Religious Education of the Young (c.1901). The Free Age Press Leaflets No. 4. Christchurch, Hampshire: Free Age Press.
'A Reply to the Synod's Edict of Excommunication' (1901) **RSE**. In *On Life and Essays on Religion*. Translated by A. Maude. 1934. London: Oxford University Press, pp. 214–225.

'What is Religion and Wherein Lies Its Essence?' (1902) **WR**. In *On Life and Essays on Religion*. Translated by A. Maude. 1934. London: Oxford University Press, pp. 226–281.

Recollections (1902–1908) **RE**. In *Recollections and Essays*. Centenary edition. Translated and edited by A. Maude. 1937. Oxford University Press (for the Tolstoy Society). London: Humphrey Milford, pp. 1–67, vol. 21.

'The Restoration of Hell' (1903) **ROH**. In *On Life and Essays on Religion*. Translated by A. Maude. 1934. London: Oxford University Press, pp. 309–330.

'Church and State' (1904). In *On Life and Essays on Religion*. Translated by A. Maude. 1934. London: Oxford University Press, pp. 331–345.

A Calendar of Wisdom (1904–1908) **CW**. Paperback edition. Translated by P. Sekirin. 1998. London: Hodder and Stoughton.

'I Cannot be Silent' (1908). In *I Cannot be Silent: Writings on Politics, Art and Religion by Leo Tolstoy*. Edited by W. G. Jones. 1989. Bristol: Bristol Press, pp. 202–212.

'The Teaching of Jesus' (1908) **TOJ**. In *On Life and Essays on Religion*. Translated by A. Maude. 1934. London: Oxford University Press, pp. 346–409.

'On Upbringing' (1909) **OU**. In *Polnoe sobranie sochinenii*. [Complete Works] 1936. Moscow: Khudozhestvennaia literatura, pp. 62–69, vol. 38. Excerpts translated by Anya Wells.

'The Wisdom of Children' (1910) **WC**. In *Recollections and Essays*. Tolstoy Centenary edition. Translated and edited by A. Maude. Oxford University Press (for the Tolstoy Society). 1937. London: Humphrey Milford, pp. 446–493, vol. 21.

Biographical sources

Addams, J. (1910) **JA**. 'Tolstoyism'. In *Twenty Years at Hull-House*. New York: Macmillan, pp. 259–280.

Behrs, C. A. (1893) **BS**. *Recollections of Count Leo Tolstoy*. Translated by C. E. Turner. London: William Heinemann.

Birukoff, P. [Biryukov] (1906) **BK**. *Leo Tolstoy, His Life and Work: Autobiographical Memoirs Letters and Biographical Material Vol. 1 Childhood and Early Manhood*. Compiled by P. Birukoff and revised by L. Tolstoy. London: William Heinemann.

Bulgakov, V. F. (1971) **VB**. *The Last Year of Leo Tolstoy*. Translated by A. Dunnigan. London: Hamish Hamilton.

Goldenveiser, A. B. [Goldenweiser] (1923) **GW**. *Talks with Tolstoi*. Translated by S. S. Koteliansky and V. Woolf. Richmond: Hogarth Press.

Morozov, P. V. (1982) **PVM**. 'An extract from the reminiscences of a teacher at Yasnaya Polyana school.' In *Tolstoy on Education: Tolstoy's Educational*

Writings 1861–1862. Selected and edited by A. Pinch and M. Armstrong; translated by A. Pinch. 1982. London: Athlone Press, pp. 185–187.

Morozov, V. S. (1982) **VSM**. 'Extracts from the reminiscences of a pupil at Yasnaya Polyana school.' In *Tolstoy on Education: Tolstoy's Educational Writings 1861–1862*. Selected and edited by A. Pinch and M. Armstrong; translated by A. Pinch. 1982. London: Athlone Press, pp. 188–221.

Schuyler, E. (1901) **SL**. 'Count Leo Tolstoy Twenty Years Ago.' In *Selected Essays*. London: Sampson Low, Marston and Company, pp. 205–299.

Tolstoy, A. (1933) **CAT**. *The Tragedy of Tolstoy*. Translated by E. Varneck. London: George Allen and Unwin.

Tolstoy, A. (1953) **AT**. *Tolstoy: A Life of My Father*. Translated by E. Reynolds Hapgood. New York: Harper and Brothers.

Tolstoy, I. (1972) **IT**. *Tolstoy, My Father: Reminiscences*. Translated by A. Dunnigan. London: Peter Owen.

Tolstoy, S. (1922) **ST**. *The Autobiography of Countess Sophie Tolstoy*. Translated by S. S. Koteliansky and L. Woolf. Richmond: Hogarth Press.

Tolstoy, S. (1961). *Tolstoy Remembered by His Son*. Translated by M. Budberg. London: Weidenfeld and Nicolson.

Tolstoy, T. (1977) **TT**. *Tolstoy Remembered*. Translated from the French by D. Coltman. London: Michael Joseph.

General references

Addams, J. (1934) 'Introduction.' In L. Tolstoy *What Then Must We Do?* Tolstoy Centenary edition. Translated by A. Maude. Oxford University Press (for the Tolstoy Society). London: Humphrey Milford, pp. vii–xiii, vol. 4.

Apostolov, N. (1926) 'Tolstoy and Dickens.' In *Family Views of Tolstoy*. Edited by A. Maude and translated by L. and A. Maude. London: George Allen and Unwin, pp. 71–84.

Archambault, R. D. (1967) 'Introduction to Tolstoy on Education.' In *Tolstoy on Education*. Translated by L. Wiener. Chicago: University of Chicago Press, pp. v–xviii.

Auerbach, B. S. (1871, first published 1851) *Neues Leben: Eine Lehrgeschichte in fünf Bücher*. Stuttgart: Cotta'scher Verlag, Erster Theil S. 1–243. English excerpts quoted in the text are translated by Bertram Jörg Schirr.

Bantock, G. H. (1984) 'The Non-Interference of the School: Tolstoy.' In *Studies in the History of Educational Theory. Volume II The Minds and the Masses 1760–1980*. London: George Allen and Unwin, pp. 280–308.

Baudouin, C. (1923) *Tolstoi: The Teacher*. Translated by F. Rothwell. London: Kegan Paul, Trench, Trubner & Co.; New York: E. P. Dutton & Co.

Berlin, I. (1988) *The Hedgehog and the Fox*. London: Weidenfeld and Nicolson.

Berlin, I. (1979) 'Tolstoy and Enlightenment.' In *Russian Thinkers*. Edited by H. Hardy and A. Kelly. Harmondsworth: Penguin, pp. 238–260.

Berthoff, A. E. (1978) 'Tolstoy, Vygotsky, and the Making of Meaning.' *College Composition and Communication*, 29 (3), pp. 249–255.

Blaisdell, B. (2000) *Tolstoy as Teacher: Leo Tolstoy's Writings on Education*. Edited by B. Blaisdell and translated by C. Edgar. New York: Teachers and Writers Collaborative.

Chesterton, G. K. (1903) 'G. K. Chesterton on Tolstoy's Fanaticism.' In *Tolstoy: the Critical Heritage*. Edited by A. V. Knowles. 1978. London: Routledge & Kegan Paul, pp. 418–419.

Cohen, A. (1981) 'The Educational Philosophy of Tolstoy.' *Oxford Review of Education*, 7 (3), pp. 241–251.

Crosby, E. H. (1903) *Tolstoy and His Message*. London: Simple Life Press.

Crosby, E. H. (1904) *Tolstoy as Schoolmaster*. London: Arthur C. Fifield.

Dennison, G. (1969) *The Lives of Children: The Story of the First Street School*. New York: Vintage Books.

Dewey, J. (1897) 'My Pedagogic Creed.' *The Early Works of John Dewey, 1882–1898. Volume 5: 1895–1898*. Edited by J. A. Boydston. 1972. Carbondale and Edwardsville: Southern Illinois University Press, pp. 84–95.

Dewey, J. (1908) 'Religion and Our Schools.' In *The Middle Works of John Dewey, 1899–1924. Volume 4: 1907–1909*. Edited by J. A. Boydston. Carbondale and Edwardsville: Southern Illinois University Press, pp. 165–177.

Dewey, J. (1910) 'Tolstoi's Art.' In *The Later Works of John Dewey, 1925–1953. Volume 17: 1885–1953*. Edited by J. A. Boydston. 1985. Carbondale and Edwardsville: Southern Illinois University Press, pp. 381–393.

Dewey, J. (1929a) 'Foreword to Helen Edna Davis's Tolstoy and Nietzsche: A Problem in Biographical Ethics.' In *The Later Works of John Dewey, 1925–1953. Volume 5: 1929–1930*. Edited by J. A. Boydston. 1985. Carbondale and Edwardsville: Southern Illinois University Press, pp. 398–401.

Dewey, J. (1929b) 'The Russian School System.' In *The Later Works of John Dewey, 1925–1953. Volume 17: 1885–1953*. Edited by J. A. Boydston. 1985. Carbondale and Edwardsville: Southern Illinois University Press, pp. 487–511.

Dewey, J. (1934) 'A Common Faith.' In *The Later Works of John Dewey, 1925–1953. Volume 9: 1933–1934*. Edited by J. A. Boydston. 1985. Carbondale and Edwardsville: Southern Illinois University Press, pp. 1–58.

Edwards, R. (1992) 'Tolstoy and John Dewey: Pragmatism and Prosaics.' *Tolstoy Studies Journal*, 5, pp. 15–37.

Eikhenbaum, B. (1982a) *Tolstoi in the Seventies*. Translated by A. Kaspin. Ann Arbour, MI: Ardis.

Eikhenbaum, B. (1982b) *Tolstoi in the Sixties*. Translated by D. White. Ann Arbour, MI: Ardis.

Gandhi, M. K. (1982) *An Autobiography or the Story of My Experiments with Truth*. Translated from the original Gujarati by M. Desai, Harmondsworth: Penguin.

Greenwood, E. B. (1995) 'Tolstoy, Wittgenstein Schopenhauer: Some Connections.' In *Tolstoi and Britain*. Edited by W. G. Jones. Oxford: Berg, pp. 239–249.

Gustafson, R. F. (1986) *Leo Tolstoy: Resident and Stranger*. Princeton: Princeton University Press.

Kant, I. (1788) *Critique of Practical Reason*. Translated by L. W. Beck. 1956. Indianapolis: Bobbs-Merill.

Kramer, R. (1976) *Maria Montessori: A Biography*. Oxford: Basil Blackwell.

Kumar, K. (1997) 'Mohandas Karamchand Gandhi.' In *Thinkers on Education*. Edited by Z. Morsy. UNESCO Publishing/Oxford & IBH Publishing, pp. 507–515, vol. 2.

Kupersmith, P. and Nolan, T. J. (2006) 'How a Meeting between an American Rabbi and Count Leo Tolstoy Resulted in the Founding of an American College.' *Tolstoy Studies Journal*, 18, pp. 70–74.

LeBlanc, R. D. (2009) *Slavic Sins of the Flesh: Food, Sex, and Carnal Appetite in Nineteenth Century Russian Fiction*. Hanover and London: University Press of New Hampshire.

Lucas, V. (1979) *Tolstoy in London*. London: Evans Brothers.

Makarov, S., Morozov, V. S. and Tolstoy, L. (May 1862) 'He Feeds You with a Spoon and Pokes You in the Eye with the Handle.' In *Tolstoy on Education: Tolstoy's Educational Writings 1861–1862*. Selected and edited by A. Pinch and M. Armstrong; translated by A. Pinch. 1982. London: Athlone Press, pp. 248–261.

Maude, A. (1902) *Tolstoy and His Problems*. London: Grant Richards.

Maude, A. (1904) *A Peculiar People: The Doukhobors*. London: Grant Richards.

Maude, A. (1917) *The Life of Tolstoy Vol. 1 The First Fifty Years*. Seventh edition. London: Constable and Company.

Maude, A. (1918) *Leo Tolstoy*. London: Methuen.

Maude, A. (1929) *The Life of Tolstoy: The First Fifty Years*. Tolstoy Centenary edition. London: Humphrey Milford.

Medzhibovskaya, I. (2008) *Tolstoy and the Religious Culture of His Time. A Biography of a Long Conversion*. Plymouth, UK: Lexington Books.

Monk, R. (1991) *Ludwig Wittgenstein: The Duty of Genius*. London: Vintage.

Morozov, V. S. (September 1862) 'The Life of a Soldier's Wife.' In *Tolstoy on Education: Tolstoy's Educational Writings 1861–1862*. Selected and edited by A. Pinch and M. Armstrong; translated by A. Pinch. 1982. London: Athlone Press, pp. 262–270.

Mossman, E. (1993) 'Tolstoi and Peasant Learning in the Era of the Great Reforms.' In *School and Society in Tsarist and Soviet Russia*. Edited by B. Eklof. Houndmills, Basingstoke: MacMillan Press, pp. 36–69.

Murphy, D. (1992) *Tolstoy and Education*. Dublin: Irish Academic Press.

Neill, A. S. (1973) *Neill! Neill! Orange Peel! A Personal View of 90 Years by the Founder of Summerhill School*. London: Weidenfeld and Nicolson.

Pring, R., Hayward, G., Hodgson, A., Johnson, J., Keep, E., Oancea, A., Rees, G., Spours, K. and Wilde, S. (2009) *Education for All: The Future of Education and Training for 14–19 Year Olds*. Abingdon: Routledge.

Rousseau, J. J. (1762) *Emile or on Education*. Translated by A. Bloom. 1991. Harmondsworth: Penguin.

Rousseau, J. J. (1781) *The Confessions*. Translated by J. M. Cohen. Harmondsworth: Penguin.

Russell, B. (1937) *Education for Democracy*. London: Association for Education in Citizenship.

Russell, B. (1961) *History of Western Philosophy*. Second edition. London: George Allen and Unwin.

Shaw, G. B. (1929) 'Review of A. Maude's *The Life of Tolstoy*.' Reprinted as an introduction in A. Maude. *The Life of Tolstoy: First Fifty Years*. Tolstoy Centenary edition. London: Humphrey Milford, pp. vii–xii.

Shestov, L. I. (1900) 'Shestov on Tolstoy's Lack of Compassion.' In *Tolstoy: The Critical Heritage*. Edited by A. V. Knowles. 1978. London: Routledge & Kegan Paul, pp. 387–394.

Simmons, E. J. (1973) *The Routledge Author Guides: Tolstoy*. London and Boston: Routledge & Kegan Paul.

Tolstoy, A. (1935) *I Worked for the Soviet*. Translated by the author in collaboration with R. Yorkes. London: Allen and Unwin.

Troyat, H. (1968) *Tolstoy*. Translated from the French by N. Amphoux. London: W. H. Allen.

Wagner, P. A. and Sobotka, B. (1986) 'Tolstoy: The Teacher.' *The Educational Forum*, 50 (2), pp. 183–190.

Wittgenstein, L. (1961) *Tractatus Logico-Philosophicus*. Translated by D. F. Pears and B. F. McGuinness. London: Routledge & Kegan Paul.

Yegorov, S. F. (1997) 'Leo Tolstoy.' In *Thinkers on Education*. Edited by Z. Morsy. UNESCO Publishing/Oxford & IBH Publishing, pp. 647–660, vol. 4.

Index

Addams, J. 152, 154, 155
Anna Karenina 3, 43, 49–51, 113
ant brothers 11–13
Archambault, R. D. 146–7
Armstrong, M. 147
art 49, 92
Astapovo 64
Auerbach, B. 21–5, 27, 171–2
Azbuka 40–2, 93, 96–9

Bantock, G. H. 150
Baudouin, C. 144–5
Baumann, E. 22–5, 27, 159, 171, 182
Behrs, S. (Tolstoy's brother-in-law) 45, 47
Behrs, S. (Tolstoy's wife) 38, 46, 64, 65
Berlin, I. 145–6, 181
Berthoff, A. E. 150
Bible, The 38–9, 87, 120, 167 *see also* Gospels, The
Blaisdell, B. 148, 155
Boyhood 13–15
Buddha 57–8, 131
Bulgakov, V. 65, 128

Calendar of Wisdom, A 49, 56, 64–5, 130–4
Caucasus 19–20, 33, 122
censorship 63, 140–1
Chertkov, V. 62, 65, 142
Childhood 12–13, 19
Christianity 4, 52, 55, 60, 63, 98, 119, 154, 178
Cohen, A. 149
communists 157
Confession, A 19–21, 48, 55, 60
Confessions, The (Rousseau) 20, 21
Contemporary, The 19, 109, 140
Cossacks, The 19, 21, 33, 54, 112
Crosby, E. H. 143–4, 155

curriculum 46, 71, 73, 79, 85–96, 106, 123–4, 163–6

Death of Ivan Ilych, The 53, 169
Delaware Valley College 155–6
Dennison, G. 158
Dewey, J. 144, 147, 151, 152–5
Dickens, C. 26, 38
Doukhobors 62, 63, 142–3, 155

Edwards, R. 152–3
Eikhenbaum, B. 34, 38, 42–4, 108
Emile 20–1
Eugen *see* Baumann, E.

fables 5, 34–6, 49, 97
Fedor Ivanovich Kessel 13
Freire, P. 150, 151, 164
Fyedka *see* Morozov, V. S.
'He Feeds You with a Spoon and Pokes You in the Eye with the Handle' 34–6

Gandhi, M. K. 61, 152, 160–1
geography 85, 87, 136, 180
Germany 25–6, 70, 173
God 71, 98, 117, 119, 121, 127, 132
Goldenweiser, A. B. 165, 170, 177
Gospels, The 39, 56, 61, 87, 158, 182

Harris Manchester College, Oxford 131
history *as a school subject* 13–14, 15, 30, 33, 83, 85–7, 129

indoctrination 38, 163–6

Jesus (Christ) 44, 54, 58, 116, 130, 134–5
Justice of the Peace, Tolstoy's role as 2, 31, 37 *see also* Zemstva

Kant, I. 50, 55–6, 71, 131
Karl Ivanych 13–14
Kazan University 17–18, 111
Krauskopf, J. 155–6
kumys 3, 36, 172

Languages *as a school subject* 123, 125
Levin
   his attitude to education 29, 113–14, 125
   his conversion 49–51, 125
'Life of a soldier's wife, The' 36, 90, 97
Literature
   the teaching of 34–6, 42, 89–93
   Tolstoy's view of 1–2, 20, 32–4, 40, 44, 49, 181
London 26, 142, 165
love 11, 160, 180

Mathematics 15, 30, 45, 46, 98, 123, 164
Maude, A. 62, 142–3, 154–5
Maude, L. 62
Montessori, M. 150, 152
Morozov, P. V. 31, 43
Morozov, V. S. (Fyedka) 29, 31, 33–7, 75, 90, 97, 177
Moscow Literacy Committee 42–4
Mossman, E. 144, 150
Murphy, D. 178–9
Music, the teaching of 18–19, 88–9, 124

Neill, A. S. 147–9, 152, 158
New Azbuka 41–2, 93, 98–9
Nicholas
   his experience of education 12–17, 109
   his moral and spiritual development 119–20

'On the Education of the People' (1862) 70–5
On Life 55, 57–60, 123
'On Methods of Teaching the Rudiments' 93–6
'On Popular Education' (1875) 99–101
Orthodox Church, the Russian 58–61, 63–4
'On Upbringing' 128–30

Pestalozzi, J. H. 21, 72, 144, 152
Pfuhl, General 27, 169
Pharisees 58–60
Pierre
   his conversion to freemasonry 51–2
   his attitudes towards education 113
Pinch, A. 109, 146–7
progress, Tolstoy's view of 25–6, 43, 59, 104–5
'Progress and the Definition of Education' 104, 105
progressive educators 151–5
'Project of a Plan for the Establishment of Popular Schools' 105–8

'Religion and Morality' 51, 53–4, 58, 168
religious education 118–19, 127, 129, 154, 161, 166–8
Religious Education of the Young, The 119, 142
'Restoration of Hell, The' 116–17
Resurrection 48, 62–3, 155
Rousseau, J. J. 20–1, 45, 72
Russell, B. 145
Russian Books for Reading 41–2, 96–9, 146

'School at Yasnaya Polyana, The' 30–4, 75–8
Schuyler, E. 22, 27, 40, 139
science 32, 105, 116–17, 123, 126–7, 132
scribes 58–60
'Should We Teach the Peasant Children to Write, or Should They Teach Us?' 36, 90–3
Sobotka, B. 149–50
Steiner, R. 151–2
St Jerome 14, 169
St Thomas 14

'Teaching of Jesus, The' 44, 134–5
'Temporary Method for Learning Music' 18
Tolstoy, A. L. 64, 65, 132, 156–8
Tolstoy, I. L. 40–1, 45–7
Tolstoy, N. 1, 11–12, 19, 25
Tolstoy, T. L. 45–6, 142, 152
Tolstoyanism, Tolstoyans 60–2, 142–3, 145–55

'Training and Education' 79–80
Turgenev, I. S. 19–20

university education 15–19,
    108–11

Wagner, P. A. 149–50
War and Peace 27–8, 29, 33–4, 51–3, 55,
    85, 112–13
Wiener, L. 146–7

'Wisdom of Children, The' 86–7
Wittgenstein, L. 158–9

Yasnaya Polyana estate 1, 11, 19, 36, 46
Yasnaya Polyana journal 37, 69, 78, 84,
    139–41
Youth 15–17, 119

Zemstva 2, 113 *see also* Justice of the
    Peace